A Comedian and an Activist
Walk into a Bar

COMMUNICATION FOR SOCIAL JUSTICE ACTIVISM

Series Editors

Patricia Parker, University of North Carolina at Chapel Hill

Lawrence R. Frey, University of Colorado Boulder

A Comedian and an Activist Walk into a Bar

THE SERIOUS ROLE OF COMEDY IN SOCIAL JUSTICE

Caty Borum Chattoo and
Lauren Feldman

UNIVERSITY OF CALIFORNIA PRESS

University of California Press
Oakland, California

© 2020 by Caty Borum Chattoo and Lauren Feldman

Library of Congress Cataloging-in-Publication Data

Names: Borum Chattoo, Caty, author. | Feldman, Lauren, 1977- author.
Title: A comedian and an activist walk into a bar : the serious role of
    comedy in social justice / Caty Borum Chattoo and Lauren Feldman.
    Other titles: Communication for social justice activism ; 1.
Description: Oakland, California : University of California Press, [2019] |
    Series: Communication for social justice activism; 1 | Includes
    bibliographical references and index.
Identifiers: LCCN 2019036801 (print) | LCCN 2019036802 (ebook) |
    ISBN 9780520299771 (cloth) | ISBN 9780520299764 (paperback) |
    ISBN 9780520971356 (ebook)
Subjects: LCSH: Comedy—Political aspects—United States. | Social
    justice—United States. | Mass media—Political aspects—United States.
Classification: LCC PN1929.P65 B67 2019 (print) | LCC PN1929.P65
    (ebook) | DDC 792.76—dc23
LC record available at https://lccn.loc.gov/2019036801
LC ebook record available at https://lccn.loc.gov/2019036802

Manufactured in the United States of America

29 28 27 26 25 24 23 22 21 20
10 9 8 7 6 5 4 3 2 1

Politics is not going to save this world, which requires a lot of saving . . .

Norman Lear

. . . what will save the world are the comics.

Carl Reiner

The publisher and the University of California Press Foundation gratefully acknowledge the generous support of the Richard and Harriett Gold Endowment Fund in Arts and Humanities.

Contents

Illustrations

Foreword

by Norman Lear

My career in comedy has been motivated and inspired by the delight I've taken in understanding what I think of as the foolishness of the human condition. Somehow, I knew if the laughs were there and the subject of the comedy was important to the audience, that audience would be motivated to engage in what was called water cooler conversation at work the following week. Triggering such discussion, as opposed to just making people laugh, is what the best comedy seeks to do. People think in conversations and find things in themselves that they didn't know were there. It's a learning process—a deeply human familial kind of learning process.

As they reveal in this book, *A Comedian and an Activist Walk into a Bar: The Serious Role of Comedy in Social Justice,* authors Caty Borum Chattoo and Lauren Feldman recognize that the social landscape is different when comedy is afoot. The more comedy is there to stir the mind and the emotion, the more we think and talk and feel and understand what we're going through. Comedy supplies a unique lens that can help repair the world (but only if the comedy is thoughtful and really funny). For students, activists, social justice organizations, scholars, and media professionals, this book helps explain why and how comedy matters, and why creative expression is so vital to democracy.

I couldn't appreciate these ideas more.

Acknowledgments

Many people are responsible for bringing this book to life, for which we are deeply appreciative. First, we offer profound gratitude to Lyn Uhl, our wonderfully supportive, enthusiastic, meticulous editor at University of California Press, and to Enrique Ochoa-Kaup for his patience and editorial expertise as we prepared this manuscript. We also acknowledge our anonymous peer reviewers for their careful consideration of our work. Additionally, we appreciate the launch of the new *Communication for Social Justice Activism* series helmed by series editors Patricia Parker and Larry Frey, in which this book finds its rightful home at an opportune cultural moment. Finally, we are tremendously grateful to the many comedy and social justice professionals who generously shared their time and perspectives through interviews. It is an honor to reflect their funny, thoughtful voices here.

Individually, we also thank one another, as well as the people in our lives who have supported us and this effort along the way. These acknowledgments follow.

Caty Borum Chattoo: At the School of Communication at American University, I am grateful to Dean Jeff Rutenbeck and Dean Laura DeNardis for their tremendous support and kindness, alongside many faculty and staff colleagues, especially Patricia Aufderheide, Dean Emeritus Larry Kirkman, Kristi Plahn-Gjersvold, Scott Talan, Filippo Trevisan, Lenny Steinhorn, and Rhonda Zaharna. In particular, Pallavi Kumar, director of the Public Communication division, provided an immeasurable supply of unwavering support, patience, laughter, and friendship as I co-authored this volume— and well beyond. Leena Jayaswal, my documentary partner, epitomizes light and strength, and I am grateful for her encouragement. I also thank my graduate research assistants, particularly Molly Page and Sarah Huckins.

I could not have co-authored this book and simultaneously directed the busy Center for Media & Social Impact without the talents and dedication of CMSI's Varsha Ramani, and the comedic flow of ideas from Bethany Hall, the center's first Comedian in Residence. In addition to supporters at American University, my friend and colleague Jeffrey Jones—whose pathbreaking scholarship on the intersection of comedy and political engagement played an instrumental role in this project—offered valuable ideas and feedback.

On a personal level, this book is a full-circle homage to the legendary comedy TV producer and philanthropist Norman Lear, my beloved former boss and forever mentor, under whose generous and brilliant tutelage I learned to revere the people-connecting magic of comedy and creativity and culture, and much more. I am grateful to my parents, John Borum and Christine Bolognese, and my sister and brother-in-law, Christie and Mike Dasher, and my funny nephews, Peter and Brady, for their encouragement over the years. Finally, this project was enabled by the steadfast love, kindness, and patience of Larry Chattoo, whose devotion to our family makes everything possible; I am deeply grateful for his support. This book is dedicated to my son, Elias, and my daughter, Simone, who make my world more joyful and beautiful—and hilarious—than I could have ever imagined.

Lauren Feldman: I am incredibly grateful to the Rutgers School of Communication and Information for creating a rich intellectual space for research and for giving me the opportunity to teach courses through which the ideas in this book could grow. I thank the School's Dean

Jonathan Potter and Associate Deans Mark Aakhus, Dafna Lemish, and Karen Novick, and my fantastic colleagues in the Journalism and Media Studies department, including my current and former chairs Susan Keith and Jack Bratich. Thanks especially to Melissa Aronczyk for her friendship and support.

I began researching comedy in 2004, while a graduate student at the University of Pennsylvania's Annenberg School for Communication. There, I was fortunate to have many wonderful mentors who continue to shape my scholarship in myriad ways, especially my PhD advisor Vincent Price, who first inspired my commitment to research; Joseph Cappella, who challenged me to think critically about message effects; and Michael Delli Carpini, upon whose essential ideas about the role of entertainment in politics this book builds.

This book would not have been possible without my amazing family. I owe much to my parents, Jane and Rich Feldman, who have encouraged and supported me every step of the way, and who, from my youngest days, indulged my desire to write. My sister, Julie Hamburg, is my rock, and even though she had her third baby while I was writing this book, she still found time to listen and lend her infinite wisdom. My husband Preston Rogers has been there for me through it all, and I am forever grateful for his patience, love, and exceptional comedic taste. Finally, to my daughters, Leona and Greta, this book is dedicated to you, with boundless love and gratitude for the light and laughter you bring to the world.

·   ·   ·   ·   ·

We and the University of California Press would like to acknowledge the following publishers for permission to reprint writing originally published in these works:

Some writing in the Introduction and Chapter 1 originally appeared in:

Caty Borum Chattoo, "The Laughter Effect: The [Serious] Role of Comedy in Social Change," Washington, DC: Center for Media & Social Impact, 2017, https://cmsimpact.org/comedy.

Some writing in Chapter 1 was originally published in:

Caty Borum Chattoo, "A Funny Matter: Toward a Framework for Understanding the Function of Comedy in Social Change," *HUMOR: International Journal of Humor Research* (2018), https://doi.org/10.1515/humor-2018-0004, used with permission from De Gruyter.

Some writing in Chapter 5 was originally published in:

Caty Borum Chattoo and Lauren Feldman, "Storytelling for Social Change: Leveraging Documentary and Comedy for Public Engagement in Global Poverty," *Journal of Communication* 67, no. 5 (2017): 678–701, https://doi.org/10.1111/jcom.12318, used with permission from Oxford University Press.

PART I Comedy amidst a
Contemporary Landscape of
Influence and Information

Introduction

66 *The last thing a comic wants is to be taken seriously. But I
can tell you this: You hear people say, "there's so much
suffering in the world—jokes are inappropriate." I say hunger
is inappropriate. Poverty is inappropriate. Lies and
hypocrisy from governments, that's inappropriate.* 99

    Hasan Minhaj, comedian[1]

In 2015, weeks after a scathing, viral video exposé of New York City's bail bond system and its outsized impact on poor, low-level offenders, Mayor Bill de Blasio took action. In a swift move, he took steps to correct an institutional process that Human Rights Watch and other social justice advocates had long maligned.[2] In a statement echoing the precise arguments made in the video-based muckraking indictment, Mayor de Blasio said: "Money bail is a problem because, as the system currently operates in New York, some people are being detained based on the size of their bank account, not the risk they pose."[3]

The source of the media fury that contributed to the mayor's action? A 17-minute comedy manifesto on a satirical TV news program, viewed millions of times online.

Just one month before the mayor's history-making announcement, on an episode of HBO's satirical news show *Last Week Tonight*, comedian and host John Oliver took on the bail issue with his trademark eye-popping fervor as an outraged, bemused social justice advocate. Oliver alternated between silly ("Jail can do for your actual life what being in a marching band can do for your social life. Even if you're just in for a little while, it can

3

destroy you.")[4] and serious ("Increasingly, bail has become a way to lock up the poor, regardless of guilt").[5] Millions of YouTube views and social media shares later, amplified by attention from media outlets including *Salon*,[6] the *Washington Post*,[7] *Reddit*, and others, New York City officials changed the city's bail protocol, immediately impacting thousands of poor and low-level offenders in the short term, and many more in the long run.[8]

Was this a home run for comedy? Is comedy a promising way to meaningfully engage audiences and policy decision-makers on pressing social justice issues? Perhaps. But perhaps it's not so simple.

Consider another story: A few years into the social media era, the U.S. Centers for Disease Control and Prevention decided to try a new approach to a public health marketing campaign. Rather than imploring the American public to follow typically somber instructions to prepare for a looming natural or human-caused disaster, the agency's strategists launched a humorous campaign, "The Zombie Apocalypse." The effort focused heavily on social media engagement with funny messages, relying on the metaphorical connection between a real-life disaster and an apocalyptic zombie attack.[9]

Researchers concluded that the public health campaign was an attention-grabbing, social-media-sharing success: Thanks to its social media strategy, more than 5 million people engaged directly with the campaign.[10] However, the researchers also revealed a distinct juxtaposition. In a deeper analysis, looking beyond the metrics of reach, the research team found that people exposed to the comedic zombie risk messages, relative to more serious risk messages, were significantly *less* likely to take protective actions in the face of an impending disaster.[11] Behavior change, at least in this instance, was too high a bar for comedy to reach.

The two stories illustrate the promise and paradox—and complexity—of contemporary comedy in service of serious social challenges. On the one hand, perhaps it's not revelatory to claim, based on anecdotes alone, that comedy can cut through the clutter of today's unrelenting digital supply of information. In the midst of a niche-driven media environment short on the shared cultural watercooler moments of the analog age, comedy's ability to pick up viral steam is invaluable. Comedy has the potential to preach beyond the choir, even as it also often mobilizes a base of like-minded thinkers. Comedy may even be able to help set a media agenda in ways that impact policy, as illustrated in the bail story. On the other hand, to ascribe monolithic, one-size-fits-all characteristics onto comedy—and its ability to contribute to social change—risks possible backfiring. Comedy comes in distinct forms, it is often culturally specific, and its appeal for communicating serious issues depends on many factors, not least of which are the roles of the audience and the issue itself. The construct of "social change" in the context of comedy and media also is not monolithic; instead, it exists on a practical level as a continuum that includes building public awareness, shaping individual attitudes and behaviors, shifting social norms and practices, encouraging public engagement, setting a media agenda, and influencing policy.

LOCATING CONTEMPORARY MEDIATED COMEDY IN THE CONTEXT OF SOCIAL JUSTICE

The twenty-first century finds us within a dramatic transformation in information, entertainment, and technology—and, simultaneously, an era of social justice activism augmented by digital advocacy. Thanks to a confluence of factors, comedy may be in the midst of its newest golden era of experimentation and influence, both in the United States and around the world. In the still-evolving digital era, the opportunity to consume and share comedy has never been as available. And yet, despite its vast cultural imprint, comedy is a little-understood vehicle for serious public engagement in urgent social problems. Moreover, in the midst of a merger of entertainment and news in the contemporary information ecology, a revolutionary transformation in entertainment media business practices and technology, alongside a decline in perceptions of trust in government and traditional media institutions,[12] comedy may be a unique force for change in pressing social justice challenges, such as global poverty, immigrant rights, gender equality, and climate change, to name only a few. Simultaneously, the post-9/11 sociocultural moment is characterized by renewed demands for social justice and equity, exemplified by social movements such as the Movement for Black Lives and #MeToo. Both the activism and cultural expression empowered by digital media converge to position comedy as a source of influence on today's social justice issues.

With the growth of entertainment in the streaming era, mediated comedy is finding new outlets beyond traditional gatekeepers, and the present-day entertainment marketplace is embracing and reflecting new voices and cultural identities. As a result, the digital media landscape has witnessed a surge of comedy. The contemporary mediated comedy menu includes an array of genres—some legacy, established forms, and some that emerged in the digital era—including satirical news, long-form sketch programs, scripted TV sitcoms, streaming comedy stand-up specials, short-form online videos destined for viral spread, documentary storytelling, and podcasts. The present-day U. S. comedy ecology includes a heavy dose of social-issue consciousness: through overt social justice commentary and topics in commercially successful comedy entertainment on legacy TV like NBC, HBO, Showtime, and Comedy Central; through new voices and audacious reflections on social justice issues on risk-taking streaming networks like Netflix and Amazon; through a rise in YouTube-enabled comedy; and through comedy producers like Funny or Die.

We position digital-era mediated comedy as a powerful influencer in contemporary social justice issues based on several specific ideas:

The entertainment marketplace for contemporary mediated comedy is embracing humor that includes social justice challenges. From a media industry perspective, mediated comedy's current moment is characterized by upheavals in economics, production, distribution, and consumption. The digital entertainment ecosystem is dominated by the upstarts—including Netflix and other streaming outlets—that have the power to shape and demonstrate a massive audience marketplace for diverse comedic voices that overtly take on social justice issues. Amanda Lotz articulated the authoritative cultural power asserted by the new streaming, niche-dominated TV environment, coining the term "phenomenal television" to describe "a particular category of programming that retains the cultural importance attributed to television's earlier operation as a cultural forum despite the changes of the post-network era" that limit its reach to a narrowcast audience.[13] Phenomenal television—new watercooler-moment entertainment—is characterized by its ability to cut through media clutter and reach incongruous, or unexpected, audiences due to its resonance with particular themes and discourses circulating in the culture and its attention to issues of social importance.[14] This is a useful characterization for our own articulation of comedy and social justice. Phenomenal TV projects may naturally tend to incorporate social justice topics because of their attention to matters of contemporary cultural, civic importance.

TV comedy sketch programs that skewer social issues such as race, gender politics, and class include the long-running *Saturday Night Live*, which reasserts its cultural legacy with each decade. Among other notable examples, legacy TV network ABC memorably portrayed the historic wedding of a gay couple, Mitch and Cam, on its hit sitcom *Modern Family*. Streaming networks like Amazon Studios have welcomed new voices and social-issue perspectives through scripted episodic programming like *Transparent*. Netflix has become a home for on-demand stand-up comedy specials; for example, its culturally acclaimed, Peabody Award–winning 2017 hit, *Homecoming King*, featured comedian Hasan Minhaj talking about his experiences of racism as an Indian American immigrant in the United States.[15] TV is not the sole domain of comedy that embraces social justice topics, however. Podcasts and online sites, like Funny or Die, are also influential sources.

As a far-reaching projector of cultural values and narratives, contemporary mediated comedy can serve as a site of cultural resistance. Comedy's prominent role and popularity in the dominant system of popular culture—the shared location where "we absorb the majority of our beliefs, ideologies, and cultural narratives"[16]—provides its central position of influence. Comedy is watched, shared, and discussed by millions of people in the digital age. Such reach matters, given that popular culture and the industrial production of entertainment is "the arena of consent and resistance. It is partly where hegemony arises, and where it is secured."[17] Dominant shared norms are fluid, and popular culture both reflects and shapes societal values and beliefs.[18]

For its part, contemporary mediated comedy—positioned prominently in the current entertainment marketplace through both reconfigured post-network TV[19] and the digital-native environment of YouTube and Funny or Die—is an engine for new ways of seeing, or an arena of resistance. The contemporary TV landscape, a dominant—but not the sole—domain for mediated comedy viewing, thus operates as a cultural institution and a cultural industry, "as a social conduit that participates in communicating values and ideas within a culture by telling stories and conveying information that reflects, challenges, and responds to shared debates and concerns."[20] To the extent that much contemporary comedy overtly includes social justice topics, it may thus provide a steady stream of cultural resistance.

Social justice topics—and diverse new comedy voices—are embraced by audiences in a cultural moment characterized by social justice struggle. Contemporary comedians are using their voices and platforms to assert their cultural identities and call out oppressive power dynamics. In turn, as a partial consequence of the shifting comedy and entertainment marketplace in the digital era, the voices of traditionally marginalized people and groups—racial and ethnic minorities, women, and sexual minorities—are not just increasingly seen in comedy, but also are rewarded by critical acclaim, media coverage, and audience buzz. For instance, after the attacks of September 11, 2001, as the United States turned the page on a new chapter of Islamophobia, Muslim-American comedians took to their microphones. In 2013, comedians Negin Farsad and Dean Obeidallah distributed their Netflix documentary, *The Muslims Are Coming!*, which featured their stand-up tour throughout the American Midwest and South, where they aimed to hilariously entertain audiences and "to combat what they call Islamophobia and to explain, reveal and connect with prejudice one passerby at a time."[21] In 2015, comedian Zahra Noorbakhsh and activist Tanzila "Taz" Ahmed launched the #GoodMuslimBadMuslim podcast to humorously address harmful Islamophobic stereotypes.[22]

Within the context of a cultural moment marked by struggle and calls for social equity, comedians themselves serve as social justice influencers in a range of ways. They are overtly calling for remedies to social problems, reframing issues in the news, asserting cultural identity, sharing experiences of discrimination and othering, and unmasking taboo topics. At a similar cultural and social justice moment, in 1960, *Time* magazine featured comedian Mort Sahl, made famous by his humorous social critique, in an in-depth article titled "Comedians: The Third Campaign," which focused on the powerful social influence of a new class of comedians as public intellectuals: "At 33, Mort Sahl is young, irreverent, and trenchant. With one eye on world news and the other on Variety, he is a volatile mixture of show business and politics, of exhibitionistic self-dedication and a seemingly sincere passion to change the world."[23] Notably, coinciding with a moment in which fewer than two in 10 Americans say they trust government, and not even half (45%) describe business leaders as honest and trustworthy,[24] a 2015 article in the *Atlantic* magazine ("How Comedians Became Public Intellectuals") asserted a similar premise:

> Comedians are acting not just as joke-tellers, but as truth-tellers—as guides through our cultural debates . . . comedians are doing their work not just in sweaty clubs or network variety shows or cable sitcoms, but also on the Internet. Wherever the jokes start—Comedy Central, The Tonight Show, Marc Maron's garage—they will end up, eventually and probably immediately, living online. They will, at their best, go "really, insanely viral." . . . . Comedy, like so much else in the culture, now exists largely of, by, and for the Internet. Which is to say that there are two broad things happening right now—comedy with moral messaging, and comedy with mass attention—and their combined effect is this: Comedians have taken on the role of public intellectuals.[25]

Satirical news, perhaps the most immediately recognizable in this context, is well documented as a source of political and civic information[26]—and an undisputed audience hit, with millions of views and shares. At its height, use of *The Daily Show* as a source of news and information—not just entertainment—rivaled that of traditional news programs, and its coverage was found to ideologically balance topics and perform a *de facto* watchdog function, particularly for civic issues, politicians, and the media.[27] Viewers' widespread embrace of satirical news has manifested in a handful of new shows—*Full Frontal with Samantha Bee*, *Last Week Tonight with John Oliver*—thus multiplying the reach of this kind of agenda-setting information and social critique packaged in comedy.

Mediated comedy in the digital era is shared widely, a public engagement mechanism and practice also central to contemporary networked social justice efforts. Within the context of a technologically engaged digital society, contemporary comedy's availability online is situated for the kind of peer sharing that also is a requirement for public engagement in social justice topics. The cultural imprint of comedy programming is amplified by the viral-sharing nature of digital-era entertainment, which allows content to reach well beyond the audiences who tune in to watch the full shows. Indeed, along with their full appointment-viewing episodes, comedy programs produce short-form video clips designed for easy online sharing. Along parallel lines, a YouTube-socialized digital audience is all too happy to share the objects of its cultural affection. How comedy's public engagement potential comes together and can manifest explicitly—based on its audience, agenda-setting, and discursive effects—is the core of the ensuing chapters. Of course, the peer-sharing, participatory properties of the digital era do not encompass the full spectrum of social-change possibilities, but they are central, parallel traits of both contemporary entertainment and social justice activism. The practices enabled by the networked culture are embedded in both digital-era entertainment and public engagement with social challenges.

Online comedy sites churn out funny short-form sketches, faux public service announcements, and other humorous treatments of the news and issues of the day. The major powerhouses garner millions of audience views among them: Funny or Die, *The Onion*, and *CollegeHumor*, along with *BuzzFeed* and *Upworthy*. In the online realm in particular, contemporary comedy's imprint lurks well beyond the traditional boundaries of entertainment: When former first lady Michelle Obama wanted to promote higher education to young people in the United States, she skipped the serious appeal and appeared in a comedic rap music video along with *Saturday Night Live* comedian Jay Pharoah, espousing the merits of getting a college degree—for *CollegeHumor*.[28] In a formal nod to comedy's reach and potential influence on U.S. policy, in 2015, Funny or Die created a department focused explicitly on producing comedy PSAs to engage policy leaders and the public in social and civic issues—including poverty, gun violence prevention, and climate change—in accessible, funny ways.[29]

ABOUT THE BOOK

A Comedian and an Activist Walk into a Bar: The Serious Role of Comedy in Social Justice is about the contemporary intersection of mediated comedy and social justice in the evolving, converged digital media age. The book illustrates how media and technological disruption—combined with newly invigorated calls for justice—have created the ideal conditions for boundary-pushing, socially critical comedy to not only thrive in the entertainment marketplace but also play a strategic role in social change efforts. We argue that mediated comedy, as a voraciously consumed and shared cultural product, is uniquely positioned to confront injustice and re-envision social reality in ways that engage and inspire.

In this context, we do not imagine comedy as a simple, tidy tactical tool for social change, as that thinking reduces it—falsely—to a lab-created mechanism able to produce predictable effects. Indeed, this is not our intent in this book. Comedy is, after all, art, with the creative serendipity embodied in such a form of artistic expression. As a widely beloved entertainment phenomenon, comedy is as old as the improv in Aristotle's ancient Greece and the physical pratfalls of vaudeville in early twentieth-century America, and as newly reinvented as the Funny or Die era of short-form online video.[30] This volume does not attempt a comprehensive full history or landscape of all entertainment comedy in the marketplace. Such a pursuit would be a different book, or, more likely, a compilation of the excellent existing works focused on comedy as entertainment. Instead, given our focus on social change, we argue that comedy's potential for public influence in the context of social issues is newly powerful in the digital media age. We concentrate on mediated comedy in distinct genres, including satirical news, scripted episodic TV, comedy documentary, stand-up comedy, and sketch.

As for social justice, when considering global problems that demand both consistent public engagement and remedy, the list is seemingly endless. From a contemporary global perspective, the closest articulation of established imperatives for social justice arrived first in the form of the United Nations' Millennium Development Goals in 2000, revisited and reconfigured 15 years later as the Sustainable Development Goals. Both sets of goals—a global to-do list—emphasize two key areas: climate change and the environment, and poverty,[31] to which we devote particular focus in Part II of the book. Throughout the book, we also reflect a range of other individual justice challenges—from civil rights to gun violence prevention to sexual assault.

As collaborators, we come to this topic from distinct professional vantage points along with shared perspectives and experiences. Together, we comprise a professional Venn diagram that includes communication scholarship, media strategy in the context of social change and justice, comedy, and creative media production—and a mentee stint with the game-changing comedy impresario Norman Lear. In this way, our lens is informed by, and reflects, scholarship, creative practice, and strategy at the heart of comedy and social justice. In our professional lives and combined body of work, we collaborate with scholars and researchers, social justice advocates, social-change communication strategists, comedians, and other creative storytellers. These intersecting perspectives underlie the book's approach and analysis.

With this premise in mind, the book stems from a series of intertwined questions, both theoretical and practical: In a niche-oriented, polarizing information ecology, how might mediated comedy be leveraged for social justice problems? How does comedy's influence work, and how can its appeal be harnessed in service of daunting, disturbing, complex social issues where public engagement can contribute to positive change? Similarly, when might comedy challenge troubling social norms, and where might it simply reinforce them? How do comedians themselves see their role in this intersection? How do social-change communication strategists and social justice leaders work collaboratively with comedy professionals? And, what are the actionable strategic recommendations and practices for scholars, students, change-makers, strategists, storytellers, and humanitarian organizations that may hope to adopt comedy in their efforts to improve the world?

In answering these fundamental questions, we locate mediated comedy—and its likely influence on social justice– within a sociocultural context at the convergence of media and entertainment, technology, and renewed social justice upheaval. We explicate five specific comedy genres—sketch, satirical news, scripted episodic TV, stand-up, and documentary—and their intersections with social justice. With this expansive focus on various comedy forms, we recognize the social-change role not only of comedy created with explicit social justice aims and targeted to narrower audiences, but also of mainstream comedy that illuminates social justice issues and has the potential for broader reach. This focus is embedded with a practical lens in mind for social-change organizations, human rights advocates, and strategists who may wish to leverage comedy in their missions, but don't know where to start or how to imagine it.

Our book is methodologically diverse and includes a range of perspectives, integrating original, in-depth interviews with comedians and change-makers that elucidate the evolving conditions and practices that support multisector collaborations, as well as comedians' conception of their role in a landscape where the lines between entertainment and activism are increasingly blurred; quantitative experimental audience research illustrating comedy's effects and its mechanisms of influence; analyses of contemporary comedic texts; as well as syntheses of existing scholarly literature. Through this approach, we offer a comprehensive, multipronged study of mediated comedy and social justice that intersects various facets of communication research—including industry dynamics, audience effects, cultural criticism, and strategic practice—in ways that we hope are valuable for scholars and practitioners alike.

The book is divided into three parts:

Part I—Comedy amidst a Contemporary Landscape of Influence and Information—provides the brief history, contemporary context, theoretical foundation, and definitions to explain how and why comedy can be a powerful force in service of today's social justice challenges. In chapter 1, "Why Comedy, and Why Now?" we illustrate the cultural, social, historical, media, and technological conditions that have given rise to contemporary social justice comedy, and we position comedy's cultural influence in the context of social justice.

Chapter 2, "Comedy's Pathways to Social Change," synthesizes interdisciplinary theory and research about the effects of comedy in social, civic, and political challenges. We locate four common forms of comedy's influence at the audience level: increasing message and issue attention, disarming audiences and lowering resistance to persuasion, breaking down social barriers, and stimulating sharing and discussion. In parallel, we highlight the broader effects that comedy can have on the wider cultural conversation through its influence on press coverage and social media discourse.

Chapter 3, "From Stand-Up to Sitcoms: Socially Critical Comedy across Genres," distinguishes five forms of comedy that leverage social justice topics and dominate the entertainment comedy marketplace: satirical news (such as *The Daily Show*), scripted episodic TV (such as *Black-ish*), stand-up (such as the Netflix special *Homecoming King*), sketch (such as *Saturday Night Live*), and comedy documentary (such as *The Muslims Are Coming!*). We situate each genre both historically and within the contemporary marketplace, describe its reach and influence, highlight notable examples, and illustrate its unique potential to engage audiences with social justice topics.

Part II—Comedy in Social Justice Challenges—focuses on how comedy has been used to communicate about two major global social justice challenges: climate change (chapter 4, "Can Laughter Help Save the Planet? Comedy's Role in Communicating about Climate Change") and poverty (chapter 5, "Beyond Poverty Porn: How Comedy Reframes Poverty and Engages Publics"). Here, we argue that comedy helps to empower and motivate audiences beyond the tragic, hopeless stories that often characterize public communication around these two issues. Using case studies of contemporary comedy examples and experiment-based audience research of comedy's effects, we show that comedy's influence on public engagement is due primarily to its ability to create entertaining media experiences and inspire positive emotions.

Part III—Leveraging Comedy for Social Change—gives voice to the comedians and social justice advocates who do this work, and in so doing, presents considerations and strategic recommendations for leveraging comedy in the pursuit of social justice. Chapter 6, "Comedians' Perspectives on the Intersections of Art and Activism," draws from interviews with comedy professionals who take on social issues in their work, including comedy performers, producers, writers, and TV showrunners—many of whom are members of traditionally marginalized gender, racial, and ethnic groups. The chapter reveals the nuanced ways in which comedians conceive of their own role—as well as of comedy more broadly—in entertainment and social change, along with their perspectives on and contributions to the evolution and diversification of the contemporary marketplace for comedic storytelling. Chapter 7, "Creative Collaborations: How Comedians and Social Justice Advocates Work Together," uses original interviews with social justice leaders and comedians to delve into cross-sector collaborations and the creative, strategic process between activists and comedians who have worked together to engage audiences in social challenges. Through case studies that illuminate these unique efforts, this chapter highlights opportunities and challenges inherent in comedian-activist collaborations, enabled by the participatory convergence culture. This chapter offers important practical considerations for activists and social change communicators who hope to work with comedians to achieve their goals.

Finally, chapter 8, "Imagining the Future of Comedy's Role in Social Justice," ties together the earlier chapters to underscore why and how comedy can engage publics with serious issues in the pursuit of social justice. It opens the door to highlight what's next by illuminating new initiatives in progress at the intersection of comedy and social change, considering unanswered questions in the arena of comedy and social change, and offering directions for future research and professional practice for communication scholars and practitioners as well as social justice advocates.

And so: Why comedy, and why now?

1 Why Comedy, and Why Now?

66 I sat in six months once at a Southern lunch counter. When they finally served me, they didn't have what I wanted. 99

Dick Gregory, comedian[1]

When comedy writer Lena Waithe walked onto the stage to receive her Primetime Emmy Award in 2017, she made TV history. For the first time, almost three-quarters of a century after the first Emmy commemorated television achievement,[2] the Outstanding Writing for a Comedy Series honor was awarded to an African American woman.[3] Bestowed for Waithe's work on the "Thanksgiving" episode of the comedy hit *Master of None*, several elements converged to create a noteworthy cultural moment.

The episode shared an autobiographical recounting of the writer coming out as a lesbian and gaining acceptance from her family, an experience showcased narratively on the show as a montage of successive family Thanksgiving gatherings.[4] The story itself also was not a typical TV portrait seen in years past. That Waithe's real story was spotlighted as comic fodder on season two of the critically acclaimed, award-winning show is not incidental. Known for its hilarious, incendiary social commentary on cultural identity, the immigrant experience, and racism in America,[5] *Master of None* was a breakout hit from Netflix, the undisputed Hollywood power player that continues to shape audience consumption habits and upend entertainment economics.[6] That behemoth Netflix is a digital-native network—which poses an "existential threat" to traditional

Figure 1 Comedy writer Lena Waithe accepts her award for Outstanding Writing for a Comedy Series for Netflix program *Master of None* at the 2017 Primetime Emmy Awards.

SOURCE / CREDIT: Michael Buckner / Shutterstock.com.

Hollywood and legacy TV networks—also is not incidental.[7] Netflix is known not only for reconfiguring audience behavior, but also for being the place where a new level of creative control lies in the hands of the story-tellers, where its executives have made a competitive bet on "generating programming people will want to watch and cannot get anywhere else."[8] The Lena Waithe moment, then, is best understood within a broader soci-ocultural context—characterized by seismic shifts in media consumption patterns and content changes in the streaming entertainment media era,[9] amidst ongoing demands for social justice and equity. In her Emmy Awards speech, which elicited a standing ovation from her entertainment industry peers—and virtual applause in the form of tweets, amplified by news media coverage in the U.S. and around the world[10]—Waithe addressed her "LGBTQIA family" directly:

> I see each and every one of you. The things that make us different—those are our superpowers. Every day when you walk out the door and put on your

imaginary cape and go out there and conquer the world, because the world would not be as beautiful as it is if we weren't in it. And for everybody out there that showed us so much love for this episode, thank you for embracing a little Indian boy from South Carolina and a queer black girl from the South Side of Chicago.[11]

The recognition Lena Waithe, *Master of None,* and Netflix received in the 2017 Emmy Awards exemplifies the contemporary moment at the convergence of digital media, a changing entertainment media system, comedy, and social justice. Such an occasion did not occur in a cultural vacuum. Instead, we argue that today's comedy is both a product of and contributor to a changing information and entertainment environment—and a cultural moment characterized by social justice upheaval. This chapter begins by characterizing the media and cultural conditions that have given rise to a new era of social justice comedy. Simultaneously, this era also has altered the processes and influences of social justice activism. The chapter then defines comedy, explicates its functions in the context of social change, and positions contemporary comedy and social justice within a sociohistorical context.

THE CONTEMPORARY LANDSCAPE OF INFORMATION AND INFLUENCE

A Reimagined Information Ecology

In a rapidly shifting media landscape, we are reimagining the cultural panorama of influence. Information is sliced, shared, parodied, and re-created. Admired truth-tellers are found beyond elected officials and legacy news outlets.[12] Publics are more actively engaged in their media environment than ever before, at least in terms of their ability to choose when, where, and what mediated content to consume, share, and create. The rapid shift from the analog era of the twentieth century to the digital era of the twenty-first is characterized by several major developments: the rise in internet availability and use, the adoption of tablets and smartphones, an increase in connectivity afforded by social media, and a transformation in the delivery of entertainment. Consequently, we are living in a moment also distinguished by niche media and news,[13] an explosion of new entertainment, and the continued blurring of information and entertainment.[14] Against such a backdrop, new forms and possibilities for influence—for both comedy and social justice activism, and the intersection of the two—emerge.

The Pew Internet and American Life Project references "three technology revolutions"[15] in Americans' media lives in the twenty-first century: the dramatic rise in broadband or internet access at home; smartphone ownership;[16] and social media use.[17] Around the world, the pattern is similar, as internet access continues to rise exponentially.[18] Although the digital transformation was heating up in years prior, 2004 marks the starting line of perhaps the most rapid and dramatic shift in entertainment and information delivery—and audience behavior. As the first transformative players on the social media scene, Facebook launched in 2004 and opened to a noncollege audience in 2006,[19] followed by YouTube in 2005[20] and Twitter in 2006.[21] Social media was—and continues to be—a game-changer in the digital media revolution as individuals are newly able to consume, produce, and widely share information.[22] When smartphones came along, with the first iPhone and Android phones in 2007, the transformation accelerated.[23] Simultaneously, possibilities emerged for new forms of entertainment—created and curated for audiences that now expect to discover and share long- and short-form entertainment and information anytime and anywhere.

In the digital age, mediated entertainment has undergone transformative changes in industrial production and distribution. Power dynamics of once-bedrock film and traditional TV networks have shifted as the streaming era's influential digital-native competitors are reshaping audience consumption norms. Media scholar Amanda Lotz characterizes the shift in television as "extraordinary and on the scale of the transition from one medium to another, as in the case of the shift from radio to television."[24] Further, the broader system of entertainment media has morphed, as Lotz summarizes: "The audience's experiences with computing and the emergence of the mobile phone as a sophisticated portal screen technology better thought of as a 'pocket computer' than a 'phone' are now as important to understanding television as the legacy behaviors of domestic viewing. Various industrial, technological, and cultural forces have begun to radically redefine television."[25]

In 2010, when Netflix evolved from a mail-order-DVD service to streaming top-tier entertainment content[26]—and again in 2013 when it streamed its first bona fide, originally produced hit, *House of Cards*—the beginning of the digital-media entertainment metamorphosis began in earnest. As a digital-native entertainment company, Netflix is free of both the demands for safer mass-audience content and the regulatory constraints of the three-network "network era" of the 1950s through the 1980s, as well as the "multichannel era" of cable's expansion in the 1990s.[27] Accordingly, Netflix has been able to provide bold new content and, along the way, change audience consumption habits—giving us entertainment we want, when we want it, in as many episodes as we can handle at one time. Now with more than 100 million members in 190 countries,[28] Netflix's experiment in streaming and new content has clearly paid off; in 2017 alone, viewers watched about 140 million Netflix hours a day, with the vast majority accounted for by Netflix original programming, not content acquired from legacy networks.[29] Jumping on the new entertainment-delivery bandwagon, Amazon provided streaming entertainment starting in 2012,[30] with original content following quickly in 2013.[31] A little more than a decade after its launch as a host for amateur user-generated material, YouTube began developing new original entertainment content.[32] In the era of entrepreneurial innovation, streaming networks are taking risks with new content—including comedy that increasingly takes on social justice topics.

Audience behavior moves in tandem with the redefined entertainment environment and digital media culture. Viewers by the millions have shown their affinity for viewing and sharing short-form material—like comedy—via YouTube and social media. In fact, according to Lotz, "late-night talk and comedy shows seemed to make the most effective use of asynchronous possibilities, as the unexpected gaffes in guest interviews or uncommonly humorous bits were widely shared and viewed in the following days and often effectively archived indefinitely."[33] That digital technology has provided mechanisms for easy sharing is not the full story of new digital entertainment's influence, of course, nor is the now-routine protocol of entertainment brands uploading their funny and engaging bits on YouTube. Rather, "the circulation of media content . . . depends heavily on consumers' active participation," according to scholar Henry Jenkins.[34] His "participatory culture" perspective embraces the active engagement of the public in creating content, re-creating it, and generating new meaning through social interactions—media-enabled public engagement.[35] Between new networks borne of the digital age, user-generated material discovered by audiences, and social sharing, the ability and willingness of audiences to discover and search and watch and share is, indeed, part of the transformation. For its part, comedy—and comedy enabled for social justice—fits squarely within the participatory culture's digital media revolution.

Influence in a Converged, Niche Media Environment

In the frenetic digital age—where views, peer-to-peer shares, follows, and likes can set the legacy media agenda[36]—news and entertainment media, and their influence on civic life, have become inextricably blurred.[37] Just as news often deals in gossip and frivolities, entertainment increasingly takes on serious topical issues. Given the theoretical and practical challenges of distinguishing between news and entertainment, political communication scholars Bruce Williams and Michael X. Delli Carpini find it more useful to characterize media content as either civically relevant or irrelevant, based on its "utility" for democratic engagement.[38] In so doing, mediated comedy that deals with civic topics can be more readily taken seriously as influential public affairs media.

Additionally, in the digital media era, audiences have the ability to create their own customized entertainment and information diets. It is, increasingly, an era of the niche media consumer, which has implications for both news and entertainment consumption, as well as for those who wish to engage broad publics through media. Media scholar Natalie Stroud has examined the partisan divide in news exposure, which she calls "niche news." Stroud's research shows that citizens' choice of like-minded news media can have polarizing effects on public opinion and political behavior;[39] yet, such niche news also can inspire partisans to be actively civically engaged, therefore affording it "a place in a democracy."[40]

Entertainment media also exist in a similar niche moment, but humor scholar Amber Day asserts that such an environment opens up additional possibilities for new, riskier comedy content. Specifically, competitive networks are more willing to engage in controversial comedy material—such as satire that takes on social justice issues—since they do not necessarily aim for the mass-appeal audiences of earlier eras.[41] As we elucidate in this book's introduction and in the comedy history section of this chapter, comedy has always existed—and continues to do so—as bolder niche material as well as mainstream mass-audience fodder. Indeed, we argue that comedy's dual niche and mass appeal contribute to its influence in social justice efforts; niche comedy that is sought by like-minded audiences may mobilize groups for collective action, and at the same time, other mass-appeal comedy (as in network sitcoms) has the ability to reach beyond the echo chamber of like-minded thinkers.[42] Reaching beyond niche audiences is thus both a challenge and an opportunity when it comes to comedy and social justice. The information and entertainment revolution does not happen in a cultural void, of course, as parallel changes in social justice activism in the digital era continue to ripple out.

SOCIAL CHANGE AND ACTIVISM IN THE INFORMATION AGE

Defining Social Justice and Social Change

History is characterized by sweeping moments of social upheaval that endeavor to expand equity and human rights through changes in law and policy. However, as history also shows, social change is embodied not only in formal laws and policies, but also in shifts in social norms, forged through public opinion, attitudes, and perceptions about individuals, groups, and issues—who is worthy of attention and who is not, who is visible and who remains unseen. As a concept, social justice embraces "values such as the equal worth of all citizens, their equal right to meet their basic needs, the need to spread opportunity and life chances as widely as possible, and finally, the requirement that we reduce and, where possible, eliminate unjustified inequalities."[43] In practice, social justice is synonymous with active, civically engaged efforts to ensure that all people—regardless of inequitable circumstances of birth, physical ability, gender, socioeconomic class, sexual identity, race or ethnicity—have access and opportunity to pursue healthy lives free of unfair treatment.

As a phrase, "social change," in the context of clarifying mediated comedy's possible role, is deliberately broad and inclusive. While the study of social change exists in disparate professional and scholarly arenas, we use a broad definition of "social change" from scholars Arvind Singhal and Everett Rogers, given their focus on the role and influence of entertainment media and narrative: "The process in which an alteration occurs in the structure and function of a social system. Social change can happen at the level of the individual, community, and organization or a society."[44] This articulation invites us to consider a full spectrum of social-change outcomes and their relationship with media and mediated narratives, from raising awareness and changing attitudes and behaviors at the individual level to macro-level shifts in social norms, media agendas, and institutional policy.

Social Change in a Networked Media Culture

Throughout history up to the present day, struggles to achieve social justice and social change are characterized by the central role of publics and the myriad groups and organizations that comprise civil society. Publics—individuals who come together to solve common challenges—provide a crucial check and balance on inherent institutional power structures, such as government and business.[45] Active public engagement is critical to identifying problems, expressing ideas about solutions, and pushing for change in individuals, institutions, and prevailing narratives. Alongside active publics, nonprofit advocacy organizations serve in a vital collaborative position, acting as a professional hub for social justice efforts: "Nonprofit organizations, interest groups and advocacy organizations are crucial conduits for the articulation and representation of the legal, political and policy interests of groups such as women, people of color, and low-income people, who have traditionally been underserved by the two major political parties and underrepresented within the electoral system."[46] Efforts for social change are thus characterized by noninstitutionalized outsiders attempting to shift a status quo that is usually enforced by privilege of dominant social hierarchy and institutions. Scholars of social movements assert that the act of changing a status quo usually requires "noninstitutionalized methods," such as protest—mediated or physical—but also often includes institutionalized means of action, such as formal advocacy and lobbying by organizations.[47]

In the social media era, practices and technologies for civic engagement have evolved. Individuals and groups engage with decision-makers, the broader public, and media in ways that have weakened traditional gate-keepers and enabled previously underreported issues to break through. Scholar Manuel Castells calls this the era of the "networked social move-ment," in which the two-way interactive style of social networks like Facebook and Twitter have rendered social justice movements, such as the Arab Spring and Occupy Wall Street in 2011, inherently more participa-tory and democratic.[48] According to Castells, networked social move-ments are deeply reliant on media and are characterized by several key traits: They are networked in both offline and online ways, often begin-ning with an online call to action that translates into media coverage and offline activity such as a march or protest; they can be simultaneously local and global given the reach of social media; they are viral and partici-patory.[49] Similarly, W. Lance Bennett and Alexandra Segerberg argue that social movements are increasingly based on a "logic of connective action," whereby digital media act as organizing agents, and movements coalesce when individuals share their personal stories, experiences, and reasons for taking action on social media.[50] Scholar Zeynep Tufekci emphasizes the digital-era power of the attention economy—that is, a transformed ability for individuals and groups to set and command a media agenda and atten-tion to social justice topics—as a characteristic and practice of contempo-rary social movements.[51]

In addition to efforts to engage publics and decision-makers through direct calls to action, the work of social change also requires shifting the cultural narrative. Entertainment storytelling—which encompasses comedy—sits within a massive cultural stew of mediated stories and icons and images, thus acting as a contributor to the "civic imagination," which scholar Henry Jenkins defines as "the capacity to imagine alternatives to current social, political, or economic institutions or problems," and, at the same time, to "imagine oneself as an active political agent."[52] According to Jenkins, popular culture, by harnessing the power of stories, increas-ingly offers the resources needed to fuel the civic imagination. When

media audiences create connections between entertainment narratives—
including comedy—and the real world, this can provide a way for publics
to not only envision a more just society but also to act on that vision.
Comedy can help realize the civic imagination, by offering both a new perspective on social reality and a form of social critique. It is, therefore, in
lockstep with social justice. Comedy—as a rabidly shared and avidly consumed form of cultural narrative that can introduce new perspectives and
new voices in the digital age, and can offer a creatively deviant lens on a
problematic status quo—contributes to a new societal portrait by which
people shape and interpret meaning.

Within this vibrant, participatory media and civic culture, the power of
cultural narrative in social justice is profound. Social justice advocates are
leveraging this understanding and the new voices enabled by the streaming, YouTube era, by partnering with storytellers and creating their own
narratives, and by working with entertainment programs that are already
popular in the audience marketplace. In chapter 7, we spotlight contemporary strategic, creative collaborative social justice efforts in the context
of comedy.

COMEDY AND SOCIAL JUSTICE: DEFINITIONS, CULTURAL INFLUENCE, HISTORY

Defining Comedy

The earliest known definition of comedy comes from Aristotle's work espousing the dual cathartic forces of tragedy and comedy; the Greek philosopher's
articulation of wit, around the fourth century BC, is "a means between buf-
foonery and boorishness," and a sense of poking fun at what is so disgraceful
it becomes laughable.[53] In Aristotle's view, humor derives from feelings of
superiority when we encounter those who are less virtuous than us. Notably,
Aristotle's original concept of comedy envisioned a mechanism that allows a
culture to reflect a mirror on itself and to offer a lens for critique.[54] Comedy,
then, is a kind of societal "corrective"—a new perspective on the status quo.[55]
Early comedy of Aristotle's time began in improvisation, an embodiment of
artistic freedom that continues today in the production of mediated comedy.
Many centuries later, psychologist Sigmund Freud focused similarly on

comedy's societal purposes in his seminal book, *Jokes and Their Relation to the Unconscious*: to raise taboo topics in the culture, to challenge existing social conditions, and to act as a form of catharsis.[56] From the beginning, comedy was understood as an active, artistic way to see a dominant state of affairs in a new way—and indeed, to critique it.

Outside of Aristotle's superiority theory of humor and Freud's interpretation of humor as catharsis, a third conceptualization—reflected in many contemporary understandings of comedy, and one that we take up more fully in chapter 2—underscores incongruity.[57] Philosophy scholar Simon Critchley explains that "humour is produced by a disjunction between the way things are and the way they are represented in the joke, between expectation and actuality."[58] In other words, to feel amused enough to laugh, the audience must be able to recognize both the status quo and the incongruent, unexpected reinterpretation of the status quo that comedy offers. Comedy is a sophisticated form of cultural expression, then, that requires both a comedian's and an audience's understanding of a state of affairs in order to process—and find funny—the humorous contortion of reality. Perhaps not surprisingly, given this context, comedy also has been positioned as a mechanism used by powerless groups and people to resist and poke fun at prevailing ideologies.[59]

Cultural Influence of Comedy in the Context of Social Justice

Several scholars, spotlighted here, position comedy as a positive change agent due to the power of its distribution and its fun and entertaining qualities, and thus, its ability to spread ideas.[60] They conceptualize comedy as a megaphone for alternative perspectives and social commentary,[61] and as a route to cultural citizenship and identity for groups and people who are traditionally marginalized.[62] In this broad cultural view, comedians have the potential to influence norms in a positive direction.[63] To consider comedy's ability to provide a voice for alternative views and social commentary, we first acknowledge that communities operate within dominant cultural hierarchies, value structures, and norms. And thus, providing an alternative lens grants a kind of reflective check and balance.

In this context, theorist John Limon conceptualizes American stand-up comedy as abjection and revolt—rejecting dominant ideology.[64] Similarly, theater scholar Sophie Quirk articulates comedy as "an important form of social comment and dispute."[65] Comedy, then, provides a way for a counterculture to express "deviant ideas" and acts as a form of resistance to a prevailing dominant status quo.[66] Scholar Lawrence Mintz emphasizes the social challenge inherent in all jokes, which "contain a critique of the gap between what is and what we believe should be."[67] Moreover, because the new ideas are presented as "only a joke," humor can bypass usual frames of societal acceptance, creating a temporary state in which dominant norms or power dynamics can be reexamined.[68] Notably, this perspective does not require comedians' explicit intentions to influence social issues; all comedy has the raw ability to be influential as alternative social commentary. In other words, comedy doesn't need to be regarded as "social justice comedy"—comedy intended to overtly help reimagine social issues—to be impactful. Whether intentional or not, comedy has the potential to influence, and "all comedians participate in a process which challenges and renegotiates societal norms, whether or not they, themselves, intend or acknowledge it."[69]

Related to challenging dominant norms and societal structures, scholars have examined comedy in the context of social change by considering representation and cultural identity. Traditionally marginalized people—as a function of race, ethnicity, gender, socioeconomic status, sexual orientation and identification—face disproportionate challenges related to justice, discrimination, and inequity; thus, asserting cultural identity and inclusion is a meaningful step toward broader social change. Through this lens, comedy allows traditionally marginalized individuals to proclaim their cultural identities to a dominant culture;[70] critique stereotypes in order to create new identity narratives;[71] express "a critical perspective otherwise unavailable to mainstream audiences;"[72] overtly skewer and confront problematic assumptions about groups;[73] and, in the case of race and ethnicity, "engage in critical self-reflexivity and embrace meaningful social change by revealing concrete examples of white privilege and racism."[74]

Despite giving voice to alternative views and traditionally powerless individuals, comedy can often also simply reinforce dominant culture. Philosopher Critchley provides a cautionary note about the limits of what he calls the "comedy of recognition," which "simply seeks to reinforce consensus and in no way seeks to criticize the established order or change the situation in which we find ourselves."[75] Indeed, as film and TV scholar Bambi Haggins asserts, in comedy, "the mobilization of stereotypes contains the potential to confront *and* conform to popularly, if silently, held racial stereotypes."[76] Political communication scholar Mary Stuckey makes a similar point in the context of political engagement, arguing that "contemporary stand-up comedians can challenge the system, and in so doing, can unite an audience as a people. At the same time, their comedy can have the opposite effect, increasing national divisions and exploiting the partisan divide."[77] Considering that the entertainment marketplace for mediated comedy has historically been dominated by white, male voices[78]—although the portrait is changing incrementally—this is a point worth remembering. A partial solution is an entertainment and public marketplace shift that welcomes and rewards comedy voices who offer diverse racial, ethnic, and gender perspectives. Indeed, this evolution is in play, as we illustrate throughout the book.

Culture scholar Rebecca Krefting considers the intersection of social change, cultural identity, and comedy through a distinct characterization of humor—"charged humor," meaning "comic performers who intentionally produce humor-challenging social inequality and cultural exclusion,"[79] such as Hari Kandabolu and W. Kamau Bell, among others, whose paths were paved by comedians of the mid-twentieth century. She explains the distinction in terms of intention and content:

> Some jokes are tears in the fabric of our beliefs. They challenge the myths we sustain about how fair and democratic our society is and the behaviors and practices we enact every day to maintain that fiction. In other words, we are all supposed to be equal, but social, economic, and political forces collude to maintain inequality. Jokesters unmask inequality by identifying the legal arrangements and cultural attitudes and beliefs contributing to their subordinated status—joking about it, challenging that which has become normalized and compulsory, and offering new solutions and strategies.[80]

Krefting's concept of "charged humor" is rooted in the theory of cultural citizenship, which asserts that many individuals in a society or community, regardless of legal status, "have not been granted full rights as citizens based on age, sexuality, race, religion, and ability."[81] This inequality, grounded in formal structures and informal cultural norms, is persistent and calls for societal challenge through corrective messages and more inclusive representation; part of this corrective process of "building cultural citizenship involves taking control of a public image created by others to maintain hierarchies; it is about empowering otherwise marginalized social identities."[82] Entrenched in the concept of "the other"—who belongs and who doesn't—comedy that intentionally challenges dominant norms has the potential to foster change by influencing attitudes and beliefs and by humanizing marginalized groups who are often the objects of othering.[83] This form of humor is often, although not exclusively, embodied in the material of alternative or lesser-known comedians. Yet socially conscious humor also can be located firmly in the mainstream; Krefting uses Chris Rock as an example: "It is activist humor, even if the speaker may not be a formal activist and is simply using the stage as a platform to advocate on behalf of a political cause or social issue."[84]

Notably, Krefting recognizes the potential for charged comedy to contribute to social change by helping to evolve audience attitudes, beliefs, and behavior.[85] However, she also acknowledges that the effectiveness of comedy in the context of social change can be difficult to measure. While Krefting situates comedy as a potential vehicle for social change, she calls for research to understand the impact of comedy on audiences in a more explicit way. We agree, and we offer support for this idea in this book; indeed, chapter 2 focuses entirely on synthesizing what we know from existing research, chapters 4 and 5 offer new empirical evidence for comedy's influence, chapters 6 and 7 offer perspectives of comedians and social justice advocates, and we call for further explorations in chapter 8. As scholar Quirk posits, it would be difficult to imagine that attitudes and beliefs aren't influenced by comedy about social issues in a longer-term "ethereal" sense, the gradual ebb and flow of public opinion.[86] But how and why these shifts can happen, and how overt change can be fueled by comedy—and the role social justice advocates can play as collaborators— are matters for this book's later chapters.

Comedy History in a Sociocultural Context

Historically, the U. S. entertainment marketplace has been shaped by the popularity of comedy as a simultaneously mass- and niche-oriented genre of audience amusement, but it also has been fashioned by game-changing comedians who created art by making fun of dominant power structures and hierarchies. Throughout the second half of the twentieth century, changes in the business and distribution of entertainment and audience consumption patterns—and trailblazing comedy personalities—paved the way for a contemporary comedy ecosystem that has increasingly embraced social consciousness and traditionally marginalized voices. By situating the history and evolution of mediated comedy within a sociocultural con-text, we can distinguish a parallel contemporary era of comedy poised for present-day social justice activism.[87]

Today's mediated comedy finds its historical roots at the convergence of dramatic cultural change and working-class appeal. At the dawn of the tumultuous early twentieth century in the United States, vaudeville was the dominant form of entertainment, a form of live theater show com-posed of brief vignettes, broad and inexpensive enough to be appreciated by the whole family.[88] Several of today's mediated comedy forms began in vaudeville as short theatrical routines performed live on stage to the early mass audience. As vaudeville and burlesque evolved in the early 1900s, so, too, did the comedy, from sketch-based humor based on physical pratfalls and mild violence, to a new form. Performing at New York's Palace club, vaudevillian Frank Fay began a stint as a comedy emcee around 1917, among the first comedians to simply stand in one place and perform jokes.[89] Stand-up comedy was thus born, the beginning of a genre that would shape virtually every comedian, well into the next century and today. Another comedy genre, sketch comedy, also started in vaudeville with acts like Buster Keaton and Groucho Marx.[90]

Radio was the next major mediated home for comedy, during and after the Great Depression.[91] Radio comedy stars, who then became the earliest TV comedy stars, started in vaudeville, including Milton Berle, Bob Hope, and George Burns.[92] As radio's dominance as a primary home-based entertainment mechanism ended and TV took off in the 1950s, executives at the broadcast networks of TV's network era—ABC, NBC, CBS—needed material to fill their channels. Comedy was an immediate audience sensa-tion on TV, introducing programs that helped to shape today's mediated humor forms: sketch, scripted sitcom, and late-night programs featuring comedy acts. Indeed, many of TV's early big hits were comedy programs, including the sitcom *I Love Lucy* with comedienne Lucille Ball; *Texaco Star Theater* with vaudeville comedian Milton Berle; *Your Show of Shows* with Sid Caesar, a sketch comedy program; *Colgate Comedy Hour* with Jerry Lewis and Dean Martin; and *The Ed Sullivan Show* and *The Tonight Show*, both of which introduced new and emerging stand-up comedians to national audiences.[93]

Notably, radio and TV, fueled by an economic system supported by advertising and mass audiences, came along with content regulation from the newly created Federal Communications Commission (FCC). Content in the early network era of TV was thus characterized by "least objectionable programming,"[94] which limited the potential for comedy with overt social commentary. However, through the formative TV years—the 1950s through the 1970s—comedy laced with explicit social critique partially found its way to audiences through a route of media adaptation, exploiting new forms of distribution and pushing the boundaries of gatekeeper-controlled traditional entertainment.[95] For instance, live performance venues in New York became the places for comedians to hone their art. Their risqué material then cycled back into early TV variety shows as comics were "discovered" through their live acts.[96]

In turn, a heyday of comedy records in the 1950s through the 1970s allowed some of the era's most socially critical comedians—Redd Foxx, Richard Pryor, Lenny Bruce, and Dick Gregory—to find audiences for such salacious topics as racism, inequality, and politics.[97] Conformity imposed by mass-audience radio and early TV coincided with, and likely shaped, alternative distribution mechanisms, including both live performance clubs and comedy records. This adaptation, seen in the early days of mediated comedy through the present day's internet era, reveals how comedians gradually drive market forces and help shape audience acceptance of, and demand for, comedy that pushes social boundaries. Historically, then, mediated comedy with social critique has always existed as both mass-audience marketplace fare, as in the case of TV network sitcoms and sketch comedy, as well as material that thrives with niche-audience demand, as in live shows and records—and today, online streaming and podcasts.

Comedy's game-changing impresarios of the late 1950s, 1960s, and 1970s established the roots for a contemporary intersection of comedy and social justice. Comedy rebels' creative material and social justice proclivities did not occur in a sociocultural bubble, of course, as demands for social equity and justice converged during the social movements of the 1960s and 1970s.[98] In this way, social upheaval and calls for social justice intertwined historically with comedy, paving the road for today's new comedy voices to take on social issues.[99] Mort Sahl, Lenny Bruce, Dick Gregory, and the Smothers Brothers are widely attributed by scholars, historians, and comedians as game-changers in this regard[100]—followed by George Carlin and Richard Pryor—known for openly discussing racism and social inequity—as well as other, more contemporary comedians.[101]

Historians generally credit stand-up comedian Lenny Bruce, whose frequent charges of obscenity and indecent content in live comedy regularly landed him in jail, as a notable early comedy talent known for overtly skewering established norms through social critique of racism and inequality, along with other topics.[102] His new brand of social critique "showed the possibilities of an art form that suddenly seemed cool and consequential."[103] In turn, Bruce helped to influence 1960s and 1970s sketch comedy, newly formed humor theater groups that were shaped to be socially critical and uncensored against the backdrop of the civil rights and antiwar movements of the day, such as Chicago's The Second City, New York's The Premise,[104] and The Committee in San Francisco.[105]

Dick Gregory, the trailblazing, commercially successful African American stand-up comedian, explicitly talked about racial justice and civil rights in his routines. In fact, Gregory's work at the intersection of comedy and social justice goes much further than Bruce's. He is as well known—perhaps better known—for his activism in the civil rights era. Media scholar Bambi Haggins writes of Gregory:

> In 1960, the clean-cut comic, dressed in the conservative manner that replicated the civil rights protestors of the era (a dark suit and tie), had broken the color line when he brought socio-politically charged black humor to the comedy club mainstream. By 1963 Gregory, whose comedy confronted racial inequality, was using his celebrity to bring attention to the struggle: Gregory was on the front line, leading the first wave of black teens and children in the Children's Crusade of the Birmingham protest.[106]

Just as comedy helped to spotlight the struggle for racial justice, the civil rights movement also shaped comedy. According to Haggins: "The civil rights movement not only transformed multiple black ideologies—social and political practices, as well as black thought—but it also changed the nature of black comedy . . . race was placed squarely on the table in a highly discursive way."[107]

In 1970s America, amidst the tumultuous terrain of the Vietnam War, women's equality movement, and civil rights, comedy increasingly provided social commentary on the juxtaposed absurdness of reality and the ideal.[108] In the first comedy revolution of the late 1950s and 1960s, women comedians "faced a show business establishment that was not yet ready to fully embrace them" and "the comedy-club world itself didn't seem particularly welcome to women either."[109] But in the 1970s, amid the women's movement, a few female comedians, including Elayne Boosler—the first to overtly talk about gender without stereotypes—gained recognition,[110] paving a path for future comediennes like Jean Carroll and Joan Rivers.[111]

During the same time frame—and well into the 1980s—TV writer-producer Norman Lear's pathbreaking brand of socially relevant scripted TV comedy dominated Americans' living rooms with sharp satire and comedy about issues that reflected the fraught time in the country. Programs like *All in the Family, The Jeffersons,* and *Maude* delved into topics as deeply sensitive as race relations and bigotry, gay rights and identity, poverty, gender relations and equality, war, abortion, and menopause.[112] Reaching more than 120 million viewers a week, Lear's programs have been widely credited with shifting social norms, particularly around race and gender; President Clinton stated, while bestowing on Lear the National Medal of Arts, "Norman Lear has held up a mirror to American society and changed the way we look at it."[113] Lear's imprint continues well into the contemporary era, as boundary-pushing comedy TV showrunners like Ryan Murphy (*Glee*) and Kenya Barris (*Black-ish*) have cited his unflinching comedic treatment of social issues as inspiration.[114]

This time period also paved the way for social and political criticism through sketch comedy on mainstream TV, and it laid the foundation for today's satirical news programs. Decades after its vaudevillian roots, mediated sketch comedy was popularized by programs like *Rowan & Martin's Laugh-In*, a variety sketch show that was TV's most-watched in its first two seasons (1968 and 1969).[115] The program was one of the earliest precursors to *The Daily Show* format through its satirical news treatments in the "Laugh-in Looks at the News" segment, which examined and poked fun at the network news of the day.[116] Two years after the program went off the air in 1973, one of the program's writers, Lorne Michaels, created the enduring sketch comedy juggernaut that satirizes topical social and political issues, *Saturday Night Live*[117]—a show that Michaels, from inception, shaped to be "hip and dangerous."[118] The contemporary mediated stage for comedy—and the intersection with social justice topics—was thus set during this crucial time frame as the TV era came of age, against the backdrop of cultural demands for equity.

Within the context of comedy and social justice, moving forward to today and into the future, it is important to spotlight the fact that—despite some notable exceptions—the voices of women, racial and ethnic minorities, and members of sexual minority groups are generally missing from this highlighted history. There is no question that the analog media era of comedy was overwhelmingly dominated by (heterosexual) white men; comedy scholars and historians acknowledge this hegemonic reality even while articulating comedy's potential—and actual—cultural influence as a social change agent.[119] Indeed, most of history's comedy game-changers who boldly took on social justice issues, including problems and realities facing marginalized groups, were not themselves members of these communities.

In the context of show business as an industry, this is not unique to comedy, however. Historically and in the present day, white men dominate decision-making positions of power in the entertainment business.[120] How, then, can comedy be imagined as a cultural contributor to social justice when, historically speaking, the voices of those who are subject to oppression, othering, and discrimination are not included directly? This is a crucial question that we do not take lightly. We argue that the portrait is gradually changing in the digital era, although matters of equity are not nearly resolved. In fact, the emergent voices of traditionally excluded, marginalized voices—among both comedians and social justice advocates—is a subtheme of this book. We illustrate this changing portrait throughout the ensuing chapters.

Positioning comedy and social justice in a sociohistorical context reveals patterns that are notably similar to today's digital, social-media age, in terms of radical entertainment media technology shifts and calls for social justice. Each moment of upheaval in the dominant entertainment delivery technologies of the twentieth century converged with cultural shifts in which audiences both accepted—and demanded—mediated comedy embedded with social consciousness and critique. In the digital, post-9/11 era, the door has swung wide open, both for comedy and for social justice, and the intersection of the two—a cultural space where new voices emerge, and where audiences make meaning of comedy as a source of entertainment and information about the world they inhabit.

2 How Comedy Works as a Change Agent

❝ Comedy doesn't change things. Comedy changes people. People change things. ❞

> Sara Taksler, director of *Tickling Giants* documentary
> and former senior producer of *The Daily Show*[1]

In 2011, as the U.S. presidential campaign was beginning to heat up, Stephen Colbert—then-host of Comedy Central's satiric *The Colbert Report*—did what many may have considered impossible: he made campaign finance law understandable—and *funny*. He did this by legally creating his own super PAC, "Americans for a Better Tomorrow, Tomorrow." Super PACs are independent, expenditure-only political action committees that can raise unlimited contributions from corporations, labor unions, and individuals, and then use these funds to explicitly advocate for or against political candidates.[2] For campaign finance reform advocates, super PACs exemplify and exacerbate the lack of transparency in the U.S. campaign finance system and the corrupt role that money can play in democratic politics.[3]

Over the course of nearly two years—with the help of his recurring guest Trevor Potter, a lawyer and former Federal Election Commission chairman—Colbert humorously illustrated how super PACs work and why they matter and, in so doing, mocked the loopholes in the campaign finance system. For example, in one segment, Colbert and Potter demonstrated how anonymous contributions to 501(c)(4) "social welfare"

Figure 2 Stephen Colbert appeals for donations to his Super PAC on Comedy Central's *The Colbert Report.*
SOURCE / CREDIT: Comedy Central video screenshot, fair use.

organizations can be funneled to super PACs; this allows wealthy donors to evade super PAC disclosure requirements and keep their identities secret—a process that both Colbert and Potter agreed resembles "money laundering."[4] Colbert also revealed the often close coordination between supposedly independent super PACs and the candidates that they support, despite the explicit prohibition of such coordination: When Colbert himself tried to run for president, he signed control of his super PAC over to his friend and fellow Comedy Central host Jon Stewart, and gave it a new, tongue-in-cheek name, "The Definitely Not Coordinating with Stephen Colbert Super PAC."

Colbert's super PAC proved to be more than just a late-night stunt. One study found that people who watched *The Colbert Report* during the 2012 general election season knew more about campaign finance law and, as a result, were more concerned about the role of money in politics.[5] Moreover, *The Colbert Report* had a greater impact on campaign finance knowledge than any of the traditional news sources assessed in the study. Other research showed that Colbert's super PAC spurred wide media coverage and analysis of campaign finance, thereby helping to increase public attention to the issue and shape the terms of the debate.[6] At the same time, Colbert's super PAC raised more than a million dollars from his fans, most of which he donated to charitable organizations.[7]

The purpose of this chapter is to explain how and why something like Colbert's super PAC—a comedic take on a complex topic—can increase knowledge, change attitudes, shape public conversation, and even inspire action. Colbert's super PAC was incredibly effective at bringing to life a topic that otherwise may make people's eyes glaze over. Through comedy, Colbert distilled difficult concepts down to digestible nuggets, playfully critiqued the status quo, and constructed an engaging narrative. These are elements shared by much contemporary comedy that addresses social issues.

This chapter takes as its starting point the idea that comedy's path to social change works—at least in part—through its effects on audiences. Social change is a gradual process that involves large-scale shifts in norms, attitudes, and behavior over time. We recognize that a short comedy sketch or even a multiseason TV series cannot, on its own, produce sweeping change at the societal level. But it *can* galvanize attention, spark conversation, change how some people think and feel about social issues and groups, and foment activism. In turn, this incremental change—in combination with other influences—may, over the long haul, add up to a shift in majority opinion or behavior within a culture, put pressure on elected officials to change relevant policy, and/or create a broader climate for social change.

In the sections that follow, we synthesize research that illuminates the efficacy—and limits—of comedy as a vehicle for social change. We argue that at the individual level, comedy has four primary effects that are important in the context of social change: to increase message and issue attention; to disarm audiences and lower resistance to persuasion; to break down social barriers; and to stimulate sharing and discussion.[8] Equally as important as these individual-level effects are the impacts comedy can have on the broader conversation and culture around social issues, for example, by influencing press coverage and social media discourse, challenging conventional media frames, and providing visibility to alternative ideas and marginalized groups.

THE EXPERIENCE OF HUMOR: WHAT MAKES
US LAUGH AND WHY?

In order to appreciate how comedy exerts social influence, it is first necessary to understand what it is that makes something funny, as well as the
cognitive and affective processes involved in the experience of humor.
Although much has been written about the nature of humor, scholars tend
to agree that humor is typically characterized by some form of incongruity—
a conflict between our expectations and the reality of the joke.[9] According
to psychologist Willibald Ruch, "humor involves the bringing together of
two normally disparate ideas, concepts, or situations in a surprising or
unexpected manner."[10]

Scholars have advanced various theories to explain why incongruity produces humor. For example, incongruity resolution theory proposes that it
is the cognitive process of encountering and then resolving the incongruity
in a joke that results in enjoyment. According to psychologist Thomas
Schultz, the experience of humor is a two-phase process that begins with
the perception of incongruity, typically created by the punchline of a joke;
this is followed by a resolution of incongruity, when we "get the joke," often
by locating an ambiguity in the joke's setup.[11] Schultz uses the example of
an old W.C. Fields joke to illustrate this process; in this joke, someone
asked, "Mr. Fields do you believe in clubs for young people?" and he replied,
"Only when kindness fails."[12] Here, the incongruity arises because the
answer does not seem to fit with the question; however, once we realize
that "clubs" is ambiguous, and Fields interpreted it not to mean "social
groups" but "large sticks," the incongruity is resolved and laughter ensues.
Somewhat similarly, Jerry Suls has conceptualized incongruity resolution
as a form of problem solving, in which people search for a "cognitive rule"
to account for how the punchline follows from the setup of the joke.[13] Upon
identifying the rule and solving the problem, we experience pleasure.

What distinguishes humor from mere problem-solving is a playful,
nonthreatening context that signals that the incongruity is intended for
enjoyment.[14] In other words, humor requires a visual or linguistic cue
that shifts us into a playful, rather than serious, state of mind—at least
momentarily; it is only in this playful state that we are able to enjoy humor
as opposed to being irritated, threatened, or offended by it.[15] Moreover, the

joke teller and receiver must agree as to what counts as play, or else the joke will fall flat. According to Simon Critchley, "in order for the incongruity of the joke to be seen as such, there has to be a congruence between joke structure and social structure—no social congruity, no comic incongruity."[16] Some psychologists have proposed a "salience hypothesis" to account for the idea that certain shared social schema—such as knowledge of a particular stereotype—must be cognitively available to recipients of a joke in order for them to be able to successfully reconcile the joke's incongruity.[17]

Offering a somewhat different view, psychologist Michael Apter has argued that it is the creation of incongruity—not its resolution—that makes us laugh.[18] According to Apter, humor relies on cognitive synergy, in which two contradictory qualities are attributed to the same object, individual, or situation.[19] When we are in a playful frame of mind, such synergies increase arousal and are pleasurable. In cognitive synergies, one of the two opposing terms is seen as real, and the other as an appearance. According to Apter, we are encouraged to reinterpret reality in light of this duality, and crucially, in order for a synergy to be funny, our new interpretation must diminish the perceived importance of the object, individual, or situation to which the humor refers, through disparagement, trivialization, or mundanity.

As an example, we can consider Stephen Colbert's "The Definitely Not Coordinating with Stephen Colbert Super PAC," which—as noted earlier—he created when he decided to run for president and signed control of his super PAC over to Jon Stewart. Colbert's transfer and renaming of his super PAC creates a synergy—in this case, based on irony, because it conveys two opposing ideas: The ostensible message (i.e., that the super PAC is *not* coordinating with Colbert) and the real message (i.e., that the super PAC will likely coordinate with Colbert because it is now being run by his friend and colleague). The latter message is a reinterpretation of the former, based on our knowledge of Colbert's relationship with Stewart. By holding these two ideas in our mind concurrently, the legitimacy of super PACs, and specifically the notion that super PACs don't coordinate with the candidate they support, is diminished in value, and we laugh.

Importantly, according to incongruity-based theories, cognitive effort and inference-making are required in order to get the joke, and it is this cognitive elaboration—the playful processing of incongruity—that results in humor.[20] As we will see, this idea is important for understanding how comedy about social issues influences audiences. However, it offers an incomplete explanation of how we experience humor, as our response to humor is emotional as well as cognitive.

Although humor's emotional components are less well understood than its cognitive aspects, both physiological and psychological forms of arousal have long been considered central to humor.[21] In the 1970s, Daniel Berlyne theorized that when we laugh in response to humor, we do so because of the pleasure we experience when our arousal rises to optimal levels.[22] Indeed, the experience of physiological arousal during humor processing—as measured by changes in heart rate, skin conductance, blood pressure, and so on—is positively associated with enjoyment and perceived funniness.[23] According to Rod Martin, humor elicits a distinct positive emotion—which he identifies as "mirth"—that is accompanied by increases in arousal and is expressed by laughter.[24] Empirical studies confirm that the experience of humor increases positive affect; in one study, watching 20 minutes of stand-up comedy was comparable to 20 minutes of exercise in terms of its effects on positive well-being.[25]

In sum, humor is both intellectually satisfying and emotionally gratifying. It occurs when we encounter an incongruity or cognitive mismatch that results in a reinterpretation, and usually a diminishment, of the subject of the humorous material. In the playful and shared social context of humor, the cognitive effort and arousal involved in processing the incongruity is enjoyable and elicits positive feelings of mirth and, often, the expression of laughter. In the sections that follow, we will convey how these elements of humor implicate social change outcomes in response to mediated comedy. Importantly, we argue that it is not just the experience of humor itself that contributes to social change but the experience of humor as embedded in a larger mediated and cultural context.

COMEDY'S FOUR SOCIAL CHANGE INFLUENCES ON AUDIENCES

Increasing Attention

When it comes to social justice issues, particularly issues that can seem removed from everyday life—such as climate change or global poverty—

one of the foremost challenges to public engagement is getting people to pay attention in the first place. In today's media environment, where myriad messages—and issues—compete for our increasingly fragmented attention, comedy can help cut through the clutter, promoting attention to topics that otherwise may be eclipsed from public view. When Stephen Colbert used comedy to tackle campaign finance law, he took an esoteric issue that for many people likely seemed personally irrelevant—and frankly, boring—and turned it into something to which people *wanted* to pay attention.

Indeed, one of the most well-documented and consistent effects of humor is its ability to enhance attention and recall.[26] Some researchers believe that because humor is distinctive, it draws greater attention at the point of message encoding,[27] and our retrieval processes are, in turn, biased toward recalling these distinctive items.[28] Others contend that humor's attentional and memory advantages are due to the cognitive effort involved in processing humor's inherent incongruities, or because the perception of humor elicits positive emotions, which may facilitate attention and recall.[29]

Regardless of exactly why humor attracts attention and improves memory, this suggests that people will pay more attention to a Funny or Die video about health care access than to a serious PSA on the same topic. But comedy not only helps draw attention to the message itself but also to the particular issues that are the focus of the humor. Psychology research finds that positive emotions—like those experienced in response to comedy—expand attention and promote deeper thinking.[30] Moreover, as noted in the previous section, making sense of humorous incongruities requires mental effort and, to the extent that issue content is enmeshed with the humor itself, this can lead us to think about that content more deeply.[31]

Comedy also helps increase issue attention because the entertainment context—the film or TV show—within which the comedy is embedded draws people in. From the Kardashians to the latest sketch on *Saturday Night Live*, entertainment has a social currency that, at least for many ordinary citizens, is often lacking in the justice issues at the center of activism campaigns. Moreover, engaging with complex issue information is cognitively taxing; it takes time and mental energy to learn about a new problem or event. Thus, when comedy takes up serious issues, it minimizes the mental effort associated with paying attention to political information by attaching it to less demanding and more socially gratifying entertainment content.[32] Indeed, political communication scholar Matthew Baum found that although people tune in to late-night comedy shows and other "soft news" media primarily to be entertained, when they find serious issue content there, they pay more attention to the issue as an incidental byproduct of their entertainment consumption.[33] These effects are strongest among those who are ordinarily least attentive to the issue at hand, and thus for whom the cognitive demands of paying attention are highest; others do not need the extra motivation that entertainment provides.[34] But this makes comedy especially useful for reaching people who typically might not attend to social justice problems.

Comedy also can inspire people to pay more attention to and seek out information about complex issues in other nonhumorous media.[35] This is, in part, because comedy "primes" social and political issues—that is, makes them more accessible in memory.[36] For example, after watching Colbert's treatment of campaign finance, a viewer now has a cognitive schema, or template, for making sense of that issue that will help them when they encounter it again in other media. Even when comedy's treatment of an issue is not as in-depth as Colbert's, it nonetheless increases the issue's salience and provides viewers with some basic recognition that can inspire future information seeking and attention. Moreover, comedy—because of its requirements for cognitive elaboration and its elicitation of attention-piquing positive emotions—may put people in a "state of mind" that facilitates more active processing of serious issue content encountered subsequent to the comedy.[37]

Joke content itself also can prime us to pay more attention to certain aspects of an individual, group, or event than we would have otherwise, and to use these criteria when forming judgments.[38] Thus, a joke about a politician's position on the gender wage gap, for example, may make this issue a more salient consideration when deciding whether or not to vote for that candidate, or make us more likely to think about gender inequality in general. This priming effect may be particularly strong among those who are less knowledgeable about public affairs.[39] Among those who are *already* civically engaged, comedy may help signal that a particular issue warrants their time and effort. For example, in June 2014, John Oliver devoted a lengthy segment on his HBO satirical comedy show *Last Week Tonight* to explaining the importance of net neutrality. At the end of the segment, he urged audiences to comment on the FCC website in support of net neutrality; this prompted a dramatic spike in public comments, temporarily crashing the FCC site.[40] In May 2017, with net neutrality again on the chopping block, Oliver again implored his viewers to contact the FCC in defense of a free internet, and again they crashed the site.[41] Given that regular viewers of political satire programs tend to be highly civically engaged and politically progressive,[42] when Oliver primed the issue and suggested a doable response, his audience was readily spurred to action.

Does issue attentiveness translate into knowledge? Here, the evidence is mixed. Some studies suggest that audiences learn more issue-related facts when the same content is presented in a comedic context than in a serious news context.[43] Moreover, as noted earlier, *The Colbert Report* was more effective at promoting factual knowledge of campaign finance regulations than traditional news sources.[44] In contrast, other studies have found that satirical news is no better than traditional news for acquiring factual knowledge about policy issues[45] and, in certain cases, is less effective.[46] Outside of late-night comedy and satirical news programs—which have been most extensively studied in this context—research also suggests that viewers can acquire long-term factual knowledge from scripted comedy.[47]

Importantly, factual knowledge is not a reliable predictor of attitudes and behaviors,[48] and thus may not, on its own, lead to meaningful social change; nonetheless, public affairs knowledge is correlated with a host of positive social and democratic outcomes, such as participation, tolerance, and self-efficacy.[49] For most social issues, knowledge is often a necessary but insufficient ingredient for change. If John Oliver's audience did not know at least vaguely what net neutrality was and how it affects their lives, they would be unlikely to comment to the FCC. In the case of Colbert's super PAC, it was knowledge of campaign finance that provided the link between exposure to *The Colbert Report* and critical opinions toward the role of money in politics.[50] Of course, factual knowledge is only one way of "learning" from comedy. Comedy also can shape *how* we think about social issues and groups, a possibility we take up in subsequent sections.

Disarming Audiences and Lowering Resistance to Persuasion

Fomenting social change is often a matter of opening—and changing—minds about controversial issues and ideas. Thus, comedy in the service of social justice will almost invariably involve the communication of belief-challenging or threatening information—for example, encouraging people to recognize their own racial or sexist attitudes, confront gross injustice, or consider how their behaviors contribute to environmental problems. In some cases, comedy may attempt a wholesale change in people's attitudes, for example convincing them that gun reform is needed or that climate change is real, when they believe otherwise. Humor, because of its ability to draw attention, may be particularly well suited for bringing people into contact with ideas that run counter to their own beliefs. Yet humor also may help to disarm audiences, lowering their defenses in the face of social and political difference. This occurs both cognitively, by reducing message counter-arguing, and emotionally, by buffering against a perceived threat.

From a cognitive perspective, when a persuasive message cuts against our beliefs or values, we are likely to counter-argue it. Counter-arguing is the internal process by which we generate negative cognitive responses to a message, refuting or identifying flaws in its underlying premises.[51] Counter-arguing can reinforce or even strengthen one's existing beliefs and is thus an impediment to successful persuasion.[52] Typically, as our attention to and interest in a persuasive message increase, as occurs with comedy, so, too, does our propensity to critically process the message.[53] But with humor, our attention and interest are directed at "getting" the humor; we process the *joke* more deeply, not the persuasive arguments, thereby reducing our motivation and/or ability to counter-argue.[54] Consistent with this idea, Dannagal Young's research found that late-night political jokes, compared to nonhumorous versions of the same jokes, produced more thoughts aimed at humor comprehension and appreciation, and less negative thoughts directed at message arguments.[55]

Along with counter-arguing, people also resist persuasion by selectively avoiding threatening information due to inertia or fear.[56] Because of the positive emotions elicited by humor, however, audiences may be more willing to engage with threatening information when it is presented in a humorous context. Just as humor can be used as a personal strategy to facilitate coping and reduce stress during challenging situations,[57] it may serve as a buffer against feelings of fear or distress induced by persuasive mediated messages about overwhelming or controversial topics.[58] For example, if someone is uncomfortable with or feels threatened by certain socially progressive ideas—such as gay marriage or gender nonconformity—the humorous approach of a TV sitcom may make the topic more palatable by inducing positive emotions.

Humorous messages also may be able to increase specific emotions that help drive engagement with justice issues. Large-scale humanitarian and environmental crises, like poverty, genocide, and climate change, often give rise to "compassion fatigue" or "compassion fade," reflected in public indifference as the number of victims of atrocities increases.[59] Accordingly, using humor to counterbalance depressing information may be one way to promote compassion[60] and increase individuals' willingness to engage with tough issues. Humor also can increase hope,[61] which is critical for public engagement and activism around daunting social issues like climate change but is often in short supply in media coverage of such issues.[62] Indeed, as we show in chapters 4 and 5, the positive emotions elicited by comedy are key to comedy's ability to engage publics in social justice challenges.

Comedy thus provides a promising way to disarm audiences and make them less resistant to threatening or ego-challenging information. Still, this doesn't always translate into persuasive effects. While some studies show persuasive advantages of humor,[63] others show more qualified effects that depend on characteristics of the comedy or of the audience.[64] Still other research suggests that humor, while capable of changing attitudes and behavior, is not necessarily more persuasive than nonhumor.[65]

In some cases, humor about a social issue may fail to persuade because it trivializes the issue through its use of diminishment.[66] Another related factor that may limit humor's persuasiveness is what communication scholar Robin Nabi and her colleagues describe as a "discounting" cue.[67] Here, due to humor's playful context, people dismiss comedic messages about social issues as "just a joke" and thereby irrelevant to their judgments. This discounting mechanism may reduce the overall impact of the message on attitudes, even as humor minimizes counter-arguing or other forms of message resistance. However, our recent research finds that when audiences perceive comedy as having entertainment value—that is, when they experience it as funny, engaging, and inspiring—this decreases message discounting and, in turn, enhances persuasion.[68] In other words, if audiences are deeply entertained by comedy, they no longer see the message as merely a joke but as something worthy of serious consideration. Thus, comedy will be most persuasive when it is allowed to be as funny and entertaining as possible—rather than didactic and "safe." We further show in chapters 4 and 5 that perceived entertainment value is a primary route through which comedy influences public engagement with social issues.

Given humor's inconsistent persuasive effects, in the context of contemporary mediated comedy about social issues, outright persuasion might be a less feasible—and potentially less important—outcome than getting people to engage cognitively and emotionally with diverse ideas, or calling their attention to an issue in the first place. By drawing audiences in, disarming them, and lowering their resistance to messages about sensitive or dissonant topics, comedy can create an important opening for further information and engagement and, as we'll see in the next section, provide opportunities for social connections across lines of difference.

Breaking Down Social Barriers

So far, we primarily have been discussing issues and arguments, rather than the *people*—the comedians and scripted characters—who are the faces of mediated comedy. If mediated comedy is to play any role in social change, it will do so only to the extent that it provides a visible platform for voices and social groups who are outside of the mainstream culture, whether due to race and ethnicity, socioeconomic status, religion, sexual identity, or disability. Entertainment TV and film, as our primary cultural products, provide the chief mechanism through which social norms and assumptions are communicated to large audiences.[69] According to media scholar Larry Gross, mainstream film and TV are "nearly always presented as transparent mediators of reality which can and do show us how people and places look; how institutions operate; in short, the way it is."[70]

Cultivation theory, originally developed by George Gerbner in the 1970s, posits that television offers a centralized system of storytelling that shapes the perceived social reality of its audience.[71] While cultivation theory has been critiqued on various grounds,[72] it nonetheless offers a useful starting point for considering how the images of social groups constructed by entertainment media are likely to shape audience perceptions. In particular, cultivation processes are thought to be especially powerful when it comes to influencing perceptions of groups with which people have limited or no direct contact. In this view, TV offers a vicarious form of learning about marginalized or less visible social groups.[73]

This idea from cultivation theory dovetails with a prominent theory in social psychology, dubbed the contact hypothesis. The contact hypothesis proposes that positive interactions between members of diverse social groups can reduce prejudice, by providing the opportunity to learn more about the other group of people.[74] While such social contact may occur in the real world, intergroup contact via positive media portrayals—or "parasocial contact"—also can improve viewers' attitudes toward minority groups, particularly when face-to-face interaction is limited.[75] In support of this idea in the context of comedy, Schiappa and colleagues found that college students who were shown a 2002 comedy special featuring stand-up comedian and transvestite Eddie Izzard became less prejudiced toward male transvestites and could better distinguish transvestites from other social groups (like drag queens).[76] In a separate study, they found that, among heterosexual college undergraduates, more frequent viewing of *Will & Grace*—which ran from 1998 to 2006 and was the first popular TV sitcom to feature two gay male characters in leading roles—was associated with lower levels of sexual prejudice toward gay men as a result of viewers' affective bonds with the gay characters on the show.[77] The relationship between viewing and lower sexual prejudice was especially strong for those who had few gay friends or acquaintances in real life.

Albert Bandura's social cognitive theory offers an additional explanation for how mediated comedy might improve attitudes toward marginalized groups. According to social cognitive theory, people learn social attitudes and behaviors by observing others, often via vicarious experiences facilitated by the media.[78] Specifically, people may model their own treatment of others based on the behaviors of a favorite media character, particularly when they identify strongly and empathize with the character.[79] Thus, a cross-race or straight-gay friendship between media characters may help normalize these relationships for viewers from the majority group who identify with the in-group character. For example, researchers found that straight viewers of *Will & Grace* who identified closely with Grace, the show's straight female character and close friend to the two gay male characters, had more positive attitudes toward gay people.[80] More broadly, this suggests that when in-group media characters confront social stereotypes or ridicule bigotry, they can help foster more open-minded views through a modeling process.

While the effects of mediated intergroup contact can occur as the result of entertainment portrayals generally, comedy—because of the positive affect it entails—may play a particularly important role in minimizing social divides. For example, advertising research supports an "affect-transfer" process, whereby the positive affect generated by a humorous ad is transferred to the product or brand featured in the ad.[81] While this is an idea that requires more research, positive affect experienced as a result of mediated comedy similarly may transfer to a depicted community or individual comic performer. Further, humor can help reduce social anxiety.[82] Additionally, the diminishment function of humor can be used to signal that any perceived social divide is not as consequential as one may have originally assumed. To this end, one study found that a film containing disability humor was more effective than a serious film about disabilities in increasing positive attitudes toward people with disabilities.[83]

It is important to note, however, that much mediated comedy perpetuates rather than challenges social stereotypes, and research convincingly shows that disparaging humor about social groups emboldens prejudice.[84] Thus, just as comedy can provide a venue to subvert the status quo and disrupt stereotypes, it also can exploit these stereotypes and normalize prejudice. Moreover, comedy—even when directed at social or political change—may not always be received as intended, as audiences exert agency in their interpretation of humorous texts. For example, in the case of *All in the Family*, which was developed by Norman Lear in the 1970s to confront racism through humor, some high prejudice viewers identified *with* the callous bigotry of the show's lead character Archie Bunker, who the show was designed to mock.[85] And another study found that white readers of black-oriented comic strips often deflected and downplayed issues of racial discrimination depicted in the comics.[86] Selective exposure also may limit the socialization effects of comedy, particularly in the niche

TV era, as those who watch may be more likely to come from or already identify with the out-group.[87]

Despite these caveats, when mediated comedy positively portrays marginalized social groups and does so in a way that unmasks rather than minimizes racial and cultural differences, it can help foster a sense of understanding of and commonality with these groups among majority audiences. Thus, while representation is still far from perfect, it is significant that today's mediated comedy culture has diversified to include late-night comedy hosts such as Trevor Noah and Robin Thede—the first woman of color to helm her own late-night show—and scripted comedy shows like *Black-ish*, *Insecure*, and *Master of None* that explicitly confront social injustice and foreground the unique cultural experiences of their diverse characters. The connection that viewers feel with media characters and comic performers can help to ameliorate social divisions in the real world, but only if nonmajority groups are visibly and accurately represented in the mainstream.

Stimulating Sharing and Discussion

In our new media ecosystem, where social media reign and audiences are empowered to create, circulate, and respond to media content, one of comedy's most powerful levers of influence is its ability to be shared. Videos posted to YouTube or made shareable by sites like Comedy Central facilitate the spread of comedic content, and this works in concert with our own predispositions toward sharing content that makes others laugh.

Sharing is an inherently social process and is thus interpersonally motivated; as such, people want to share content that reflects favorably on themselves and enhances their social relationships.[88] One reason people share is to entertain others;[89] people also are more likely to share content that is helpful, novel, persuasive, and emotionally arousing.[90] People tend to share amusing content due to the arousal it induces,[91] and humor is considered an important predictor of what goes viral.[92] Indeed, in one analysis, humor appeared in 25 of 30 highly popular and shared videos on YouTube,[93] and during topical discussions of social issues on Twitter, humorous tweets were more likely to be retweeted and had a longer life span than other types of shared content.[94]

Several social issue campaigns have effectively used humor to increase the reach of their messages. An analysis of the Until You're Ready, AvoidtheStork.com campaign, which was designed to prevent unintended pregnancies among young women, revealed that college students who found the campaign funny were more likely to share it with their social networks.[95] The CDC's "Zombie Apocalypse" campaign—which we discussed in the book's introduction—employed pop-culture-referencing humor to generate social media buzz and spread awareness about the need for disaster preparedness, accumulating nearly 4 billion total impressions from traditional and social media coverage in just a few months.[96]

Mediated comedy is also often shared with explicit social justice aims. Geoffrey Baym and Chirag Shah analyzed how environmental advocacy groups reappropriated and circulated clips about environmental issues from *The Daily Show* and *The Colbert Report* in ways that supported their agendas for change by informing, connecting, and mobilizing their constituents.[97] The researchers tracked 10 video clips that were reposted on more than 500 different websites and more than 30,000 individual web pages. These sites were, in turn, linked to by more than 5,500 other unique sites and more than a half-million individual pages. Advocates integrated the clips into arguments, policy statements, and calls for action, using them to build affinity within like-minded networks and as discursive tools to articulate and reinforce their issue positions.

From the perspective of social change, sharing is important in several respects. First, and perhaps most obviously, sharing increases—sometimes exponentially—a message's reach, thereby amplifying its effects. Thus, if—as past experimental research suggests—humor is often equally effective as nonhumor at relaying knowledge or changing attitudes, but it is *more* likely to be seen and shared, its potential influence is much greater. Second, shared content is not just passed along neutrally; rather, it carries normative information, or social cues. An endorsement from a friend or admired social media connection can have a powerful influence on what information we think is important or useful, as well as on our attitudes and behaviors.[98] Moreover, even a modest piece of information such as the number of "likes" or shares attributed to social media content can affect people's reactions to it.[99] For example, social media comments attached to a comedy program can influence program enjoyment;[100] people are more open to reading even counter-attitudinal online content when it has been "recommended" by a high number of users,[101] and the number of views associated with a YouTube video can influence perceptions of how important most Americans think the issue featured in the video is.[102] Third, sharing is itself a form of engagement, an expression of the sharer's interest and commitment,[103] which can, in turn, foster broader participation in the public sphere.[104] Thus, someone who shares a funny clip about a social justice topic may, as a result, be more likely to participate in other ways, such as contacting an elected official or attending a protest. Finally, people share stories as a way to build and reinforce a collective identity, which is made only more potent in the social media age.[105] Thus, sharing—and sharing a joke, in particular—enhances group cohesion and helps create a sense of belonging to a common cultural experience.[106] For example, Mohamed Helmy and Sabine Frerichs detailed how the sharing of humor during the 2011 Egyptian Revolution "grew from and consolidated a shared identity"[107] and thus was integral to the larger social movement that helped topple Egypt's Mubarak regime.

Because of the affordances of digital media and humans' propensity to pass along humorous content, mediated comedy has the potential not only to reach but also to *connect* larger audiences than ever before possible. This connection is critical in the context of social change, as it contributes to a larger shared experience that can build solidarity and promote collective action. This idea is taken up more fully in the next section, where we consider how mediated comedy can reach beyond its direct audience to influence the broader public sphere.

SHAPING THE CULTURAL CONVERSATION

Thus far, this chapter has detailed the ways in which comedy can attract attention, disarm audiences, alleviate social barriers, and stimulate sharing through direct impacts on audiences. These audience effects are incredibly important; yet, they do not tell the full story. For example, scholar Amber Day cautions against looking only for direct and immediate influences of political comedy on audiences, "where the more significant impact is often felt in public discussion as a whole."[108] Day argues

that comedy's most profound effects reside in its capacity "to push periph-
eral worldviews further into the mainstream, to contest the existing framing of particular issues, and to gradually change the associations that we
collectively have of particular concepts / people / ideals, etc."[109] We agree
that comedy's potential for social change lies not merely or even primarily
in its ability to directly impact individuals—effects that can be unreliable
and are necessarily constrained to a particular audience—but also in its
ability to impact the broader public sphere, as well as to provide resources
for collective action.

One way in which mediated comedy can influence the broader cultural
conversation is through intermedia agenda-setting, which occurs when the
media's agenda—i.e., the issues that they cover—is shaped by other media,
for example when the issues reported on by elite newspapers influence the
topics covered in local newspapers or television news broadcasts.[110] While
most studies of intermedia agenda setting focus on traditional news media,
entertainment texts are likely to become "influential media" in the context
of agenda-setting when they reach a large audience, are acclaimed by other
media outlets, and when they take up serious issues that are not already
salient on the news agenda.[111] Many of today's mediated comedies fit these
criteria. Thus, as a given comedic text about an important but less well-
trafficked issue draws attention and is shared, it may help sanction journalistic attention to that issue. For example, as noted earlier, Colbert's super
PAC spawned coverage of campaign finance regulations in mainstream
news;[112] likewise, Tina Fey's *Saturday Night Live* parody of Sarah Palin
during the 2008 U.S. presidential election propelled news coverage of
Palin.[113] Additionally, one industry media analysis found that John Oliver's
coverage of lesser-known issues on *Last Week Tonight* drove coverage of
those issues in digital news outlets and had a much bigger effect on online
news coverage than the popular, but serious, *60 Minutes*.[114]

Notably, however, these agenda-setting effects not only shape *what* topics get covered in the news but also *how* these topics are covered, thereby
helping to shift the dominant framing of social issues, as "journalists take
interpretive cues from comedians."[115] For example, much of Colbert's critique of the campaign finance system was repeated in journalistic reporting on the topic.[116] Similarly, when Tina Fey parodied Sarah Palin in ways
that challenged her basic knowledge and fit for office, journalists used this

in their political coverage not only as a humorous sidebar but also as a way to introduce legitimate concerns about Palin's competence.[117] Importantly, by helping to set journalists' agendas and interpretive frames, comedy's critical perspectives on issues reach and potentially influence a much larger audience than actually watches the comedy itself.

Moreover, by shaping the larger public conversation about social issues, comedies and comedians can influence policymakers. For example, in 2012, then-Vice President Joe Biden credited *Will & Grace* for helping to shift the culture around gay rights: "I think *Will & Grace* did more to educate the American public, more than almost anything anybody has done so far. People fear that which is different. Now they're beginning to understand."[118] In 2017, Republican senator Bill Cassidy said that his support for a new health care bill would depend on whether or not it passes "The Jimmy Kimmel Test," referring to late-night comedy host Jimmy Kimmel's emotional monologue about his infant son's heart surgery and the costs borne by many families who need to care for a child with congenital heart disease.[119] Jon Stewart is widely recognized for helping to draw media attention to and ultimately secure the passage of the 9 / 11 First Responders Health Bill, following coverage of the issue on *The Daily Show* in 2010 and again in both 2015 and 2019 when he directly lobbied lawmakers on Capitol Hill to extend the bill permanently, including delivering a searing testimony to a subcommittee of the House Judiciary Committee in June 2019.[120] And there is abundant anecdotal evidence that John Oliver's issue-driven comedy has influenced not only public behavior but also policy, from the bail bond example described in the book's introduction to net neutrality to ensuring fair treatment for chicken farmers.[121]

Humor's discursive power also makes it a valuable resource for collective action. Comedy connects people and, in so doing, creates the sense that they are sharing in something larger than themselves. In particular, when humor gives visibility to underrepresented groups and exposes social inequalities, it can help build what Rebecca Krefting calls "cultural citizenship" by affirming the collective identities of and, in turn, empowering marginalized groups.[122] In the context of social movements, this— coupled with humor's ability to reframe the terms of debate—can be a tool for resisting oppression. From the 2000 Serbian Optor movement that brought down Milosevic[123] to the 2011 Egyptian Revolution that dismantled the Mubarak regime,[124] humor has served as a catalyst for change, used by activists to build social support and solidarity as well as a means of opposition.

In this way, comedy can become more than a sum of its parts. Today's media platforms grant comedians incredible reach, which can help translate comedy's cultural power into political power—affecting not only the broader journalistic discourse but policymaking itself. At the same time, comedy can be a practice of empowerment that strengthens and mobilizes marginalized communities, ultimately serving as a tool of resistance. Yet, comedy is not without its limitations, to which we turn in the next section.

PARADOXES OF HUMOR: CONCEPTUALIZING COMEDY'S LIMITS FOR SOCIAL CHANGE

In August 2017, days after a group of white nationalists marched on the campus of the University of Virginia, inciting violence that resulted in the death of a young woman, *Saturday Night Live* veteran Tina Fey, a University of Virginia alumna, made a surprise return to *SNL*'s "Weekend Update." With her characteristic snark, Fey called out the hate groups, as well as President Trump for his reticence in condemning them, and then, she offered her solution—to eat cake:

> I know a lot of us are feeling anxious and we're asking ourselves, like, what can I do? I'm just one person, what can I do. So, I would urge people this Saturday instead of participating in the screaming matches and potential violence, find a local business you support, maybe a Jewish-run bakery or an African American–run bakery. Order a cake with the American flag on it . . . and just eat it.[125]

Then, fork in hand, Fey proceeded to devour and maim a sheet-cake while humorously ranting to co-anchor Colin Jost, ultimately claiming "sheet-caking is a grassroots movement." As #sheetcaking trended on Twitter, some audiences reacted positively,[126] finding humor in Fey's cathartic suggestion and therapeutic solidarity in her appeal to a larger sense of national despair. Others, however, were critical, accusing Fey of being tone-deaf and exclusionary to those who do not have the privilege to merely eat cake in the face of oppression[127] and, more generally, for suggesting "turning inward" to the day's social and political problems rather than offering any real solution.[128]

This example, while emblematic in many ways of the contemporary cultural and political moment, also highlights several of the challenges and tensions inherent in conceptualizing comedy as a tool for social change. First, humor is nearly always subjective, and is socially and culturally dependent.[129] What one person finds funny, the next may find offensive or juvenile, and what makes people laugh in one particular time and place may fall flat when the backdrop changes. As discussed earlier, humor is privy to selective perception, whereby people read media texts through the lens of their own social identity and values.[130]

Tina Fey's cake-eating complacency in the wake of Charlottesville is consistent with another common critique of comedy, which is that it can serve as a distraction from—rather than a means of engaging with—harsh societal truths. In this vein, communication scholars Roderick Hart and Johanna Hartelius have critiqued Jon Stewart's brand of satire on *The Daily Show*, claiming that Stewart "makes cynicism attractive," teaching us to "cop an attitude" rather than confront the hard work of politics.[131] Although research has shown that *The Daily Show*'s audience is particularly civically and politically engaged,[132] thus undermining the cynicism charge, Hart and Hartelius's critique is of a piece with other arguments about humor's limitations. Humor scholar Paul Lewis wrote that by reducing real problems to a joke, "humor can support denial and evasion, drawing observers . . . away from urgent issues by enticing them to enjoy a little laugh about a subject and dismiss it from consciousness."[133] Others see humor as "unreliable in reaching serious aims," arguing that its ambiguity and playfulness can subvert aggressive critique.[134] And, in 2016, Malcolm Gladwell, in his podcast series *Revisionist History*, aired an episode exploring what he called the "satire paradox," in which he argued that most contemporary satire is *too* accessible, *too* funny to effectively challenge problematic norms; rather, according to Gladwell, "satire works best when the satirist has the courage not just to go for the joke."[135]

Fey's sketch also raises the question of comedic intention. A common refrain among comics—Fey included—when their comedy is criticized is that it was "just a joke."[136] Popular comedians typically see themselves first and foremost as entertainers, and even those who take up social issues often report that it is comedy, not activism, that guides them.[137] And in fact, some viewers responded to the criticism of Fey's "sheetcaking" by asking why humor can't be left to be just humor, why it's not okay if something just makes us laugh, particularly in a moment when we *need* to laugh.[138] In our view, comedy's influence on social change can happen with or without the intent of the comedian. Yet, there can be tension between what makes (some of) us laugh and what mobilizes or unites us. This speaks to a real conflict between the authenticity and creativity of humor and the strategic aims of advocates who endeavor to use comedy intentionally for social change, a topic that we will address explicitly in later chapters.

Finally, the polarized response to Fey's sketch highlights yet another quandary of comedy. As John Meyer argues, humor often can be divisive and "may serve to unite one group against another."[139] In social change, this may serve a critical aim, as was the case with the protestors in Egypt's Tahrir Square or when John Oliver rallied his audience in support of net neutrality; yet, it also can be used to "push away the 'other' and to show that they or their opinions are beyond the pale of common values being invoked."[140] Because of the social specificity of humor, because it requires identification between the audience and comic in order to "get" the joke, it very easily can create an us versus them mentality. Consequently, while mediated comedy—because of its attention-grabbing qualities and its capacity to be shared—has the potential to reach beyond the choir with messages of social change, this potential may not always be realized.

This chapter thus reveals a multitude of paradoxes: Humor can help us confront and deny social problems; it can attract and repel, and it can bridge social divides just as it can ostracize and malign. Here, we join other scholars who recognize the paradoxes of humor.[141] Yet, we argue that comedy, particularly in the current era of technological and social justice upheaval, is nonetheless uniquely positioned for engaging diverse publics with social issues. Humor's advantages for attention and recall, its capacity to disarm, to lower social barriers, and to go viral are built into its DNA and are assisted in social change efforts by the affordances of digital media and the memetic style of contemporary social movements. And as we detail in subsequent chapters, comedy offers an antidote to several particular communication challenges posed by key contemporary social justice issues. We thus view comedy as an important and—at least where strategic communication is concerned—underused tool for facilitating social change.

While we tend to take an optimistic view of comedy's potential, we also are not naïve in thinking that humor can solve all of society's ills, or that comedy is always an effective route to engaging the public with society's problems; it most certainly should not be the *only* route. At the end of the day, comedy may be more effective in drawing attention than in changing behavior, and better suited for rallying the troops than winning over the other side. Yet comedy *can* change behavior and *can* persuade; it all depends on the comedy itself and the audience it reaches. Different types and forms of comedy have different functions and will elicit different audience reactions. In the next chapter we consider more deeply the various genres of mediated comedy about social issues—their history, their production and distribution, their content, and their role in social change.

3 From Stand-Up to Sitcoms

SOCIALLY CRITICAL COMEDY ACROSS GENRES

"Comedy calms people down and makes people feel better because they are having fun conversations. And people's defenses come down, and you can say something real to them. I think that's why comedy works so well."

Negin Farsad, comedian and director of *The Muslims Are Coming!* documentary[1]

As 2015 came to an end, a Cleveland grand jury issued a decision about the legal fate of a police officer who had killed an unarmed 12-year-old African American boy, Tamir Rice, as he played outside with a toy pellet gun in late 2014: There would be no charges.[2] The same month Rice was fatally shot, another grand jury delivered an identical judgment in a different tragedy. This time, it was the case of a police officer in Ferguson, Missouri, who shot and killed Michael Brown, an unarmed, black 18-year-old.[3] Albeit miles apart, the similarities—unarmed black boys killed at the hands of police officers—were evident.

Coinciding with the grand jury announcement in the Rice case, Kenya Barris, creator and showrunner of the ABC comedy sitcom hit, *Black-ish*, was hard at work writing what he has described as "maybe my most important episode."[4] For Barris, the boy's fatal shooting and the grand jury decision infused an urgency and meaning into his idea for an episode that would mirror the patterns dominating the news: "It really sort of put an impact and effect on the words that I was putting into the script and also the feeling behind it . . . That, for me, was just such a tragedy."[5]

Figure 3 The Johnson family discusses racial discrimination in the "Hope" episode of
ABC's *Black-ish*.
SOURCE / CREDIT: Hulu video screenshot / fair use.

In the February 2016 episode of *Black-ish*, titled "Hope," the on-screen
African American Johnson family discusses a fictional case of an unarmed
black teenager who is shot and killed by police. The episode—set entirely
within the Johnsons' living room—offers the audience an intimate look at
a family of color grappling with this frightening topic. We watch as the
family members debate how to talk with the youngest children about the
case, whether the teenaged children should participate in protests in
response to the news that there will be no grand jury indictment, and—
more broadly—how they should make sense of a world where police brutality targeting black people is a frequent occurrence. In some of the episode's darker humor, the family members are confused about the location
of the latest incident, since there have been so many similar cases. The
dialogue and points of reflection were inspired by Barris's own family's
conversation: While watching the TV news, the nine-year-old fictional
Jack asks, "Why are all these people so mad?," just as Barris's young son
did during news of the protests in Ferguson after Michael Brown was shot
and killed.[6]

Barris has emphasized in press interviews that he did not want to polit-
icize the show. Instead, he aimed to create a combination of comedic

entertainment value and social change: "I hope nothing more than that [the audience] got some laughs, and that it sparks a conversation between them and their family or them and their friends and those conversations spread out into something else. The best scenario would be that it motivates some change."[7] Yet Barris also recognized the delicate balance involved in producing comedy about charged issues: "We didn't want to have it so joke-heavy that we trivialized the situation and the seriousness of the topic they were talking about. We really just tried to make sure we gave ourselves enough balance to still get the point across but at the same time, give people an entry point where they felt like they could get into it and not be bummed out the whole time."[8]

This approach seems to have succeeded. On social media, tweets emphasized "television gold" and reacted to the episode's cultural importance, including viewer sentiments like: "This is the best and deepest episode I have ever seen. I felt the same way 8 years ago," and "I love how Blackish uses every family member to show the different opinions the black community has on these tough topics."[9] Later in 2016, *Black-ish* was nominated for three primetime Emmy awards, including "Best Comedy Series," attributed in part to a second season that tackled social justice issues— albeit without sacrificing comedy and entertainment value—with the "Hope" episode at the fore.[10]

Black-ish's success highlights several key ideas about the broader landscape of mediated comedy in the context of social change. First, *Black-ish* represents a resurgence of mainstream and niche mediated comedy material infused with present-day social justice topics in the mold of Norman Lear's groundbreaking work from the 1970s and 1980s. Barris, who cites Lear as a direct influence on his sitcom style, noted in an interview with NPR that this moment does, indeed, feel like a rebirth: "For some reason, television went through this amazing hibernation of not talking about things."[11] Although sitcoms about black families are not new, *Black-ish* differs from some of its notable predecessors like the 1980s *The Cosby Show* in its willingness to explicitly address issues of racial difference and discrimination.[12]

Moreover, the authenticity of the comedy in *Black-ish* originates from the voice, perspective, concerns, and experiences of an African American creative decision-maker whose writing engages wide audiences beyond a community's inside conversation. Airing on legacy network ABC means that *Black-ish* can reach a broad, multiracial, potentially "incongruent" audience[13] that may not view the world in lockstep with Barris. As of the 2016–17 season, according to Nielsen data, 80 percent of *Black-ish* viewers are not black,[14] thereby increasing the likelihood that at least some of the show's viewers will not be aware of particular aspects of racial justice.

However, infusing a painful racial justice topic into a sitcom is not without risk for a program on a network like ABC that strives for mass appeal. Barris had pitched a similar episode to the network two years prior, when his show was new, but he was discouraged then from telling jokes about police.[15] Barris's status as an acclaimed, successful comedy showrunner in the second season of a bona fide network hit meant that he could attempt a risky move, at least in the context of a mainstream legacy network typically less willing to support controversial topics. Yet even so, ABC shelved a subsequent episode that tackled race relations in the context of NFL players' "take a knee" protests, and in July 2018, Barris announced that he was leaving ABC Studios. Soon after, Netflix announced a three-year, $100 million production deal with Barris, offering him more freedom to take on contentious social and political issues and to deviate from the constraints of the network sitcom format.[16] Nonetheless, today—amid broader, ongoing conversations about social justice—a combination of changing audience demographics, increasing diversity among creative decision-makers, new distribution channels, evolving industry practices, and critical and audience rewards for justice topics will likely encourage more mainstream entertainment storytelling in the direction of *Black-ish*.

Scripted episodic comedy, of which *Black-ish* is an example, is one of several contemporary mediated comedy genres where social justice themes resonate. This chapter describes five distinct genres of mediated comedy that are prominent in the entertainment marketplace and encompass most—although not all—examples of comedy's treatment of social issues: satirical news, scripted episodic TV, stand-up, sketch, and documentary. For each genre, we offer a definition and situate it historically, provide evidence of its cultural reach, offer examples, and highlight its ability to engage audiences with justice topics in distinct ways.

SATIRICAL NEWS

Satire uses humor to spotlight and skewer the absurdness or inherent injustice of a situation, typically targeting powerful people and institutions in an effort to challenge and reform the status quo.[17] According to scholars Jonathan Gray, Jeffrey Jones, and Ethan Thompson, "it is the ability to attack power and pass judgment on the powerful while doing so in playful and entertaining ways that makes satire a particularly potent form of political communication."[18] Moreover, satire does not merely go after those in power, but it does so in a way that is intended to awaken and provoke the audience, encouraging them to reckon with often uncomfortable social realities.[19] Although a negative, critical form, satire's goal is positive social change.

As a genre of mediated comedy, the satirical TV news format—with roots in Rowan and Martin's *Laugh-In* and *Saturday Night Live's* "Weekend Update"—has become increasingly popular over the past two decades and is keenly emblematic of today's "discursively integrated" media age, where information and entertainment are inextricably entwined.[20] Its basic formula—a funny host who comments on news and issues of the day while incorporating various combinations of TV news clip montages, politician sound bites, correspondent features, interviews, and field segments—is reflected in a range of satirical programs, both in the U.S. and around the world. Using parody, a form of satire rooted in imitation, the shows' hosts adopt the pretenses of a TV news anchor in order to ridicule multiple layers of institutional hypocrisy—including news media framing of and official responses to political events—while championing the interests of marginalized groups.

In the U.S., the formula is directly embodied in the Comedy Central juggernaut *The Daily Show*—hosted by Jon Stewart from 1999–2015 and now helmed by South African comic Trevor Noah—along with newer incarnations hosted by former *Daily Show* correspondents, including Comedy Central's *The Colbert Report*, which aired from 2005–14; *Full Frontal with Samantha Bee* on cable network TBS; *Last Week Tonight with John Oliver* and *Wyatt Cenac's Problem Areas*, both on HBO; and *Patriot Act with Hasan Minhaj* on Netflix. These programs both challenge political power and spotlight social justice topics, from immigration to transgender rights to student loan debt.

Contemporary satirical news programs have come to play a prominent role as public sources of news and information, particularly among young people. For example, during the presidential election year of 2004—just as *The Daily Show* was gaining political and cultural momentum—21 percent of Americans under 30 said they regularly "learn" about the election campaign from comedy shows like *The Daily Show*, a level similar to what that age group reported for newspapers and the evening TV news.[21] Lynn Schofield Clark and Regina Marchi, in their ethnographic study of teenagers' media use, found that young people often first learned about current events from satirical news programs and that these were among the sources that they found most informative.[22]

Although satirical news programs of *The Daily Show* variety are, by their hosts' own admission, not journalism,[23] it is these programs' close relationship to—and often ridicule of—mainstream journalism that distinguishes satirical news from other genres of mediated comedy. Indeed, some scholars have conceptualized satirical news, particularly *The Daily Show*, as an alternative form of journalism, one that interrogates power, exposes flaws in contemporary news practices, and engages in productive dialogue with its interview guests.[24] Because satirical news shows are not constrained by journalistic conventions, they can speak truths and hold politicians and media accountable in ways that traditional news programs often cannot. Likewise, *The Daily Show* and its ilk often provide a counternarrative to conventional news framing, and correct gaps and deficiencies in news coverage of controversial issues. For example, in the early 2000s, *The Daily Show*'s coverage of the Iraq War—dubbed "Mess O'Potamia"—invoked frames of insurgency and civil war well before these appeared in the mainstream press.[25]

Because satirical news explicitly and consistently connects to and comments on current events, often as they unfold, this genre has particular potential to expand viewers' attention to and knowledge of public affairs and motivate civic and political behaviors related to specific issues, as we discussed in chapter 2. At the same time, satirical news can play a powerful media agenda-setting role, elevating and reframing social justice topics that otherwise may be obscured, and offering activist organizations the opportunity to piggyback on these topics' newfound attention. For example, programs like John Oliver's *Last Week Tonight* dive deeply into issues that highlight structural inequalities and power imbalances. Some of Oliver's most popular segments—on topics such as the corruption of televangelists,[26] government surveillance practices,[27] problems with the Miss America pageant and scholarship program,[28] and America's deficient sexual education system[29]—exceed 15 million views on YouTube. With this level of engagement, Oliver is able to contribute to and even create a national discussion about less visible issues, spurring broader media coverage and attention.[30] Oliver's program is also unique in that he often directly—and successfully—advocates for action from his viewers,[31] such as asking them to comment to the FCC in support of net neutrality.[32] These calls to action can work synergistically with ongoing policy advocacy efforts. For example, in response to Oliver's net neutrality segment, Tim Karr, senior director of strategy for Free Press—an organization founded in 2003 to advocate for internet freedom—told *Bloomberg News*: "'Oliver gave us a great moment to rally around, and a hilarious video to share.'"[33]

Yet satirical news carries its own risks for engagement as well. Because satire is an inherently aggressive form that seeks to disturb the status quo, it can all too easily veer away from the terrain of comedy and into the territory of outrage;[34] satirical news that is too vicious or demeaning to its comedic targets may risk alienating viewers and further entrenching people's existing attitudes. When this is the case, satirical news may do little more than preach to the (liberal) choir. Indeed, according to a 2014 survey by the Pew Research Center, 72 percent of Americans who reported getting news from *The Daily Show* in the past week were liberal, compared to just 6 percent who were conservative.[35] Thus, contemporary satirical news in the U.S. may not be well suited for changing minds around deeply polarized political topics. Still, it can contribute to social change by uncovering important issues, rallying the like-minded, and driving the broader agenda and conversation.

Around the world, satirical news also has increased in marketplace popularity and willingness to explicitly highlight social justice challenges, particularly in global regions faced with restrained media and political freedoms, where satire offers a form of popular resistance. Indeed, the cultural impact of *The Daily Show* is seen today in its imitators in the U.S.

and around the globe, as much as in its continued scrutiny of media, politicians, and social problems. For example, in 2011, Bassem Youssef, a surgeon-turned-satirist, launched a self-created YouTube-channel, which he soon developed into a TV program, *Al-Bernameg*, comically skewering then-President Mohammed Morsi as well as other government officials on the heels of the country's populist revolution. Often dubbed "Egypt's Jon Stewart," Youssef adopted the format and techniques of *The Daily Show*, localized to the Egyptian context.[36] Yousef's show was embraced by millions of Egyptians, who rallied around and were empowered by its humor; yet, Youssef's bold and critical comedy angered many government leaders and politicians. Facing arrest and intimidation, Youssef canceled the show in 2014 and left the country amid safety concerns.

SCRIPTED EPISODIC TV

As an enduringly popular genre of television, scripted comedy is dominated by the sitcom, or "situation comedy," a half-hour fictional episodic series that gets its name from the core narrative scenario, whereby a comedic situation arises and is resolved within the program time.[37] With episodic TV storytelling, viewers' relationships with characters and situations unfold and deepen over time; this opportunity for ongoing engagement is a meaningful characteristic that distinguishes this genre of comedy. As audiences become more involved with characters over the course of multiple episodes and seasons—particularly in the humorous context of a TV sitcom where viewers often laugh along with the shows' stars—this fosters parasocial relationships and social modeling that can reduce social prejudice and bias,[38] as we described more fully in chapter 2. Engaging narratives also can psychologically "transport" audiences into the imagined world of the story, facilitating attitude change consistent with the narrative's premises or conclusions.[39] In the digital era, where on-demand content allows for binge-watching that is even more immersive and involved than traditional weekly viewing,[40] connections to characters and transportation into a storyline— and their effects on persuasion—are likely to be intensified.

Moreover, with scripted comedy, any intention to persuade is obscured,[41] as social justice content is seamlessly woven into characters' conversations and plot development. Over time, what may have once been seen as unconventional or taboo can become normalized through long-term media portrayals,[42] particularly when couched in a nonthreatening comedic landscape. Indeed, as one of the oldest and most popular genres of TV, the sitcom plays a role in shaping our conception of what is "normal" or "ideal" in society. Thus, by allowing viewers to see a gay couple or immigrant family, for instance, embedded in ordinary, relatable, funny situations, scripted comedies can help cultivate broader acceptance of these groups while also empowering viewers who see their own experiences reflected in these stories.[43]

In general, sitcoms of the early TV era, while important for solidifying the audience popularity of the form, were mostly dominated by banal humor, often centered around white, suburban family life.[44] TV writer and producer Norman Lear's groundbreaking work in the 1970s and 1980s represented a historical turning point in scripted episodic TV comedy and its potential to fuel social change. Not only did his half-hour comedy shows—including *All in the Family* and the spin-off *The Jeffersons*, along with *Maude* and several others—focus squarely on topics of the day, along with little-seen individuals (African American, gay) and social issues (racism, abortion), but they also attracted enormous audiences. In the mid-1970s, an episode of the top-rated *All in the Family* averaged 50 million viewers, 60 percent of the American viewing public.[45]

Whereas 1990s television comedy was dominated by *Seinfeld*, widely dubbed a "show about nothing," scripted TV comedy in the 2000s floundered on broadcast networks, with few breakout "must-see" hits, as once-stable legacy TV was disrupted by cable and the internet.[46] Yet during this same time, original scripted television was experiencing a renaissance on cable, and by 2015, with the rise of on-demand internet-distributed television and streaming apps, business and production practices shifted to accommodate the growing desire for high-quality TV content, including comedies, catered to narrower niche audiences, thus permitting a surge of experimentation and diversity harkening back to Lear's era.[47] Between just 2012 and 2017, the number of original scripted series on TV rose by 69 percent—adding nearly 200 new series—owing largely to the rapid expansion of programming on streaming platforms, although sizable increases occurred across cable and broadcast as well.[48] During the

2015–16 season, comedy comprised the largest genre of shows streaming from digital platforms.[49] At the same time, the casts of scripted TV programs have slowly become more diverse, with greater inclusion of women, LGBTQ characters, people of color, and people with disabilities among series regulars—although these groups are still vastly underrepresented relative to their actual makeup in the U. S. population.[50] Women and people of color also are better represented among scripted TV creators and writers, particularly for digital shows; yet, these creative roles are still dominated by white men, and TV directors have seen no improvements in representation.[51]

Amidst this growth in new—and newly diverse—scripted TV content, the last decade has seen an abundance of TV comedies that confront social issues and foreground conversations about gender, race, and cultural and class identity. On broadcast networks, in addition to shows like ABC's *Black-ish* and NBC's *The Carmichael Show* that take up issues of racism, police brutality, and gun violence, CBS's *Mom* deals with themes of addiction and recovery, ABC's *Speechless* portrays a family with a teenage son who has cerebral palsy, and ABC's *Fresh Off the Boat* humanizes the immigrant experience in its depiction of a Taiwanese American family—the first Asian American sitcom family since 1994's *All American Girl*.[52] And ABC's long-running and award-winning *Modern Family* has helped to normalize gay marriage with its portrayal of Cam and Mitchell, who were wedded in the show's 2014 season finale, watched by 10.2 million viewers.[53] While these storylines are often softened and simplified to fit the formulaic structure of the prime-time network family sitcom, and can sometimes resort to reductive stereotypes,[54] they nonetheless are helping to shift the entertainment landscape by offering popular portrayals of social justice topics and marginalized groups that reach wide audiences (at least by today's standards).

As niche fare, scripted comedies on cable and streaming platforms have wider license than those on legacy broadcast networks to take on edgy social topics and experiment with form, often embracing darker and more serious storylines that defy genre conventions. For example, on premium cable, Issa Rae's Peabody Award–winning HBO program *Insecure* explores the social and racial dynamics that contextualize the contemporary black female experience. Examples on basic cable include the sex-positive, feminist comedy *Broad City* on Comedy Central; *The Last O.G.* on TBS, starring Tracy Morgan, whose character returns to a gentrified Brooklyn following a 15-year prison stint; and FX's Emmy Award–winning *Atlanta* about black life in Atlanta, which stars creator Donald Glover as Earn, a homeless Princeton dropout who is trying to manage his cousin's rap career. *Atlanta*, which has an all-black writers' room and provides unflinching portrayals of racism in America, is the most-watched comedy in FX's history.[55]

Among streaming platforms, Netflix has developed a host of socially critical comedies, including *Master of None*, which spotlights the American immigrant experience, and *Orange Is the New Black*, which broke ground with the racial and sexual diversity of its female cast and has exposed problems of mass incarceration and injustice in the prison system while also humanizing the female inmates. On Amazon, *Transparent* is the first sitcom with a transgender protagonist and the most trans-inclusive series across broadcast, cable, and streaming networks.[56] Also on Amazon, *The Marvelous Mrs. Maisel* chronicles a 1950s housewife turned stand-up comic as she challenges the male-dominated comedy scene, a scene that in many ways remains unchanged today.[57] Adding to the new comedy heyday are the reboots—on legacy networks and streaming platforms alike—of once-beloved hit sitcoms from the 1970s through the 2000s, including *One Day at a Time*, *Will & Grace*, and *Murphy Brown*, all of which deal with political and social issues.

In spite of shows like *Transparent* and *Atlanta*, the corporate TV networks, including the streaming platforms, continue to prioritize the stories of white, straight men; portrayals of women, the LBGTQ community, and ethnic minorities, while increasing, still do not embody the full diversity of these groups.[58] On the web, however, independent production and development practices have given rise to a range of culturally specific and fan-driven comedy series that authentically reflect the lived experiences of marginalized groups. As Aymar Christian describes in his book *Open TV*, independent producers make and market their own shows, relying on crowd-funding and utilizing the open distribution of the web "to create stories for communities perceived 'too niche'—of too little value—for television and theatrical distribution."[59] The web also can be a pipeline for mainstream success: Some web comedy series have gone on to be developed by legacy networks, such as *Broad City* on Comedy Central and *The Misadventures of Awkward Black Girl*, which served as the basis for HBO's *Insecure*—offering producers stability and scale but sacrificing the full creative autonomy afforded by the indie TV market.

STAND-UP COMEDY

Although stand-up comedy has roots in the American vaudeville era,[60] the form has since expanded around the world, and today is performed in venues ranging from intimate comedy clubs, bars, and coffeehouses to large concert arenas, for live audiences as well as mediated for audiences at home. The format is simple: A comic stands on stage and entertains the audience with jokes and social commentary, using minimal or no props. Many current U.S. comedy TV performers were trained through stand-up, including Amy Schumer, Trevor Noah, and Hasan Minhaj to name but a few.

Fundamental to stand-up is the role of the audience. Scholar Ian Brodie sees stand-up as a "form of talk. It implies a context that allows for reaction, participation, and engagement on the part of those to whom the stand-up comedian is speaking. When it is mediated through broadcasting and recording, an audience present to the performer is included in that mediation."[61] Stand-up comedy is, therefore, a collaborative act, "performed not to but with an audience."[62] Stand-up comics build intimacy with their audiences through conversational interactions, connecting to us through a process of recognition and the universality of their experiences. In turn, comics' rapport with their audience gives them permission to push boundaries and say things that may not otherwise be seen as acceptable in a public arena. As media scholar Bambi Haggins argues in her analysis of Chris Rock's stand-up comedy, "creating this sense of intimacy, regardless of the venue, is vital for a comic like Rock, whose material will, at some point or another, challenge the sensibilities of the audience."[63]

Another related distinction of stand-up comedy as a genre is that it allows for and even requires personal disclosures by the comic. According to Brodie, "most stand-up comedy implies a level of performed autobiography."[64] Scholars of stand-up comedy emphasize the importance of the comic persona, which, according to Bambi Haggins, is constructed from a comedian's life story in intersection with the broader culture.[65] According to Haggins, the "core" of a comedian's comic persona is articulated via stand-up comedy;[66] thus, a stand-up performance is the comic at their rawest, most honest self. This first-person perspective makes stand-up comedy a powerful and natural vehicle for social critique.

Speaking from personal experience, stand-up comics from marginalized groups are in a unique position to expose injustices and challenge stereotypes. Yet stand-up comedy is more than a lecture or confession; comics use humor to make their lived experiences more relatable and humanizing to their multiple audiences—some who share their social or cultural identity and some who do not. For example, in the face of rising Islamophobia following 9/11, Muslim American stand-ups like Maysoon Zayid and Azhar Usman told jokes about "flying while Muslim," which functioned to expose the absurdity of being stereotyped in American airports.[67] Such jokes exemplify what scholar Jaclyn Michael calls "insider to outsider" humor, which "socially critical comics use to change misinformed or negative social attitudes."[68] Marginalized comedians also often use self-deprecatory humor, allowing them to shift "from victim to perpetrator," and, in so doing, "undermine the power of people who laugh at them."[69]

Moreover, when comics open themselves up for scrutiny over the course of a 30-minute or hour-long performance, they create a powerful connection with the audience. Research in psychology has established the importance of self-disclosure for creating intimacy in interpersonal relationships,[70] a process that easily can be extended to the interaction between stand-up comics and their audience. The bond developed between a comic and audience is where stand-up comedy derives its greatest potential as an agent of social change and public engagement. Through this bond comes empathy and understanding, which can reduce stigma and foster more positive attitudes.[71]

The mediation of stand-up comedy allows it to reach beyond the walls of clubs and coffeehouses, broadening its potential for social influence. Since the 1950s, stand-up comedy has been mediated on records, radio, and late-night TV, and beginning in the late 1970s, an hour-long stand-up special on HBO was seen as a comic's big break. Yet in terms of sheer reach and accessibility, stand-up comedy's influence may be even more profound today than in earlier decades, given its availability in formats like YouTube, Vimeo, SoundCloud, iTunes, Spotify, podcasts, and other streaming audio and video platforms. Netflix has revealed a particular commitment to stand-up comedy; in addition to its many original stand-up feature specials, it also distributes half-hour and even 15-minute stand-up programs in its "The Standups" and "The Comedy Lineup" collections, respectively.[72] And HBO remains an iconic platform for stand-up, with recent specials from Michelle Wolf, Jerrod Carmichael, Sarah Silverman, and Tig Notaro, among others. In 2018, HBO adapted the *2 Dope Queens* podcast, hosted by Jessica Williams and Phoebe Robinson, into a series of live comedy specials featuring stand-up sets from lesser-known comics, many from underrepresented communities.

Recent specials on Netflix and HBO have showcased the various ways in which stand-up comedians—because of the deeply personal nature of their stand-up and the way in which they privilege the telling of their story—can illuminate social justice issues, reframe marginalized groups, and spur audiences to see or understand things from new perspectives. For example, Hannah Gadsby, in her much-discussed 2018 Netflix special *Nanette*, uses stand-up as a vehicle to expose and challenge the homophobia and sexism she has faced as a queer, "gender not normal" (in her words) female throughout her life, especially while growing up in a small town in Australia's Tasmania. Chris Gethard, in his 2017 HBO special *Career Suicide*, transparently chronicles his experiences with chronic depression, including a suicide attempt at age 21, using humor to help undercut the stigma attached to mental illness. Hasan Minhaj's 2017 Peabody Award–winning Netflix special, *Homecoming King*, uses personal comic storytelling to illuminate the realities of racism and xenophobia. In his stand-up set, Minhaj invites his audience to share in his emotional, often hilarious journey as an Indian-American Muslim growing up with immigrant parents amid racism and intolerance in post-9/11 America. In Ali Wong's Netflix specials *Baby Cobra* (2016) and *Hard Knock Wife* (2018)—both of which she performed while extremely pregnant—she offers a subtler social critique, using jokes about bodily fluids and oral sex to confront gender double standards, challenge assumptions about the female experience, and normalize the complicated relationships many women have with parenthood, work, and sex.

SKETCH COMEDY

Decades after the physical comedy sketches of vaudeville, mediated sketch comedy evolved against the backdrop of the late 1950s and 1960s movements for equality and social justice in the United States. Leading sketch comedy troupes included Chicago's The Second City, New York's The Premise, and The Committee in San Francisco.[73] With improvisation as the core generative practice, sketch allowed comedians of the time not only to entertain, but—perhaps more importantly—to take on divisive and socially critical issues, such as racial justice and the war. Thus, improvisation-based sketch comedy, whereby an ensemble of theatrical comics rehearses and performs brief scenario-based vignettes generally based on contemporary issues, comes from a socially conscious, activist motivation—an ethos that continues today among many sketch comedy performers.[74] The fertile training ground of The Second City has fostered decades of sketch-based talent and productions: Tiny Fey, Amy Poehler, Steve Carell, Stephen Colbert, Keegan-Michael Key, and many other contemporary comedians honed their craft with The Second City before achieving fame in mediated forms of sketch, scripted comedy, and satirical news.[75] Other prominent sketch theaters, among them The Groundlings and Upright Citizens Brigade, also continue to shape and prepare comedians for successful media careers.[76]

As a genre of mediated comedy, sketch is a nimble format that allows comics to construct humorous situations and satirical narratives around a seemingly endless range of identities, issues, and events. Unlike scripted comedies that must sustain an episode or season-long story arc, or stand-up that is necessarily rooted in the personal perspective of the comic, the structure of sketch gives it freedom to take up myriad social and political topics. Because of this flexibility and likely also owing to sketch comedy's origins in social justice activism, contemporary sketch comedy functions as an inherently risk-taking form. Audiences understand and even expect that sketch comedy will confront controversial issues in irreverent and often subversive ways. Moreover, the short-form, vignette-style of comedy sketches means that they are untethered from a larger narrative, making them highly sharable in the digital media era.

Over the last 40 years, no media entity has been more synonymous with sketch comedy than *Saturday Night Live* (*SNL*), created in 1975 by executive producer Lorne Michaels for NBC as a place for cutting-edge, countercultural humor. Politics has long been central to *SNL*'s brand; its political sketches—particularly during presidential election years—bring in the show's largest audiences. Its 2016–17 season featuring Alec Baldwin as Donald Trump averaged 11 million viewers per week—a 23-year high.[77] As Jeffrey Jones notes, *SNL*'s sketch format distinguishes its political content from satirical news and other TV comedy because it can reenact real political events such as debates, press conferences, and speeches, reinterpreting the actual words and actions of politicians to highlight their absurdity.[78]

Yet over the years, *SNL*'s identity as a countercultural voice has struggled against network TV's economic imperative to attract a mass audience. Thus, its humor often stays socially and politically safe, trafficking largely in celebrity and popular culture—and even when taking up politics, reserving its critique for politicians' personalities and other superficial characteristics rather than their policies and governance. Jeffrey Jones has argued that *SNL*'s political humor may even help make politicians more likeable, rather than challenging the status quo.[79] Despite these constraints, *SNL* has delivered its share of biting sociopolitical critique. For example, in the 1980s, Eddie Murphy wrote sketches that blended nonthreatening racial humor that appealed to mainstream white audiences with black-oriented critiques of racism and inequality.[80] And Tina Fey's 2008 parody of vice-presidential candidate Sarah Palin effectively highlighted Palin's lack of fit for office and negatively shifted perceptions of Palin among young viewers.[81] Sketches about Trump have been damning enough to activate his Twitter ire, although some research suggests that his tweets attacking *SNL* counteract any critical influence of the show's humor.[82]

While lacking *SNL*'s longevity, other TV sketch comedy shows have dealt more effectively with issues of race and gender than *SNL*, which has a reputation for marginalizing women and people of color. The Emmy Award–winning *In Living Color*—which aired on Fox in the early 1990s—was created and produced by black comic Keenen Ivory Wayans, featured a majority black cast, and focused on black culture and issues of race and class. *Chappelle's Show*, from comedian Dave Chappelle—which aired on

Comedy Central in 2003–4, with a truncated third season in 2006—pointed an unflinching spotlight on the ignorance and hypocrisy of racism, including his viral episode focused on the character Clayton Bigsby, played by Chappelle, a leader of a white supremacist group. More recently, half-hour TV programs such as Comedy Central's *Inside Amy Schumer* and *Key & Peele*, both recipients of prestigious Peabody Awards, were known for taking on gender and racial politics, respectively.

Online, sketch comedy is discovered by audiences and shared virally in short-form, most prominently from Funny or Die, CollegeHumor, UCB Comedy (from Upright Citizens Brigade), and SCTV on YouTube from The Second City team, although independent YouTube vloggers also often incorporate sketch into their repertoires. Epitomizing the booming era of short-form online videos, the comedy website Funny or Die was created in 2007 by a group of comedians and producers, including Will Ferrell, Adam McKay, and Chris Henchy.[83] Supporting both user-generated content and Funny or Die–produced videos, the site is known for its comedy sketches, often featuring celebrities, and has built an enormous web comedy platform—averaging more than 100 million video views per month[84]—and a commanding social media presence. According to long-term creative director Andrew Steele, its ethos, from the beginning, has been oriented toward "attack[ing] power, whatever form that takes."[85] Indeed, Funny or Die has found viral success with topical political humor. For example, in a 2014 video, actress Kristen Bell parodied Mary Poppins, singing in support of a federal minimum wage increase. As a recurring web series, Funny or Die's Emmy-winning *Between Two Ferns* is a sketch-style, faux talk show hosted by Zach Galifianakis, who conducts awkward, mostly improvised interviews with celebrity guests meant to poke fun at the artifice of the talk show genre. In March 2014, when President Obama needed help encouraging young people to sign up for health insurance through the Affordable Care Act, he appeared on *Between Two Ferns*, resulting in a 40 percent traffic increase to healthcare.gov.[86] Piggybacking on its success in the political realm, in 2015, Funny or Die opened a Washington, DC, office to create content explicitly focused on politics and civic issues. Between 2015 and 2018, the office developed 40 different political projects.[87]

DOCUMENTARY

Documentary is a genre of nonfiction mediated storytelling, defined as "the creative treatment of actuality" by social reformer John Grierson in the 1930s.[88] The genre, a reflection of real life, is artistically creative and often maintains a public interest focus.[89] Some—but certainly not all— documentaries endeavor to illuminate social justice issues with the hope of advancing social reform.[90] Indeed, of the genres considered in this chapter, documentary offers the possibility for the most in-depth and complex exploration of a single issue. In the digital era, social-issue documentary stories are often accompanied by a strategic public engagement campaign designed to incite public support and action around a change in the status quo.[91] Documentary's potential to engage viewers persuasively is attributed, at least in part, to its depiction of real life,[92] as well as its ability to engage audiences emotionally.[93]

Social-issue documentary film and TV programming is found across a wide variety of platforms and networks, including HBO, Showtime, CNN, PBS, Discovery, National Geographic, iTunes, Amazon, Netflix, Vimeo, YouTube, and more. Thanks to streaming networks and YouTube, audiences in the digital era are more readily able to discover, access, and watch documentary storytelling. Short-form documentaries are also found on journalistic sites, including the *New York Times'* Op-Docs series, where independent documentary makers are invited to reflect editorially on topical issues.

Comedic social-issue documentaries, while less dominant than a somber approach, have clear audience appeal and value in social justice work. Writing in 1999, documentary scholar John Corner argued that comedy and irony can be used to critical advantage in documentary:

> The linking of documentary purposes to comic and sometimes farcical devices can generate an affective power which the more committedly "sober" tradition of programme-making . . . is hard put to achieve. Perhaps the possibilities here offer some of the most interesting lines of current development for documentarists wanting to retain a radical, questioning edge in their work while attracting large audiences within an increasingly competitive television marketplace.[94]

Michael Moore is the most well-known documentary filmmaker who employs a comedic approach. Moore has produced eight full-length political documentaries, including his first film *Roger & Me*, which chronicled the decline of his hometown, Flint, Michigan, after General Motors closed its plants there; *Bowling for Columbine* about U.S. gun culture and violence, which won the 2002 Academy Award for Documentary Feature; and *Fahrenheit 9/11*, which critiqued U.S. involvement in the Iraq War under President George W. Bush and stands as the highest grossing documentary of all time.[95] Moore popularized what Amber Day calls the satiric documentary style, which "combines the playful, satiric style with unabashed polemic, resulting in a product rooted simultaneously in mass culture entertainment and political activism, guerilla theater, and documentary exposé. These elements are brought together through a narrative centered around the filmmaker's own personal quest, tracking his interactions and explorations."[96] Although Moore's ethics as a filmmaker have often come under scrutiny, his style of documentary—combining humor and politics, entertainment and activism—has unquestionably helped to popularize the form.[97]

Other notable examples of comedic documentary include *Blue Vinyl: The World's First Toxic Comedy*, a 2002 documentary, which combined humor and investigative reporting to uncover the health and environmental hazards of polyvinyl chloride (PVC), as one of the filmmakers, Judith Helfand, tries to convince her parents to replace the vinyl siding on their home. The 2010 documentary *Bag It* follows an "everyman" named Jeb as he illuminates our dependence on plastic bags—exploring their origins, their final resting places in landfills and oceans, and their ecological impact. For advocacy groups and policymakers working on efforts to scale back Americans' use of plastics, the film was an effective mechanism for social change, and the comedic approach has, at least anecdotally, been recognized as a key element in its public engagement success.[98]

Perhaps unsurprisingly, several funny social-issue documentaries have been about comedy itself. *The Muslims Are Coming!*, a 2013 comedy documentary created by and starring comedians Negin Farsad and Dean Obeidallah, follows a group of Muslim American stand-up comics as they tour the United States, using comedy to confront and attempt to change negative perceptions of Muslims in America. The 2014 film *Stand Up Planet*, discussed at length in chapter 5, uses stand-up comedy as a way to explore issues of global poverty in India and South Africa. The 2016 documentary *Tickling Giants*, directed by Sara Taksler—a longtime senior producer at *The Daily Show*—explores the intersections of comedy and free speech through the story of Bassem Youssef, the host of an enormously popular but politically controversial news satire show in Egypt, who was ultimately forced to leave his country because he critiqued his government. *The Problem with Apu*, released on cable's truTV in 2017, focuses on creator and comic Hari Kondabolu, as he deconstructs the problematic South Asian–American stereotypes embedded in *The Simpsons* character Apu, voiced by white actor Hank Azaria.

Further blurring the boundaries between comedy and other formats, comedian W. Kamau Bell hosts Emmy Award–winning *United Shades of America*, an ongoing docuseries on cable news channel CNN, in which Bell travels throughout the country and visits with different communities to explore issues of race and identity. He has met with people who have very different views from his own, such as members of the Ku Klux Klan, as well as many groups "whose voices," according to Bell, "aren't heard enough,"[99] including refugees, Sikhs, the disability community, Native Americans at Standing Rock, and Chicago residents working to end gang violence in their neighborhoods. Reflecting the media hybridization of the contemporary era, the program is part news reporting, part documentary, and part critical comedy.

COMEDY GENRES IN THE CONTEXT OF SOCIAL CHANGE

While most comedy is created to make us laugh, comedy about social justice also makes us think—about the unfairness and systemic inequities plaguing our society, the abuses of the powerful, and the ordinary everyday injustices faced by marginalized groups. As comedians push the boundaries of what might be seen as socially acceptable, they challenge audiences to imagine social issues in new ways. Yet within this broad understanding of what constitutes socially critical comedy, there exists tremendous variation. This chapter strived to organize this variation into a coherent framework, articulating key genres of mediated comedy and illustrating how they function distinctively in the context of social change.

Satirical news shows comment directly on current events, exerting agenda-setting power to both elevate lesser-known issues and provide alternative framings for well-trodden topics, while using humor to make complex issues more digestible. Given their overtly critical lens, satirical news programs may be best suited for mobilizing like-minded audiences, rather than persuading those who hold an opposing view. *Scripted comedies* offer relatable characters and absorbing storylines that both reflect and help change the culture. Together, humor and a compelling fictional narrative provide an entry point through which audiences are invited to connect emotionally and empathize with individuals that they may not encounter in their daily lives, helping to challenge stereotypes and promote tolerance toward marginalized groups. Because social justice content is integrated naturally into ongoing storylines and conversations between characters, scripted comedy is a valuable way to reach audiences who may be resistant to persuasion in other formats. *Stand-up comics* provide social critique and give voice to marginalized identities through their personal insights and experiences, leveraging their intimate connection with their audience to shift perspectives and generate a broader conversation. *Sketch comedy*, whose history is rooted in the counterculture, is inherently boundary-pushing and offers a flexible format that readily can take on myriad topical issues in the social justice space. Sketch comedy's short form also renders it easily shareable in the digital age. In *documentaries*, which provide serious immersion into a single topic, comedy disrupts the typical somber portrayal of social realities, attracting and mobilizing larger audiences and pushing new ideas into mainstream discourse, thus often acting as a source of counternarratives. Mediated comedy about social justice also is not limited to these genres, although they are often the foundation for comedy in other formats. Editorial cartoons and comic strips, comedy podcasts, vlogs, feature-length films, and late-night comedy talk shows all incorporate elements of the comedy genres presented in this chapter while taking on social justice issues.

Importantly, each genre of mediated comedy outlined in this chapter provides unique strategic opportunities for interventions in social justice that are increasingly being leveraged by activists and advocacy groups.

Comedy documentaries offer a format familiar to activists and can be used fairly readily by advocates as an engagement tool through local screenings and other mechanisms. Partnerships with Funny or Die and Onion Labs offer formalized mechanisms for creating and distributing strategic comedy messages that use sketch and satire. At the same time, the openness of the web has paved the way for scripted comedy serials that have overt activist intentions, such as *Halal in the Family*, a sitcom parody designed to critique anti-Muslim bias. Yet even with existing entertainment products, there are opportunities for advocates to partner with creative decision-makers. For example, comedy writers are often looking for new storylines and ways to accurately and thoughtfully incorporate contemporary social issues. In response, some nonprofit and advocacy organizations make collaboration with the entertainment industry an integral part of their strategic practice, convening meetings with entertainment writers to pitch story ideas and brief them on topics that might be of interest. Even when advocates do not have the opportunity to influence the creative process directly, they can piggyback on the spotlight that mediated comedy shines on social issues. For example, topical clips from satirical news shows or independently produced short-form sketch videos about justice topics can be lifted up by advocacy groups and shared with their networks to galvanize supporters and raise the profile of particular issues and arguments. In subsequent chapters, we explore in depth the intentional ways that activists are increasingly interfacing with the various genres of mediated comedy and the creative minds behind them to affect social change.

PART II Comedy in Social Justice
Challenges

4 Can Laughter Help Save the Planet?

COMEDY'S ROLE IN COMMUNICATING ABOUT
CLIMATE CHANGE

*❝Save the planet?! We don't even know how to take care of our-
selves yet! We haven't learned how to care for one another,
and we're gonna save the fucking planet?!❞*

George Carlin, stand-up comedian[1]

In April 2016, in the throes of the U.S. presidential campaign season, if
you were one of Funny or Die's 15 million followers on Facebook, a video
may have come through your news feed featuring a cadre of older actors
and comedians—Cloris Leachman, Ed Asner, M. Emmet Walsh, Michael
Lerner, and Bill Cobbs—seemingly delighting in the fact that they don't
care about climate change. The video opens with Cloris Leachman: "I'm
actress and notable famous person Cloris Leachman. And I gotta say it
feels wonderful not caring about climate change." We also hear from Ed
Asner: "Worry about climate change? It's an after-I'm-dead problem. I
still have while I'm alive problems ... like finding comfortable shoes."
These septua- and octogenarians aren't worried about sea level rise:
Leachman sarcastically quips, "Ooh the big bad ocean is going to rise up
and swallow half of Florida," to which Bill Cobbs replies, "Good. That
takes care of our country's Florida problem." While arguably great comedy,
the video—now with more than 6.5 million views and 94,000 shares on

Figure 4 Cloris Leachman in the Funny or Die video "Old People Don't Care about Climate Change."
SOURCE / CREDIT: YouTube video screenshot / fair use.

Facebook—ends with a serious call to action: "Old people don't care about climate change. That's why you have to. Vote climate."[2]

The video was created as a partnership between online sketch comedy and pop culture institution Funny or Die and Defend Our Future—the Millennial-focused environmental advocacy arm of the Environmental Defense Fund—as part of Defend Our Future's broader strategy to motivate young people to not only turn out to the polls but also to prioritize climate change when voting.[3] The video functions as satire, skewering the blinkered perspective of those who downplay the importance and dire consequences of climate change. It also calls attention to the generational cleavage around climate change. Today's youngest citizens will bear the brunt of a changing climate, and polls show that, in the U.S., they tend to worry about climate change and support action to address it more so than older generations;[4] yet, they typically vote at starkly lower rates.[5] The video reminds young people that it's up to them to step in and make a difference. Here, Defend Our Future gambled that satirical comedy about climate change would not only be attention-grabbing but also empowering to young people in the lead-up to the 2016 election. Was this a sensible gamble? Can comedy help engage the public around climate change, and if so, how?

For decades, scientists and activists have issued dire warnings about climate change, yet have been unable to create the public and political will to support decisive action that can help avoid the worst climate impacts. Defend Our Future's embrace of comedy signals a growing recognition among advocates and entertainers alike that comedy may be one way to help climate change break through into the public imagination. As climate change becomes an urgent reality yet remains a relatively low political priority among most U.S. policymakers and the public, and is often given short shrift by many mainstream news outlets, comedy has emerged as an important space for discussing climate change—most prominently in satirical news shows but also in sitcoms, fictional films, documentaries, sketch, stand-up, and strategic advocacy campaigns like Defend Our Future's.

This chapter argues that in the face of a crisis as complex and consequential as climate change, comedy offers a valuable, if often underused, pillar of communication—one that can engage attention, offer a sense of hope and agency, and in some cases, overcome partisan resistance. In this way, comedy may help to encourage wider public acceptance of climate solutions and foster the public engagement needed to pressure policymakers to act more aggressively.[6] Below, we first offer a brief review of climate change and its impacts. We then describe central challenges to public engagement with climate change and how comedy can contribute, before describing key examples of contemporary mediated comedy focused on climate change. The chapter concludes with results from an original experimental study that illustrate the benefits and trade-offs of comedic approaches to climate change communication.

CLIMATE CHANGE AS A SOCIAL PROBLEM

Global climate change refers to ongoing, system-wide changes to our global climate. The most notable way that our climate is changing is via an increase in average surface temperature, but climate change also encompasses shifts in precipitation and wind patterns, rising sea levels, ice melt, and ocean acidification. The scientific community widely agrees that human activities—primarily, the burning of fossil fuels but also deforestation and certain agricultural practices—are contributing to increases in heat-trapping greenhouse gases, such as carbon dioxide and methane, in the earth's atmosphere, and that this buildup is fueling temperature rise.[7]

As of 2015, global average surface temperatures have risen by one degree Celsius compared to pre-industrial levels (i.e., since 1880), and increases continue apace. The four warmest years on record have occurred since 2014, with 2016 ranking as the hottest.[8] Many scientists identify two degrees of warming as a critical threshold beyond which we will see dangerous impacts of climate change, although a 2018 report by the UN Intergovernmental Panel on Climate Change warned that severe effects and widespread suffering would be felt with just 1.5°C of warming and as soon as 2040.[9] We already have a taste of what our new climate reality will look like: Recent years have delivered bigger, slower moving, and wetter hurricanes bringing record rainfall and flooding, such as Hurricanes Harvey, Maria, and Florence; devastating floods from Malawi to Texas to India; massive wildfires in the western U.S. and in Greece; intense heat waves across Europe, Asia, North America, and northern Africa; and droughts in California, South Africa, and Australia—extreme events that scientists say are intensified by climate change.[10] In turn, climate change is threatening public health, not only because of extreme weather that puts people in harm's way, but also because of its degrading effects on air quality, which contribute to asthma, allergies, and other respiratory and cardiovascular illnesses; the spread of infectious diseases such as malaria and Lyme disease; increases in water and food scarcity due to drought, contamination, and other factors; and the rise in mental health problems as people deal with the stressors of climate change.[11]

Climate change, then, is fundamentally a human issue. It has been described as the "defining social justice issue of our time,"[12] not only because of generational disparities, discussed in this chapter's introduction, whereby younger generations will shoulder the burden of a problem passed on by their elders, but also due to the socioeconomic inequalities that shape vulnerabilities to climate change. The populations and parts of the world most threatened by climate change—from residents of low-lying, small-island states to Indigenous people living in the Arctic—are some of the world's poorest and have the least developed governments;[13] they also have contributed least to the causes of climate change. Within developed countries like the U. S., the communities that will suffer most are those that already are marginalized: poor people, communities of color, immigrant groups, Indigenous people, people with disabilities, women, children, older people, and people with preexisting or chronic medical conditions.[14]

Solving the climate crisis requires massive collective action and behavior change at the global level. The Paris Agreement, negotiated through the United Nations Framework Convention on Climate Change (UNFCC) and established in December 2015—although it lacked binding targets for emissions cuts—nonetheless signaled the possibility of widespread international cooperation to keep global temperature rise to well below two degrees Celsius above pre-industrial levels, while also recognizing the human rights and equity dimensions of climate change. However, in 2017, President Trump announced plans to withdraw the U. S.—the world's biggest carbon polluter—from the Paris Agreement.[15] In the first two years of his presidency, Trump also reversed a number of steps taken by the Obama administration to mitigate climate change.[16] In the face of these political setbacks, grassroots organizing and public engagement have never been more critical.

PUBLIC ENGAGEMENT WITH CLIMATE CHANGE

Despite the profound dangers climate change poses, it is not an issue that figures prominently in the American public's consciousness. In 2019, only 44 percent of Americans rated climate change as a top national priority, putting it at the bottom of a list of issues gauged by the Pew Research Center.[17] Just about three in ten Americans say they are very worried about global warming,[18] while few Americans follow news about global warming very closely[19] or discuss the issue regularly with their friends and family.[20] And only 13 percent of Americans say that they have contacted their elected officials to urge them to take action to reduce global warming.[21] This relatively low level of public concern for and engagement with climate change is due primarily to the intersection of three factors: the nature of climate change itself, the politicization of the crisis, and the way climate change is typically communicated.

First, the process of climate change is relatively abstract, invisible, and diffuse. For example, we can't see how our everyday activities—such as running the air conditioner or driving to work—contribute to climate change, even as they do. We also can't easily observe the climate changing, even if we occasionally experience extreme weather that could be linked to a warming world. Compounding this problem is the fact that the worst climate impacts may not be felt for a generation, and present climate impacts continue to be most visible in remote polar regions. As a result, climate change remains a perceptually distant issue, both in time and space,[22] and therefore lacks the relevance and immediacy that other public issues—like health care access or economic concerns—have. At the same time, climate change is a complex, "super wicked" problem that evades simple or straightforward policy and technological solutions.[23] Individual actions, like driving less or using less electricity in our homes, are helpful, yet insufficient. In order to slow climate change, the world needs to come together and embrace disruptive changes to the social and economic status quo. This is no small task, and is rendered all the more challenging by a rapidly ticking clock. Climate change is thus an issue that is at once both distancing and overwhelming, with a problem and solution that both feel out of reach to the average individual. In turn, people respond by pushing it from their minds.

Secondly, within the United States, the issue of climate change has become inextricably linked with political identity. Since the 1990s, as political elites have become more divided along partisan lines on climate change and other environmental issues, they have cued the public to follow suit.[24] Democrats are now the party of environmental concern, while among Republicans, the perceived threat to business and industry posed by the reality of climate change has spurred climate skepticism and even outright denialism. This uncertainty about climate change has been stoked by a well-organized denial movement—composed of fossil fuel corporations along with conservative think tanks, media, and politicians—that has cast doubt on the science of climate change and undermined efforts to advance climate mitigation policy.[25] Even though, today, the majority of Americans agree that climate change is real and human-caused, partisan divisions persist: In 2018, 90 percent of liberal Democrats said that global warming is caused by human activities, compared to just

28 percent of conservative Republicans.[26] This tribal mentality is a barrier to effective communication, as partisans respond to new information not with open-mindedness but with motivated reasoning—a tendency to accept arguments and evidence that reinforce one's existing beliefs and to ignore or refute those that don't.[27] Thus, efforts to promote engagement with climate change are often met with resistance, if not hostility, by conservative Republican audiences.[28] More broadly, simply talking about climate change can be contentious and polarizing.

Finally, news media often fail to communicate about climate change in ways that encourage people to engage with the issue. Just as climate change is a difficult issue for the public to grasp, its complexity and incremental nature make it challenging for news media to cover, as it doesn't fit well either with journalistic norms that emphasize drama and novelty or with industry economics that prioritize eyeballs and ratings.[29] Thus, climate change has mostly occupied the sidelines of U.S. news coverage, particularly on TV. When news outlets do cover climate change, they often focus on scientific uncertainty and political disagreement. Indeed, through at least the mid-2000s, leading U.S. news organizations engaged in "false balance," giving roughly equal attention to perspectives that both supported and challenged established climate science.[30] Although journalists have largely self-corrected,[31] they still tend to emphasize partisan conflict.[32] This makes it difficult for the public to see the personal relevance of climate change.

At the same time, much climate change communication—in news, entertainment, and activism—has focused on doom and gloom. For example, network TV news broadcasts have often used a narrative of "climate tragedy" that emphasizes the disaster wrought by global warming;[33] in contrast, journalists have spent less time covering the role of ordinary people in the fight against climate change.[34] Moreover, from Al Gore's 2007 Oscar-winning documentary *An Inconvenient Truth*—with its tagline "the most terrifying film you will ever see"—to journalist David Wallace-Wells's 2017 landmark *New York Magazine* article, "The Uninhabitable Earth," which vividly depicted worst-case climate change scenarios and became the most read article in the magazine's history,[35] the most popular and widespread imagery and narratives about global warming have trafficked in fear and dread. Indeed, an entire genre of "cli-fi" films has emerged in recent years, many of which, in the mold of the 2004 blockbuster *The Day after Tomorrow*, focus on stories of apocalypse, dystopia, and disaster.[36] Yet fear-based imagery and appeals can be overwhelming and immobilizing,[37] especially if they are not balanced with more hopeful narratives.[38]

A ROLE FOR COMEDY?

While comedy is certainly not a cure-all, it may help to correct for some of the deficiencies in existing communication approaches and offer a way into a problem that—despite its urgency—has yet to register as a priority for many Americans. As a form of climate change communication, comedy offers several distinct benefits. First, it provides a way to engage public interest in and attention to an issue that many people are not actively following. The facts, statistics, and future-oriented projections that underlie scientists' understanding of climate change are unlikely to compel public interest in an issue that already seems distant and overwhelming, whereas comedy and funny stories connect with people on a personal, emotional level and thus can help make climate change seem more relatable. By linking climate change to everyday concerns, comedy also can provide new ways of thinking about the issue. Given that less than 10 percent of Americans are truly dismissive of climate change and unlikely to change their beliefs,[39] communication efforts are best spent trying to reach and motivate those who are ambivalent about the issue or who are complacent about taking action. Particularly for the sizable swath of Americans who are indifferent toward climate change, comedic and narrative-based communication approaches can help make the issue seem more interesting and accessible.[40] In fact, several studies have found that comedy about climate change was most engaging and persuasive for individuals who had less initial interest in the issue.[41]

Even those Americans who are most engaged with and worried about climate change—now the largest segment of the public[42]—lack a sense of efficacy, meaning that they feel ill equipped to effectively help fight climate change and, as a result, are less likely to take action.[43] More generally, climate change is profoundly depressing and, therefore, disengaging.

Comedy offers a way through the fatigue and despair. While much comedy is not, in fact, hopeful—it instead highlights society's shortcomings—it packages its critiques in humor and entertainment, thereby creating a positive connection with a topic that otherwise may seem hopeless and not worth investing effort in. In this way, comedy can be empowering and activating. In support of this idea, one study found that a short-form comedy video about climate change, delivered in the context of a faux weather report, increased viewers' willingness to take political action, particularly among younger audiences.[44]

Comedy also may be able to help overcome the partisan rancor that characterizes climate change by broaching the issue in a nonthreatening way. People like to laugh, and they seek out opportunities for entertainment. Thus, even otherwise resistant audiences may listen to a message or story about climate change if they perceive laughter as a payoff. Moreover, as discussed in chapter 2, comedy can reduce counter-arguing, which means that skeptical audiences may be less likely to reject information about climate change when it is presented through jokes and humor. In short, comedy can help disarm audiences and make the topic of climate change more palatable.

Finally, comedy can say what other media can't or won't; comedians, for example, are not encumbered by professional journalistic norms and thus can call out hypocrisy and highlight the absurdity of climate politics in ways that traditional journalists and more serious media cannot. Comedians also can communicate about climate change without seeming preachy or condescending. Environmentalists are often perceived as eccentric and aggressive, which can interfere with their efforts to promote social change;[45] thus, comedy, particularly when it is embraced by environmental advocates, offers a more approachable and less didactic way to engage people with climate change.

Yet comedy about an existential challenge like climate change is not self-evident. What is it about climate change that can be mined for laughs? Perhaps the easiest targets for climate change humor are the so-called deniers or skeptics who don't accept established climate science. While such low-hanging fruit may be effective for rallying the liberal troops, it may work less well for bringing new folks into the fold and for reducing political polarization. People don't like to be attacked, even if it's done in a funny way; thus, humor focused on other aspects of climate change may be needed to help broaden public engagement. For example, comedy also can locate the absurdity in the flawed logic of political leaders and the ridiculousness of global climate politics writ large, the self-serving rhetoric and actions of the industry actors most responsible for climate change, the excesses of human consumption and the disregard with which we treat our planet, the disconnect between the reality of climate change and public perceptions or engagement, the way our lives will be changed by climate change, proposed solutions to climate change, or the problematic ways that climate change is often communicated in the media. The next section reviews some of the ways that climate change has been represented in contemporary mediated comedy.

CLIMATE CHANGE IN MEDIATED COMEDY

In recent years, climate change has appeared—albeit irregularly—as a topic across all genres of mediated comedy. Rather than attempt an exhaustive accounting of comedy's treatment of climate change, we highlight several key examples that illustrate the various functions of comedy in climate change discourse: as political critique and counternarrative, as explainer, as a reflective mirror, as a tool of empowerment, as an attention hook, and as comic relief.

Among mediated comedy genres, satirical news programs have taken up climate change most enthusiastically. Climate change, as an issue that often is both inadequately covered by the news media and handled ineptly by elected officials, is ripe for comedic treatment by satirical news hosts for whom the news media and politicians are favorite targets. As progenitors of the contemporary genre of satirical news, Comedy Central's *The Daily Show with Jon Stewart* and *The Colbert Report* established an early and consistent track record of covering climate change;[46] in fact, in 2007, the Pew Research Center found that *The Daily Show* devoted a greater proportion of its "news hole" to the topic of global warming than did the mainstream press.[47] For the most part, coverage on both shows explicitly affirmed the reality of climate change and decisively rebutted climate skeptics, including those in government.[48] Indeed, an analysis of more than 180 segments between the two programs found that Republican politicians and climate skeptics were the most frequent targets of the hosts' climate-related humor.[49] Thus, unlike some traditional news outlets, *The Daily Show* and *The Colbert Report* took a clear stand on climate change and, in so doing, may have influenced viewers to accept that climate change is happening, as one study found.[50]

Other news satire hosts have carried on this tradition. For example, Trevor Noah, the current host of *The Daily Show*, frequently covers climate change, and in October 2017, Samantha Bee devoted an entire episode of *Full Frontal* to the issue, using her opening monologue to connect climate change to the hurricanes and wildfires experienced in the U.S. that year—something that few traditional news broadcasters did.[51] John Oliver's coverage on *Last Week Tonight* has been particularly notable; in 2017, *New Republic* journalist Emily Atkin dubbed Oliver "the best climate change reporter on television."[52] In 2017 alone, Oliver did a long segment disassembling President Trump's rationale for withdrawing from the Paris climate agreement; another on the coal industry, in which he exposed Trump's empty and misguided promises to bring coal jobs back; and still another that took on the flawed National Flood Insurance Program (NFIP) following the spate of hurricanes in the United States.

Whereas traditional news about climate change is often hamstrung by its brief, fragmented, and sometimes conflictual coverage, Oliver offers impressive factual depth on relatively untrodden topics related to climate change science and policy, while using humor both to engage his audience's attention and to punctuate his arguments. For example, Oliver comically explained how the NFIP was created in 1968 by Congress as a temporary fix, based on the unfounded expectation that at-risk homeowners would eventually relocate out of flood zones: "That's not how people work. We will gladly accept huge risks to our personal safety for the sake of a discount. That was the entire premise behind the McDonald's dollar menu."[53] Moreover, Oliver highlights solutions, warding off any cynicism that might be implied by his dismal assessment of our political leaders. For example, in his Paris Agreement segment, after lampooning several state-level Republican politicians' uninformed interpretations of climate science, he issued a call to action: "If your local reps resemble those guys in any way, you are going to need to work to get them out of office as soon as you can."[54] In his coverage of the NFIP, he concluded the segment with suggestions for reform, including providing people financial help to move out of high-risk flood areas.

Oliver also has taken to task climate skeptics and the media who enable them. A standard format for covering climate change on cable TV news outlets, such as CNN, is the split-screen "he said, she said" interview, where one guest accepts established climate science and another contests it, giving the false impression that scientific opinion on climate change is evenly divided, or at least widely debated. In a 2014 episode, Oliver satirized that misleading news format when he invited Bill Nye, "The Science Guy," to ostensibly debate a climate change denier, only to then welcome to the stage 96 climate scientists who agreed with Nye and two people who agreed with the skeptic, allowing for what Oliver termed "a statistically representative climate change debate."[55] Here, Oliver used comedy to critique typical news media representations of climate change as well as the broader notion that the reality of climate change is up for debate.

Outside of satirical news, several one-off episodes in popular sitcoms have incorporated climate-related topics, humorously highlighting the importance of environmental action. For example, in a 2014 episode of ABC's *Modern Family*, Jesse Eisenberg guest starred as Mitchell and Cam's overzealous eco-friendly neighbor, Asher, who chastises Mitchell for not being "green" enough. When Asher stops by to ask Mitchell to stop running his air conditioner all the time, Mitchell explains, "My partner runs a little hot," to which Asher quips, "Not as a hot as our planet." When Mitchell retorts that he drives a Prius, Asher responds, "My car runs on reclaimed cooking oil." As the episode unfolds, Mitchell's efforts to impress his neighbor with his greenness culminate in a series of comic blunders. Ultimately, Mitchell admits, "I like to think that I'm greener than I am, but maybe I just want the credit without doing all the hard work that you do."[56] Fans of *Modern Family* likely relate to Mitchell, and the episode thus may encourage them to more carefully consider the environmental impact of their own everyday behavior. Mitchell's naïve understanding of his own behavior, brought into comic relief by his neighbor, also critiques the notion that an individual action (like driving a Prius) can address the climate crisis and underscores the need for broader societal changes.

NBC's *30 Rock*, created by and starring Tina Fey, took up the issue of climate change in two episodes, season 2's "Greenzo" and season 4's "Sun

Tea," both of which aired during NBC's "Green Week." These episodes are notable in that they explicitly critiqued shallow corporate efforts to address climate change—including that of NBC's Green Week. For example, in "Greenzo," fictional NBC network executive Jack Donaghy (played by Alec Baldwin) hires guest star David Schwimmer as the network's environmental but "business friendly" mascot: "Greenzo! Saving the Earth while maintaining profitability."[57] Yet Greenzo quickly gets carried away with his planet-saving power and goes off corporate message, both criticizing the staff's environmentally unfriendly habits of leaving lights and computers on ("You act like you care but you do nothing") and in a *Today Show* appearance, his corporate boss ("Did you know that there are people out there with the power to heal Mother Gaia, but they're paralyzed with greed? I'm talking about big companies and their two-faced, fat cat executives").[58] Jack then tries to replace Greenzo with Al Gore, who appears in a cameo as himself, but Gore refuses to endorse Jack's message that "big business is good for the environment." Instead, Gore explains, "If your network really wants to demonstrate a commitment to the environment . . . you can have a character in prime time making a passionate argument to the American people that we need CO_2 taxes to replace the payroll taxes. Your parent company can lobby Congress and the President to pass the [Kyoto] Treaty and save the climate!"[59] Similarly, in "Sun Tea," Jack has been tasked with reducing his show's carbon footprint. Al Gore again appears, playing a custodian installing fluorescent light bulbs, which he notes use less power than regular ones but are, on their own, insufficient for addressing climate change: "If we're going to solve the climate crisis we've got to change more than the lightbulbs and the windows. We've got to change the laws and policies through collective political action on a large scale."[60]

An October 2018 sketch on *Saturday Night Live* raised a mirror to many citizens' lack of concern about climate change. In the episode following the release of the IPCC's report warning that the world has just over a decade to act in order to avoid the worst effects of climate change, "Weekend Update" co-hosts Colin Jost and Michael Che satirized the American public's muted response. Jost explains, "Scientists basically published an obituary for the Earth this week, and people were like, 'well, what does Taylor Swift think about it'?" Che admits: "The story has been stressing me out all week. I just keep asking myself, why don't I care about this? I mean don't get me wrong, I one hundred percent believe in climate change; yet, I'm willing to do absolutely nothing about it." He goes on to suggest that to get people to care, you need to tell them that climate change is going to take away things that matter to them—for Fox News viewers, "all the flags and Confederate statues"; for black people, "Atlanta"; for white women, "all the yarn."[61] Here, the comedians' relatable responses to the dire IPCC report provide a vehicle for viewers to consider their own reactions and perhaps recalibrate them to better reflect the urgency of climate change.

Comedy also can provide hopeful frames about climate change that serve as a model for and potential motivator of individual and collective action. In the 2009 documentary *No Impact Man*, filmmakers Laura Gabbert and Justin Schein followed Colin Beavan, a husband and father living in Manhattan with his family, as they embarked on a comedic personal experiment to live a full year with no net environmental impact, giving up modern-day conveniences such as electricity, driving, and take-out food, and dramatically minimizing their waste. The comedy arises, in part, from Beavan's everyday interactions with his wife, Michelle Conlin, who initially struggles with the sacrifices required of sustainable living and questions whether Beavan will be seen as a "fringe whacko."[62] As their family navigates the challenges of contemporary life without the efficiencies to which they've grown accustomed, the audience is invited to share in and laugh along with their weaknesses and mistakes, as well as in their rewards, such as the health benefits, outdoor adventures, and deeper social relationships afforded by their new lifestyle. Scholar Marilyn DeLaure argues that the film offers a comically framed performance of green identity with which ordinary people can relate and, in turn, a model that they may want to emulate, at least in part.[63] Through comedy, low carbon living becomes more approachable. In DeLaure's view, "comedy enables us to see ourselves not as helpless victims in a doomsday scenario, but as imperfect actors who are both guilty contributors to the problem and agents responsible for its amelioration."[64]

Spotlight California, a 2016 documentary web series, exemplifies how comedy can be used both to illuminate and counterbalance deeply serious content about environmental issues. The film—also discussed in chapter 7—was developed by the progressive advocacy organization NextGen America (formerly NextGen Climate), founded by billionaire philanthropist Tom Steyer. The series consists of five 9-minute episodes hosted by comedian and actress Kiran Deol, who is filmed as she travels through California chronicling how the state's environmental problems, such as drought and pollution, are impacting residents. The series highlights the inadequate policy response to California's environmental issues, while also exposing the contributory role of the oil and gas industry. While much of the documentary's content is serious and fact-filled, the comedy derives from Deol's chemistry with the people she meets and from her spontaneously comic reactions to the information she hears. Ali Hart, who produced the web series, describes its creative approach as "doc-forward with humor," where "the focus was on the storytelling and bringing in humor where we could."[65] For example, in episode 3, Deol visits Los Angeles, where she explores air pollution's disproportionate impact on low-income and immigrant communities. She interviews Manuel Pastor, director of the USC Program for Environmental and Regional Equity; when he describes himself as a "social scientist," Deol jokes, "So, you're like the party scientist?" Pastor responds, "I'm thinking I am in an ethnic studies program; so, maybe I am a fiesta scientist."[66] On the other hand, an interview with a tearful mother whose young daughter suffers from ongoing health challenges as a result of the air pollution from local oil refineries contains no humor. Thus, the comedy functions primarily to draw attention to and offer comic relief from the documentary's otherwise somber content.

These examples illustrate the myriad ways to make climate change funny and engaging. Yet they also reveal some shortcomings in comedy's treatment of climate change. While much comedy about climate change comes from satirical news programs, their coverage is often, but not always, politically antagonistic, and explicitly calls out deniers and skeptics, including Republican leaders. As we have emphasized in earlier chapters, viewers outside the liberal choir may not be receptive to this type of humor. At the same time, both *Modern Family* and *30 Rock*'s storylines about climate change situate environmentalism as a target of ridicule. Even as these episodes comically highlight the need for stronger collective action to address climate change, they also derive humor from stereotypic portrayals of environmentalists as sanctimonious and intolerant. Moreover, while Al Gore's appearances on *30 Rock* reinforce a serious message of environmental action, Gore—although an icon of climate activism—is an incredibly polarizing figure within America's politicized climate debates,[67] and unlikely to be seen as a trusted messenger by those who don't share his politics. Still, it is notable that climate change has become a story arc on network comedy TV in any capacity—as well as a sketch topic on *Saturday Night Live*. We see this as a critical step toward integrating discussions of climate change more broadly within our culture and, in so doing, portraying concern about climate change and support for its solutions as a widely shared value. Shows like *Modern Family* and *SNL* are not ordinarily concerned with climate change and thus can reach unexpected audiences with funny, relatable arguments for climate action, just as satirical news programs and comedic documentaries offer audiences who are perhaps already predisposed to care about climate change new ways to think and feel about and engage with the issue.

AN EXPERIMENTAL TEST OF COMEDY'S EFFECTS ON PUBLIC ENGAGEMENT

Despite these examples, aside from satirical news—which has been relatively well researched in this context—we know little about how contemporary mediated comedy designed to encourage public engagement with climate change actually influences audiences. To help shed deeper light on how popular marketplace approaches to comedy may work to engage and mobilize audiences around climate change, we conducted a messaging experiment that compared the effects of two short-form comedy sketches about climate change from Funny or Die—which has become a prominent source of climate change comedy—with a short video news segment from CNN, as well as with a Funny or Die sketch unrelated to climate change, which served as a control condition. We wanted to address two key questions: (1) Can short-form comedy content help boost viewers' political engagement with climate change? and (2) What are the cognitive and affective pathways through which comedy engages audiences, compared to serious didactic messaging? With this second question, we were interested in the extent to which comedy increases political engagement with climate change because of its ability to create an enjoyable and entertaining media experience, foster positive emotions like hope, and reduce message counter-arguing. We also aimed to answer a third question: (3) Does comedy's influence on engagement depend on viewers' political orientation? In particular, does politically targeted climate change humor that explicitly calls out "deniers" work equally well across the political spectrum, or is it alienating to conservative Republicans?

For the study, we selected two Funny or Die sketches that were broadly similar but differed in the targets of their humor (i.e., politically explicit vs. not). The first was the "Old People Don't Care about Climate Change" sketch described at the outset of this chapter, which satirically mocks the sentiment that older people don't need to care about climate change, because they won't be around to see its effects. The second comedy video, "Climate Change Denial Disorder" ("CCDD"), also satirizes people who aren't concerned about climate change but does so in a more politically targeted way. The video, released in 2015, parodies a direct-to-consumer pharmaceutical ad, opening with a voice-over narrator asking, "Does your parent, grandparent, or political representative suffer from climate change denial disorder? CCDD is a rapidly spreading disease that world health officials say if left untreated could destroy the entire planet."[68] The sketch stars actor and environmentalist Ed Begley, Jr., as a senator afflicted with CCDD, who is depicted as so far removed from reality that he is shown rowing a boat in a parking lot, which he mistook for the water. The video mocks the inane arguments that climate skeptics often use to discount climate science and explicitly calls out the "56% of Republicans in Congress [who] have been severely infected with CCDD." The voice-over identifies Republican senators and representatives who reject climate science by name, while their names and state affiliations also scroll in text on the screen. Both videos end with a call to action that highlights the importance of political engagement with climate change: "Old People" encourages viewers to vote, whereas "CCDD" urges viewers to "help" Republicans in Congress who suffer from CCDD.

The comparison serious news video was produced by CNN in 2018 and features meteorologist Jennifer Gray delivering facts that illustrate the reality of human-caused climate change and its impacts, including video images of global heat maps, melting glacier ice, and stormy seas.[69] The unrelated control video was a Funny or Die sketch, produced in collaboration with @Overheard LA, which features actress Nina Dobrev reenacting ridiculous statements that were overheard in Los Angeles.[70] All four videos were approximately 90 seconds long.

In August 2018, we recruited 801 U.S. adults (aged 18–49) to participate in an online survey-experiment in which they were randomly assigned to watch one of the four videos and then answer questions that gauged their attitudes and behaviors relative to climate change, as well as their reactions to the video itself.[71] We examined four different indicators of political engagement: (1) political efficacy (i.e., the belief that one can personally influence the government when it comes to climate change), (2) importance of climate change when deciding who to vote for in the 2018 Congressional elections, (3) discursive action (i.e., intentions to discuss, look for more information about, and share information about climate change), and (4) political action (i.e., intentions to contact a government official, participate in a protest, sign a petition, join an organization, and/or donate money in support of action to reduce climate change). We also measured several variables that capture the potential routes through which comedy influences political engagement: enjoyment (i.e., the perception that the video was entertaining and fun to watch); emotions felt in response to the video, including hope and fear; and message counterarguing (i.e., the extent to which participants said they disagreed with or argued back against the video).

What did we find in terms of the comedy videos' ability to politically engage audiences with climate change? The videos were effective, but in different ways (see appendix A, table 1). Participants who watched the politically explicit "CCDD" video rated climate change as more important to their vote in the 2018 elections and were more willing to discuss and share information about climate change than participants who saw the non-climate-related control video. Participants who watched the "Old People" video—which comically reminded young people of their role in political decision-making about climate change—reported higher levels of perceived efficacy, indicating that they felt more politically empowered, compared to those who watched the control video. The comedy videos, however, did not differ from one another or from the CNN video in their effects on these outcomes. Also, intentions to engage in high-level political actions, like protesting or volunteering, did not vary across the video treatments.

What are the pathways through which the comedy videos influenced political engagement? To answer this question, we analyzed how the two comedy videos compared to the news video in terms of how much audiences enjoyed the videos, felt hope and fear in response, and disagreed with or argued back against the videos (see appendix A, table 1). In turn, we examined how these responses to the videos related to viewers' engagement with climate change (see appendix A, table 2). Here, we found that both comedy videos inspired more hope than the news video; hope, in turn, was a consistent motivator, positively associated with all four forms of political engagement. Similarly, audiences found both comedy videos to be more enjoyable than the news video and, as a result of their enjoyment, were more likely to say they would look for and discuss information about climate change, and to say they would take political action. Thus, both hope and enjoyment provide pathways through which comedy increases engagement (see appendix A, table 3). In contrast, people experienced more fear in response to the news video; yet, fear also was positively related to the importance people attributed to climate change in their upcoming vote, their intentions to look for and discuss information about climate change, and their willingness to take political action. Thus, the news video engaged viewers with climate change by arousing fear. With regard to counter-arguing, we found that viewers were more likely to counter-argue the comedy videos—particularly the "CCDD" video—than the news video. In turn, viewers who were more likely to counter-argue the videos were less likely to see climate change as important to their vote choice but felt more politically efficacious.[72] Ultimately, then, comedy's positive influence on engagement comes primarily from its ability to foster enjoyment and inspire hope, rather than through any direct reduction in counter-arguing.

Finally, we wanted to understand whether political orientation matters in how audiences respond to the two comedy videos compared to the news and control videos. First, we found that the videos' direct influence on viewers' political engagement with climate change did not vary according to one's political identification. This means that the comedy videos, overall, were equally effective in shifting attitudes and intended behaviors, regardless of one's politics. However, viewers' political orientation *did* influence the effects of the videos on enjoyment, hopeful emotions, and counter-arguing (see appendix A, table 4). The comedy in the "CCDD" video, which attacked climate deniers and called out Republicans, was less likely to be enjoyed and more likely to be counter-argued by conservative Republicans than the politically neutral comedy in the "Old People" video.[73] Thus, for conservative Republicans, only the "Old People" video— and not "CCDD"—indirectly encouraged political engagement through effects on enjoyment (for liberal Democrats and moderate Independents, both comedy videos boosted political engagement as a result of comedy's effects on enjoyment; see appendix A, table 5).[74] This is an important finding that reinforces our argument that humor that explicitly targets Republican climate skeptics may not help to bridge the political divide on climate change; yet, politically neutral comedy *can*. At the same time, the hopeful effects of climate change comedy were confined to liberal Democrats. Although this difference is worthy of further investigation, left-leaning audiences—who already are predisposed to care about climate change—may be more likely than other groups to see comedy as something that will inspire collective action around climate change, thus giving them more reason for hope.

Several important lessons can be gleaned from these results. First, comedy about climate change is neither monolithic in its influence nor a one size fits all approach. Watching short-form comedy about climate change can enhance political engagement with climate change, compared to not seeing any information about climate change; yet, the effects of comedy depend on the type of comedic message as well as on the outcome in question. At the same time, comedy does not work identically for all audiences; individuals' political predispositions, in combination with the political explicitness of climate change comedy, affect viewers' reactions to the videos. Thus, when using comedy strategically, it is critical to design messages with a clear goal and target audience in mind. Finally, we see that even though comedy and news do not differ in their direct effects on political engagement, they work through different pathways; this suggests that within the broader media ecosystem, comedy can serve a distinct, albeit complementary, role to more serious news-based discourse about the impacts of climate change. In particular, we found that comedy engages audiences with climate change indirectly through its effects on hope and enjoyment, whereas news works through effects on fear.[75] This finding is consistent with past research that has found both fear and hope motivate climate activism and policy support;[76] thus, the availability of both types of emotional messages is important for encouraging engagement.

Overall, our key findings are consistent with our broad theoretical expectations about how comedy works to engage audiences with climate change: by creating enjoyable media experiences that inspire hope. For a social issue that is too often portrayed and perceived as hopeless and over-whelming, this is no small feat. Further, despite a polarized political cli-mate, comedy can reach people beyond their partisan tribes. Even the most dissenting audiences—conservative Republicans—can enjoy comedy that supports taking action on climate change, particularly when they are not being attacked.

.   .   .   .   .

In closing, we return to the questions that we posed at the outset of the chapter. Did Defend Our Future make a sensible gamble when investing in comedy as a strategy to engage young voters with climate change? More broadly, does comedy offer a way to help climate change break through into the public imagination? To the first point, we have shown through our experimental research that people who watched Defend Our Future's "Old People" video felt more politically empowered as a result. Relative to a comparable news segment about climate change, the "Old People" video also made viewers, regardless of their politics, feel entertained, and made liberal Democrats more hopeful, which created a pathway for comedy to influence several indicators of political engagement. Outside of the labo-ratory, Defend Our Future's own research showed that their voter engage-ment strategy was effective: Their field-based voter registration drives—which media efforts like "Old People," seen by millions, likely helped amplify—boosted voting rates among targeted youth.[77]

Beyond Defend Our Future's tactical effort, through multiple genres of comedy, climate change is being woven into our popular culture, as comedians give us new frames of reference through which to make sense of this daunting issue. Moreover, in today's fragmented, high-choice media environment, entertainment and comedy may provide some people with their primary—if not only—way of hearing about climate change. While we urge comedy performers and writers to broaden the target of their humorous critique beyond climate deniers, particularly if their goal is to reach outside a liberal Democratic audience, we are encouraged by the wide and increasing range of mediated comedy about climate change, which has the potential to galvanize public attention to and involvement with the issue and, over time, help normalize support for climate action.

Still, despite the protestations of late-night satirists, the comedy experiments of organizations like Defend Our Future and NextGen America, and the various creative ways that comedians have incorporated climate change into their craft, 2016 nonetheless ushered in a Republican president and Congress who were decidedly unfriendly to climate action. This does not mean that comedy didn't—or can't—make a difference; rather, it reminds us that social and political change occur incrementally and through multiple, reinforcing pressure points (e.g., media, organizing, voting, etc.). Indeed, following the 2018 U.S. midterm elections, which saw a surge in youth turnout that helped elect a Democratic majority to the House of Representatives, proposals for a "Green New Deal" have elevated conversations about climate change—and climate justice—and public concern about the issue is at an all-time high.[78] It's unclear what role comedy may have played in this, and there is still a long road ahead; yet, these recent shifts suggest that public engagement and outreach are having an impact. The nature of climate change as a "super wicked" problem means that it requires a variegated set of technological and policy solutions, supported by a wide menu of communication strategies. Comedy certainly should be included among these.

5 Beyond Poverty Porn

HOW COMEDY REFRAMES POVERTY AND ENGAGES PUBLICS

66 *If ever this comedy thing doesn't work out, then I've got poverty to fall back on.* **99**

> Trevor Noah, stand-up comic and host of
> *The Daily Show*[1]

On his second night in Mumbai in 2013, Indian American comedian Hasan Minhaj stepped onto the stand-up comedy stage to perform in India for the first time. He tapped slowly on the mic, theatrically poking fun at the opening silence from a curious, quiet audience scrutinizing its guest: "Is this thing on?" The night before, Minhaj, a then-burgeoning comic in the United States—a year before he would explode onto the cultural scene as a correspondent on *The Daily Show*—had confessed his nervous anticipation in an interview with young rebel Indian comedian Tanmay Bhat on Bhat's podcast: "I think I'm going to bomb," to which Bhat irreverently responded, "If you bomb, that means you suck."[2]

Perhaps wisely, Minhaj sized up the room and decided to spotlight his cultural insider-outsider status—his dual identity as American-born comic with Indian familial roots—to comedic effect. His set began:

> Oh man, OK, this is gonna be . . . this is interesting. Do you understand?
> I don't know what I'm doing here. I got off the plane, they said, "Hey, there's
> a guy, his name is Raj, he'll pick you up." I'm in fucking India, man, how
> many Rajs are there? I come out, there's 97 brown dudes saying, "sir, sir." No.
> I can't. I'm gonna believe *all* of you.[3]

With his self-deprecating opening, Hasan Minhaj won over the stand-up comedy crowd in Mumbai, a bustling metropolis where comedy audiences harbor high expectations for no-boundaries topics. In India, the new comedy scene—which comprises stand-up comedy clubs, podcasts, and web-based sketches and stand-up—provides an entertainment mechanism to talk about things that matter. As Bhat explained to Minhaj: "The internet is one of the very few places in India where you can say what you want to say. 'Cause you can't say anything on television because it's heavily censored. You can't say anything in film. 'Cause we have very strict rules. Politics plays a very huge part in our arts . . . Sometimes comics are saying stuff on stage just because they want to and because they can."[4]

To wit, Bhat's stand-up set that same night, which was met with raucous laughter from a standing-room-only crowd of Mumbai's young urban professionals, centered around taboo cultural topics: political corruption, birth control, and poverty. His poop joke pulled no punches:

> Bombay is a shitty, shitty-smelling city. That's because 54 percent of all Indians shit outside. Do you know this? 54 percent, man. And this number's been going up since 1947, did you guys know? In the '40s it was 34 percent and in the '50s it was 44 percent. This number's been going up. Basically, the British left and we started shitting outside a lot more. I think this is the best defense strategy any country could adopt. Like, make the country smell so shitty that no one will want to invade us again.[5]

With his joke, Bhat not only called out India's colonial history, he also took on a long-standing uncomfortable truth that contributes to the country's disproportionate share of a global poverty epidemic: India's death rate for children under age five is the second-highest in the world, in large part due to a sanitation problem.[6] From a global poverty perspective, the imprint of India's child mortality and poverty reality is immense.[7] According to UNICEF, while 80 percent of deaths of children under five years old occur in two regions (Saharan Africa and Southern Asia), "India and Nigeria alone account for almost a third (32 percent) of the global under-five deaths."[8] But sustained attention from the public and global leaders makes a contribution; between 1990 and 2015, the rate of daily death due to preventable conditions of poverty decreased by half,[9] in part attributed to focused global resources and public engagement through bodies like the United Nations and its member countries. Bhat's joke—and his audience's head-nodding recognition and laughter—provided a conversational portal into a sensitive topic.

For his part, Minhaj's journey was the centerpiece of a 2014 documentary film that aired in the United States and India, *Stand Up Planet*, a quest that endeavored to "follow the jokes" of international stand-up comics into the challenges of their societal circumstances. The case of *Stand Up Planet* helps us to consider and understand the role mediated comedy can play in spotlighting attention onto—and encouraging public engagement with—poverty as an expansive, complex social problem. As we present in this chapter, mediated comedy in the information age offers a strategic way to engage publics in poverty as an issue, through comedy's ability to take on taboo topics, but also through its ability to critique, reframe, call attention to, maintain a spotlight on, entertain, and offer a positive frame of hope and optimism that can motivate action. Comedy also can invite new audiences to think about an issue about which they may have voluntarily opted out, or not contemplated at all.

This chapter considers the scope of global and U.S.-based poverty, as well as the limits of leveraging only traditional somber approaches to communicate about the issue—from othering "poverty porn" to exclusive frames of doom and hopelessness, which can inadvertently perpetuate a dehumanizing lack of agency and implicit victim-blaming. Analysis of comedy's social-change attributes in the context of poverty, as well an extended case study and our original research about *Stand Up Planet*, alongside other examples of humorous treatments of poverty, provide a path by which we consider: How can comedy work in service of antipoverty activism and public engagement?

THE SCOPE OF POVERTY

Poverty is not a simple, monolithic problem. Income inadequacy alone does not encapsulate its extent or ripple effect. Instead, poverty comprises a maelstrom of chronic illness, malnutrition, and systemic inequality—a circumstance of life misfortune and structural failure, and often the legacy of discriminatory practices and institutions. Scholar Rufus Akindola articulates poverty as "more than a lack of adequate income but a combination of many forms of deprivation that together allow human capabilities to go unrealized."[10] Around the globe, about 836 million people live in extreme poverty—on an income level of less than $1.25 per day.[11] This status quo presents an ongoing challenge to all nations.[12] No sole solution to poverty exists, of course, but a collection of remedies—both global and local in scope—coalesce around the need for visible leadership and public financial support to address health, food scarcity, and shelter. From a public engagement and activism perspective, public awareness, direct financial appeals, and support for government aid have been the focus—in other words, finding ways to capture and hold attention.[13]

While extreme poverty is often framed formally within discourse and interventions concerning developing nations in the Global South—a focus of the United Nations' original Millenium Development Goals, and the current UN Sustainable Development Goals, established in 2015 to end global poverty by 2030[14]—the United States is not immune. In 2017, after wrapping up his investigation of poverty in the United States, Philip Alston, the UN Special Rapporteur on Extreme Poverty and Human Rights, concluded that the scope of the challenges in the U.S., including homelessness, unsafe sanitation practices, and criminalization of the poor, "are shockingly at odds with [the United States'] immense wealth and its founding commitment to human rights," and thus, "The American Dream is rapidly becoming the American Illusion, as the United States now has the lowest rate of social mobility of any of the rich countries."[15] According to U.S. Census data in 2016, 40 million Americans (13%) live in poverty, about 1 in 8 people.[16] Women and people of color are disproportionately represented among the U.S. poor, and 32 percent of those living in poverty are children under the age of 18.[17] In the U.S., the pattern of income inequality has increased over the past several decades, with the gap between the top and lower-wage earners continuing to widen.[18] As is true of poverty in the developing world, solutions to unemployment and underemployment, homelessness, affordable housing, food insecurity, criminalization of the poor, and health challenges in the United States are complex. Advocacy around poverty is embodied, structurally, in antipoverty public policy on the federal and state levels, such as educational opportunities for children, food assistance, health insurance, and tax policies. Economists also have argued that steady wage growth is a key solution to lifting low- and middle-income families and individuals out of poverty.[19] Still, conclusive solutions to a host of issues that encompass poverty remain fluid. The need for public awareness and support is crucial.

ANTIPOVERTY ADVOCACY AND PUBLIC ENGAGEMENT

Early visual and narrative treatments of poverty appeals are familiar—and often parodied. In 1983, the popular U.S. TV actress Sally Struthers appeared in a fundraising film and a series of televised public service announcements that implored audiences in the United States to give money to help children in the developing world. While recording a fund-raising film for a charity, Struthers noted, "I'm depressed . . . Those babies are covered with millions of flies. It makes me sick. They look so sad and sweet and so hungry."[20] Well-intentioned though the effort may have been, similar appeals are referenced in the annals of visual antipoverty public engagement work as "poverty porn,"[21] implying a lack of agency on the part of local people and promoting pity. Such a framing device may have emerged from the first televised images of poverty starting around the late 1960s—"the birth of media humanitarianism"—leading to millions of charity donations.[22] In the present day, however, advocacy, activist, and humanitarian organizations have disavowed this approach to capturing public attention, in favor of more positive appeals.[23] Poverty porn aside, however, the quandary of communicating effectively to the public about poverty, toward social change goals, remains ever-present.

The public engagement challenge is compounded by years of disempowering narrative portrayals, myths, and damaging stereotypes, all of which contribute to a kind of public inertia—a broad cultural perspective that accepts a status quo of inevitability and victim-blaming.[24] Believing the poor are lazy, ignorant, and unable or not interested in helping themselves are not only persistent negative stereotypes established early in life;[25] such negative images and ideas also contribute to poverty's perpetual state.[26] Indeed, "beliefs about the characteristics of poor people and the causes of poverty undoubtedly influence, directly and indirectly, middle-class voting behavior, social policy decisions, beliefs about welfare, and willingness as a society to end poverty."[27] Media images of the poor, across TV and news, contribute to the challenge; in American popular culture, for example, poor people are often portrayed on reality TV (e.g., *COPS*) or talk shows like *The Jerry Springer Show*, both of which reinforce negative stereotypes.[28] Moreover, a comprehensive analysis of U.S. TV and news images and narratives concludes, "for the most part, economic inequality, social class, and poverty are presented superficially or are rendered invisible by the mainstream media"; the media thus reinforce or fail to challenge existing stereotypes while also neglecting to take on structural barriers that underlie poverty.[29] Between the relative invisibility of and entrenched negative societal beliefs about poverty,[30] advocacy, activist, and humanitarian groups have their work cut out for them, particularly when it comes to fueling vocal public support for antipoverty public policy.

Indeed, at the culmination of his 2017 investigation and report about U.S. poverty, UN Special Rapporteur Alston decried what he called "caricatured narratives" of poverty in the public mind, often perpetuated by policymakers, the very decision-making individuals with the power to make change:

> I have been struck by the extent to which caricatured narratives about the purported innate differences between rich and poor have been sold to the electorate by some politicians and media, and have been allowed to define the debate. The rich are industrious, entrepreneurial, patriotic, and the drivers of economic success. The poor are wasters, losers, and scammers. As a result, money spent on welfare is money down the drain. To complete the picture we are also told that the poor who want to make it in America can easily do so: they really can achieve the American dream if only they work hard enough . . . . Some politicians and political appointees with whom I spoke were completely sold on the narrative of such scammers sitting on comfortable sofas, watching color TVs, while surfing on their smart phones, all paid for by welfare. I wonder how many of these politicians have ever visited poor areas, let alone spoken to those who dwell there.[31]

The need to shine a public spotlight on poverty through narrative approaches that can bear witness, and yet, communicate with dignity and agency on the part of individuals involved, also is a challenge. There's nothing attention-getting about poverty, unless and until moments of crisis emerge. Indeed, beginning in the 1980s, after record donations raised for charity in response to the Ethiopian famine of 1984 and 1985, global NGOs began a period of what scholar Nandita Dogra calls "development education," which centralizes a public engagement function in poverty reduction work; according to Dogra, "the broad framework of development education includes a three-pronged process of information, promotion of humanitarian values, and spurring of community action."[32] The latter component that continues in the present—public action and activism—was thus designed to encourage public audiences to engage in immediate and longer-term goals and actions, including public policy support and influence.[33]

Evolving into the present day, public engagement and activism, fostered in part by the collaborative ecosystem efforts of local governments, international humanitarian organizations, in-country NGOs, and social service agencies,[34] are required elements to promote sustained social change in poverty.[35] For example, the organization ONE facilitates policy advocacy to ensure a robust U.S. foreign aid budget, and the group also distributes short-form digital videos online to encourage individuals to donate, share, or take other supportive action.[36] Online public-interest advertising campaign videos from the likes of Malaria No More, Oxfam, and Save the Children also are designed to raise public awareness and engagement.[37]

Despite the ongoing pursuit to engage publics by disseminating visual narratives and facts, existing efforts, from long-form journalism to short-form advocacy PSAs and videos, are often relegated to a category of what scholar John Cameron calls "worthy but dull."[38] Such visual narratives thus may not serve the interests of broad public engagement and activism beyond the ranks of those already paying attention. Further, the narratives and visual frames can fail to address the structural failures and discriminatory practices that shaped and perpetuate the challenge, instead focusing on archetypical images of the poor—without agency—nearly exclusively.[39] Narrative portrayals focused on hopeless odds may lead audiences to disengage from a seemingly impossible problem[40] and also can do detriment by portraying individuals living in poverty as "the other,"[41] and thus not worthy of our attention.

But a public spotlight is crucial. Without public engagement, it's hard to imagine how a set of challenges generally rendered invisible—or characterized in negative stereotypes or "othering" narratives—can maintain the consistent attention needed to push for change. Together, then, the unique public engagement, narrative, and communication challenges around poverty comprise a set of acute needs from an activism perspective: to raise awareness and call attention, to offer frames of positive hope and optimism, and to find ways to move beyond "compassion fatigue"— feeling desensitized to a repetitive glut of crisis-oriented stories about human suffering.[42]

COMEDY APPROACHES TO FRAMING POVERTY AND ENGAGING AUDIENCES

Humorous approaches to poverty narratives can help engage and motivate publics, reframe and critique negative stereotypes, and also amplify and draw attention to serious calls to action. Moreover, comedy can encourage optimism "through the reduction of stress and the promotion of hope."[43] Perhaps most importantly, comedy serves as a mechanism to attract new audiences and motivate them by fostering positive emotions and entertaining experiences with media content. Despite this potential, poverty shows up infrequently in comedy entertainment programming. Further, an intentional, strategic use of comedy to explicitly engage audiences in poverty justice and activism is rare.[44] We highlight several examples here.

The Entertainment Comedy Marketplace and Poverty

> Across America, new and innovative ways to alleviate
> homelessness are being introduced, like banning the
> homeless because of body odor, fining them for sleeping
> outdoors, and arresting them for sitting down.[45]

A 2015 segment on *The Daily Show* opened with this acerbically sarcastic voice-over narration, juxtaposed over real-life news headlines proclaiming new poverty and homelessness measures in cities around the United States. The segment went on to skewer callous institutional approaches to poverty—that is, those that are linked to typical negative stereotypes of the poor as lazy—in a six-minute story about a homelessness initiative, Housing First, in Salt Lake City, Utah. Through comedy, the segment illuminates an institutional antipoverty approach that opposes discriminatory policies steeped in damaging portrayals of the poor as shiftless and burdensome.

In the story, *The Daily Show*'s correspondent, Hasan Minhaj, meets with one of the recipients of the program, Russell Flowers, who reminds him that "no one wants to be poor . . . everyone needs a hand sometimes," after Minhaj satirically comments on the state of the new apartment ("if you just give people these apartments, next thing you know, everyone's going to want to be poor").[46] In its treatment of the issue and interview with Flowers, *The Daily Show*'s comedic frames highlight two key narratives: the poor are not "the other," and, in contrast to the Utah program at the heart of the segment, some institutional remedies further dehumanize the poor and may not ultimately be cost-effective. The *Daily Show*'s poverty segment—which amplified the homelessness program in Utah through the millions of viewers who watched it on TV and online, as well as through the coverage it inspired in news outlets[47]—exemplifies comedy's ability to reframe poverty stereotypes, and to critique inadequate institutional solutions while highlighting promising ones.

Over the past few years, several entertainment comedy programs similarly challenged poverty stereotypes in satirical ways by critiquing the potentially dehumanizing, victim-blaming narrative framing of mainstream news and other media portrayals. For example, a 2011 segment on *The Colbert Report* humorously but scathingly criticized a report from a conservative think tank: "'A Heritage Foundation report proves that as long as 'poor' Americans have refrigerators and the strength to brush flies off their eyeballs, they're not really poor.'"[48] In 2014, *Saturday Night Live* aired a faux public service announcement on its program, titled "39 Cents," an acidic portrayal of a white, Western plea for financial help for an African village. In the story, filmed with the slow piano music and slow-motion aesthetic reference to famine relief PSAs, the "villagers" ask the PSA narrator and host, played by comic actor Bill Hader, if he even knows which African country he's in (to which he replies, "Africa!") and tell him to ask for more than 39 cents, which he says is "the price of a cup of coffee" (one of the "villagers" objects to say, "Why can't it be the price of an Arizona iced tea? They're 99 cents.").[49] The segment, which aired on *Saturday Night Live's* main program and online, attracting millions of views, makes clear the butt of the joke is not poor people themselves, but Africa's colonial legacy, along with the stereotypical portrayal of people in the Global South as passive victims.

Outside the U.S., a nonprofit advocacy organization based in Norway— SAIH Norway (Norwegian Students' and Academics' International Assistance Fund)—created an ongoing online media campaign, Radi-Aid. The campaign aims to humorously critique media narratives of Africa and the developing world, which, according to SAIH Norway, "often present an image which is lacking in nuance and focuses exclusively upon war, poverty and conflict."[50] One example of Radi-Aid's work—a short-form parody public service announcement hosted on YouTube, titled *Let's Save Africa*— presents an aid organization filming a commercial plea for help. The parody PSA, which garnered more than 1.5 million views on YouTube, "stars" a young African boy, Michael, who reveals himself to be a local actor cleverly leveraging the steady stream of such filming in his community, given that he matches the image of "the sad African."[51] (When the aid representative begins to cry as she reveals the litany of sadness in the area, he places his hand gently on hers and asks, "Is this your first charity appeal?") The end of the video implores the audience to "Donate Your Stereotypes at Rusty Radiator.com," where viewers can watch more comedy videos that critique narrative approaches that may inadvertently imply a lack of agency and encourage a new way of telling stories to empower developing countries.[52] By challenging the Global North white savior narrative, the comedic treatment not only can attract attention, but also can encourage audiences to accurately consider Global South residents as active participants in their communities, rather than passive victims awaiting charity.

Not all entertainment comedy portrayals have found their comic material by consistently targeting damaging poverty stereotypes or underlying structural and institutional challenges, however. The long-running Showtime TV program *Shameless*, which premiered in 2011 and portrays the Gallaghers, a family living in Chicago, may have perpetuated negative stereotypes at first, but is applauded by critics today for consistently showcasing a generally invisible segment of the American population—the lower class. As one TV critic put it during the show's first season: "The show plays on so many stereotypes as to be white-trash porn," even as he acknowledged the difficulty of placing poverty in the centerpiece—not a side angle—of episodic entertainment comedy.[53] As the show has evolved, critics have noted the importance of the show's portrayal of poverty by moving beyond racial tropes,[54] and spotlighting challenges that face working-class families through the ongoing episodic portrayal.[55] In a media interview, culture scholar Reece Peck applauded the show for showcasing American class divides: "In the way cities have been designed to keep the poor and the homeless out of sight, these same groups have been mostly invisible in the terrain of American TV. *Shameless* represents how poor communities carry resentment towards various upwardly-mobile class groups. It's this plurality of class antagonism that allows both conservative and liberal viewers to see their own political identities reflected and affirmed by the show."[56] By allowing a portal into an invisible group, *Shameless* may encourage more complex public consideration of poverty than the damaging archetype of laziness and handouts. Indeed, perhaps the show most saliently illustrates the complexity of poverty narratives in comedy, and the need to move beyond two extremes—the passive victim or the heroic individual who overcomes impossible odds.

The Strategic Use of Comedy for Poverty Advocacy

Antipoverty public advocacy and engagement generally focus on calls to action or appeals for support from individuals, governments, and organizations to make crisis donations or to publicly and privately endorse antipoverty policy. Serious information and humorous calls for engagement with antipoverty measures can serve reinforcing, symbiotic functions. Employing comedy to attract attention and bring audiences into a cause— to donate or take some other kind of action—works in service of a serious goal. To use this tactic effectively, however, comedy must be permitted to be truly funny—with a call to action that is distinct from the comedy.[57]

When it comes to motivating audiences to think about and advocate on behalf of daunting social issues, comedy has been leveraged primarily in recent years to raise public awareness and encourage audiences to take digital action, such as online donations. Based in the U. K., Comic Relief is a notable—and likely best-known—charitable effort that links comedy, poverty, and media, using a large-scale media campaign and comedy to attract attention.[58] Through sketch comedy bits combined with interstitial serious videos and information about extreme poverty, the organization's Red Nose Day TV special, broadcast on the BBC, has raised millions of dollars to benefit global development charities in past years.[59] Over the years, the charity expanded to include an annual event in May, Red Nose Day, which enlists celebrities and comedians to entertain and raise awareness and funds for global and U.S. antipoverty efforts, in partnership with comedy power player Funny or Die.[60] Comic Relief also leverages its mainstream media partnerships with NBC Universal in the United States,[61] along with short-form YouTube videos.[62] Through its mediated public engagement strategy from 2015 to 2017, Comic Relief has raised $145 million and benefited more than 8 million children in the United States and around the world.[63]

Similarly, in Singapore, entrepreneur Jack Sim founded the World Toilet Organization to help solve the deadly sanitation-related illnesses facing 2.5 billion people in parts of the globe without access to toilets. Sanitation, crucial to antipoverty measures, is one of the UN's Sustainable Development Goals.[64] In order to raise money to bring toilets to vulnerable corners of the world, and also to encourage behavior change, Sim, who dubbed his public antipoverty persona "Mr. Toilet," uses "potty humor" to inspire people to listen.[65] Sim uses the outrageous to open the door to a taboo conversation: "When we are children, our parents tell us not to talk about shit."[66] Traveling around the world to advocate to world leaders and to shift norms and behavior in communities in order to make toilets "a status symbol for the poor," he has strategically leveraged comedy to bring attention to a somber problem.[67] Meet Mr. Toilet, a 2012 short-form documentary about Mr. Toilet directed by Academy Award–nominated director Jessica Yu, screened online and at festivals around the world to bring attention to Sim and his campaign.[68] After more than a decade engaging world leaders and the public through humor and advocating for resources, Sim and the World Toilet Organization successfully achieved what he calls "the Nobel Prize for Sanitation"—the United Nations' official adoption of November 19 as World Toilet Day, a consensus agreement of 122 countries at the UN General Assembly in 2013.[69] The commemorative day ensures a level of global attention to the crucial sanitation antipoverty angle for the foreseeable future.

What these highlighted examples share—including both comedy in the entertainment marketplace and comedy as an explicit public engagement strategy—is an ability to shine a spotlight, jump into taboo topics, and attract and command audiences to pay attention to a broad social problem that remains complex and riddled with negative stereotypes, yet is often rendered invisible. The question remains: When audiences experience a dire social problem like poverty through the lighthearted lens of comedy, what influence can this have? Can an entertaining comedy approach to poverty inspire audiences to develop supportive attitudes or even a willingness to take some kind of action? The original production and research about the *Stand Up Planet* project offers insights.

MOTIVATING PUBLIC ENGAGEMENT IN POVERTY THROUGH COMEDY: *STAND UP PLANET*

> You can tell a lot about people by the jokes they tell. I've been doing stand up for about eight and a half years and for the majority of my comedy career, I would just kind of tell jokes . . . It was a lot of hiding behind jokes and not killing nearly as hard as I thought I should be. So, I stopped trying to be funny and started telling my story . . . And a funny thing is, I got funnier. My story had power. My struggle as a kid growing up between two worlds mattered to people. And that got me thinking. The world is full of struggle. Comedy comes from adversity. This must be one hilarious planet. What if there were young comics out there just like me, killing it in places I never imagined? Who're the Pryors and Carlins of this new global comic spring? What stories were they telling? What truth bombs were they dropping? What sacred cows were they slaying? And more importantly, how could I get in on the joke? I decided to find out.[70]

In the opening three minutes of *Stand Up Planet*, the 2014 comedy documentary, the journey's narrator and lead subject, Indian American comedian Hasan Minhaj, frames the entertainment quest. Alongside Minhaj's odyssey to learn about the world through the boundary-pushing perspectives and jokes of comedians, the documentary endeavored to inspire viewers to experience and think about their global neighbors in ways that promote human connection, not pity. *Stand Up Planet* also aimed to intervene in a set of challenges narratively plagued by frames of doom and impossibility. Created by filmmakers David Munro and Xandra Castleton, and produced by a group of independent documentary producers, including one of this book's authors, Caty Borum Chattoo,[71] *Stand Up Planet* was designed to entertain—but also to engage new audiences, both in the U.S. and internationally, around antipoverty activism with a rarely employed mediated narrative frame for the topic: comedy. The multimedia project—a two-part documentary film and TV special, along with a multipart short-form webisode series—was shaped to be funny, not sacrificing entertainment value on the way to human enlightenment and connection.

Through a research-infused storytelling strategy inspired by a model of entertainment for social change,[72] the underlying social justice activism of *Stand Up Planet* was developed to explore two particular global poverty topics: sanitation-related illness in India, and HIV in South Africa. The producing team chose India as a country focus due to its disproportionately high rate of child mortality due to sanitation-related illness,[73] along with South Africa, given its high rate of HIV infection —the highest in the world.[74] Both countries were relevant to the entertainment core of the nonfiction film because of their thriving stand-up comedy scenes.

On screen, the documentary narrative follows Hasan Minhaj as he travels through Mumbai, India, and Johannesburg, South Africa, to identify some of the funniest international stand-up comics. On his journey, Minhaj tracks the jokes and personal experiences of the comics he meets as a way to delve into the reality of poverty issues facing their home countries, which often serve as the basis for the comedians' jokes. In India, Minhaj follows the jokes and stories of Tanmay Bhat, the rebel comedian and podcaster, and Aditi Mittal, who takes on gender norms and gender-based violence through her humor. And in South Africa, comedy TV stars like Kagiso Ledega and Loyoso Gola, former hosts of *Late Nite News*, South Africa's version of *The Daily Show*, and stand-up comedian Mpho

Figure 5 Stand Up Planet documentary subjects Mmpo Popps, Hasan Minhaj, and Aditi Mittal.

SOURCE / CREDIT: Photo courtesy of KCET.

Popps welcome Minhaj into the entertainment comedy scene, where jokes about apartheid and condoms and HIV abound. Peer-reviewed research provides promising support for *Stand Up Planet*'s style of funny jokes followed by serious information; scholar Robin Nabi and her colleagues, in considering comedy's persuasive influence on serious issues, posited that a "restoration of gravity"—that is, a comedic treatment of a social issue, followed by more substantive information about the issue—may help reduce message discounting or issue trivialization while maintaining the other persuasive benefits of a funny, entertaining format.[75] *Stand Up Planet* was executed in this way; its core narrative device followed comedians' jokes into their central social issues through Minhaj's visits with people living in areas affected by extreme poverty, along with interviews with community leaders or social entrepreneurs who provided more serious insights. Importantly, the comedy was creatively unfettered.

Aside from the comedy scenes in each country, the connection with people comes as Minhaj spends alternatively light-hearted and somber on-screen time in communities in both India and South Africa. He plays soccer with Mpho Popps and kids at Grassroot Soccer, an organization in South Africa that fights HIV through stigma reduction and awareness for young people, and he spends time with families in Shivaji Nagar, a slum community in Mumbai, India—having fun with them and joking along the way. The film culminates with an international Hollywood comedy stand-up show performed at the world-famous Laugh Factory, after the comedians—American, South African, Indian—tour Los Angeles together and discuss shared poverty challenges in the United States.

Stand Up Planet premiered theatrically in the U.S. in April 2014 as part of the San Francisco International Film Festival, and on three TV networks later in the year: the independent public network KCETLink, cable network Pivot (formerly owned and operated by Participant Media, the Hollywood studio and producer of socially conscious film), and a top broadcast network in India, NDTV. According to internal viewing metrics from the Pivot and KCETLink media teams, *Stand Up Planet* reached millions of viewers in 2014 across a year of repeat broadcasts.

Stand Up Planet Research

After the documentary engaged audiences in the entertainment marketplace, a core question remained, beyond the metrics of reach: In a poverty context, can comedy engage audiences meaningfully, encouraging viewers' positive attitudes and even a willingness to take some kind of action? If comedy is able to reach a viewing audience in this way, why? What is the role of positive emotion and entertainment value—two attributes often missing from mediated narratives about poverty—in helping audiences to think, care, and take some kind of action to support antipoverty measures? Our original research about the influence and viewing effects of *Stand Up Planet* was designed with these questions at the core.

As background—and detailed in chapter 2—several factors are thought to be at work for an audience when experiencing an entertainment story about a social issue.[76] First, *narrative transportation* occurs when media audiences are temporarily absorbed into an entertaining story, becoming so immersed in and personally connected to the events of the narrative that they lose touch with their immediate surroundings and are changed as a result.[77] Because the experience of narrative transportation is both pleasurable and all-encompassing, it is likely to reduce cognitive resistance to persuasive messages embedded within the narrative,[78] and accordingly has been linked to changes in audiences' knowledge, attitudes, and behavior.[79]

Next, *emotions* also play an important role in learning and persuasion in response to entertainment storytelling. According to scholar Paul Slovic and colleagues, the concept of the affect heuristic means an audience's negative and positive feelings create a powerful route to decision-making based on short-cut emotional cues rather than carefully deliberated cognitive processing.[80] In the context of entertainment and documentary storytelling, the effects of emotions are mixed: Although some studies have found that emotions are positively related to key outcomes, such as learning and discussion,[81] others found that both positive and negative emotions in response to a fictional narrative interfered with learning and attitude change.[82]

Finally, *entertainment value* is an important factor in a media narrative's ability to engage audiences on serious social issues. When considering the role of storytelling in social change, "story" is key; mediated narratives should ideally be entertaining and not didactic in order to fuel social change.[83] As such, stories that are perceived as entertaining may be especially influential in shaping knowledge, attitudes, and behaviors around social issues. Although perceived entertainment value is less studied than other mechanisms of narrative influence, two recent analyses found that an entertainment-education initiative was more likely to foster engagement with the program topic when it was evaluated as fun, entertaining, and enjoyable.[84]

In order to understand the influence of *Stand Up Planet* as a mechanism to engage audiences in poverty through comedy, in 2014, we conducted an audience study using a pre-test, post-test experimental design. The purpose of our research was to examine shifts in U.S. audience engagement with global poverty after watching two documentaries that used different editorial approaches to the storytelling: the comedy documentary compared with a somber documentary, *The End Game*,[85] which focuses on a global poverty topic through a traditional long-form, serious journalistic approach. *The End Game* aired in the same year as *Stand Up*

Planet on Al Jazeera English. Specifically, the study examined the extent to which viewing each documentary—funny or serious—increased audiences' perceived awareness of global poverty, support for government aid, factual knowledge, and intended actions. To better understand the mechanisms via which documentaries influence public engagement with global poverty, we studied the mediating roles—or "pathways to persuasion"—of four key variables: audience perceptions of entertainment value, narrative transportation, character involvement, and emotions. By studying these mediators, we can see more clearly how and why different storytelling approaches, like comedic or serious, can influence audiences differently.

In the study, we randomly assigned a total of 1,258 U. S.-based respondents, aged 18–49, to watch one of the two hour-long documentaries online, either *Stand Up Planet* or *The End Game*. The viewers completed pre- and post-viewing survey questions that assessed their attitudes, knowledge, and willingness to take action around global poverty, along with their perspectives about the stories. We also included measures of narrative transportation, entertainment value, identification with characters, and emotional response.

What did we learn? Did the *Stand Up Planet* comedy narrative and approach engage audiences seriously? The results confirmed that both documentaries increased viewers' support for U.S. government aid to poor countries overseas, perceived awareness of global poverty issues, factual knowledge of the topics in the films, and their willingness to take some kind of action on poverty—such as signing a petition or volunteering; however, *Stand Up Planet* produced larger effects than *The End Game* on awareness, knowledge, and intended action (see appendix B, table 6). Thus, our findings highlight the motivating role of comedy when it comes to social change indicators around poverty. In other words, after watching *Stand Up Planet*, viewers felt more aware about the issue, and gained more factual knowledge—significantly more than viewers of *The End Game*. When it comes to activating audiences to do something, we found that people who watched *Stand Up Planet* also were significantly more likely to say they would take action on poverty—such as signing a petition or volunteering—than viewers of *The End Game*.

What explains the power and influence of the funny documentary, *Stand Up Planet*, in its ability to help viewers learn, support policy, and even do something to help? Looking at the pathways to persuasion illuminated the full story. In this case, experiencing positive emotions, and believing the story was highly entertaining, were the factors most at work for the *Stand Up Planet* audience. Viewers who watched *Stand Up Planet* experienced higher levels of the positive emotion of happiness and thought the story was more entertaining than viewers who watched the serious documentary, *The End Game* (see appendix B, table 6). In turn, happiness while viewing predicted viewers' changes in awareness and knowledge, while the experience of being highly entertained was positively associated with changes in awareness, support for government aid, and intended action (see appendix B, tables 7 and 8).[86] On the other hand, *The End Game*'s lesser effects on the audience were mediated by different influences; audiences who watched the serious, somber documentary were moved because they were deeply transported into the story—that is, narrative transportation—and because they experienced negative emotions (see appendix B, table 8).

What do these findings mean when it comes to producing and distributing public engagement campaigns and stories that may be well equipped to spark social change around poverty? While some prior research has suggested that entertainment and particularly comedy can distract from the perceived seriousness of social issues and thereby interfere with desirable behavior change,[87] our findings reveal an exciting new path forward for antipoverty public engagement work, which rarely leverages comedy. While our recommendation is not to replace all forms of serious storytelling and information with comedy, a positive conclusion for social-change communicators in antipoverty advocacy is to consider adding comedy to the public engagement mix, particularly because of the inherent challenges facing this social issue: dire, hopeless, and sad. Notably, perceived entertainment value—which has been less studied as a way to narratively engage audiences—was one of the most consistent predictors of audience engagement with poverty; it is thus a consideration that deserves serious attention in future work, particularly as factual, serious public engagement efforts are likely to continue in the mix of ways that NGOs and others seek to make social change. In other words, it's not enough to engage audiences with only serious facts or sad images—incorporating real entertainment through funny comedy that hooks an audience in a new way is not only strategic as a humanizing entry point, but perhaps imperative in the narrative mix for antipoverty activism and advocacy.

.   .   .   .   .

Shaping and executing antipoverty public-engagement narratives and campaigns that are designed to make people laugh and experience positive emotions requires both courage and creativity. Entertaining, funny media storytelling, with a strong focus on human stories, can be an effective advocacy tool to leverage in the pursuit of public engagement even in a social problem as sad and serious as poverty. Pairing an entertaining story with separate content that offers instructional information—along with a call to action inspired by entertainment-education,[88] such as donating to a humanitarian group or signing a petition—may be an optimal digital-era social-change communication configuration. Centrally, to engage audiences meaningfully in global poverty and other daunting social issues to which they have become desensitized, a steady stream of hopelessness as a narrative frame may be ineffective. A mixed-message media diet—including stories and frames that offer optimistic perspectives, including comedy, rather than nearly exclusively dire scenarios that can lead to chronic audience exhaustion and disengagement—offers a path to new engagement.[89]

Creating light-hearted storytelling focused on a set of social problems as daunting as poverty is not easy. In the case of poverty as a social problem, a balance must be struck in order to meet the dual needs of social-change communication—that is, a need to engage an audience to pay attention and care, but also a requirement to frame communities and individuals in ways that are empowering instead of relying on or perpetuating negative, harmful stereotypes. As the examples in this chapter illuminate, comedy—by critiquing and lampooning underlying institutional dynamics, punching up and not down, overtly opening a door to taboo topics, and inspiring feelings of hope and optimism through positive emotions that take place when watching a funny, highly entertaining story—is not just a good idea to add to the social-change campaign mix, but a crucial one.

PART III   Leveraging Comedy for
Social Change

6 Comedians' Perspectives on the Intersections of Art and Activism

"I know how to write a policy memo; no one is reading my policy memo. But I made a video that makes people laugh, and millions of people have seen it.***"***

Jenny Yang, comedian[1]

In 2011, Franchesca Ramsey was a graphic designer at the fashion brand Ann Taylor, dabbling in comedy content creation on YouTube in her spare time. Having grown up on the internet, she had been making her own YouTube videos since 2006, one year after the site was founded, honing her comedic voice with the benefit of the feedback and community of the site's rapidly growing audience. Although, in those early years, she amassed a respectable following (about 10,000 subscribers) for her YouTube channel, @chescaleigh, where she posted comedy videos infused with social commentary, as well as beauty videos with natural hairstyling tips, she was not widely known outside of that community. That was about to change.

Ramsey was selected as one of the winners of YouTube's 2011 NextUp contest; the prize was a week in Google's New York City offices, where she was mentored by some of YouTube's top creators, along with grant money to invest in her channel. Ramsey saw this as a pivotal opportunity to get serious about developing her channel. Around the same time, comedians Kyle Humphrey and Graydon Sheppard created "Shit Girls Say," originally a parody Twitter account that morphed into a web video series, which mocked, albeit in a relatable way, the stereotypical things that girls say.

Figure 6 Franchesca Ramsey in her viral video, "Shit White Girls Say . . . to Black Girls."
SOURCE / CREDIT: YouTube video screenshot / fair use.

A viral sensation, the series inspired parodies across the internet. While Ramsey mulled making her own parody, stand-up comedian Billy Sorrell created the video "Shit Black Girls Say," which Ramsey found riddled with sexist stereotypes and not at all reflective of her own identity and experiences as a black woman. Simultaneously channeling her personal frustrations with the everyday racism she often encountered, the inspiration for her video, "Shit White Girls Say . . . to Black Girls," was born. Ramsey donned a platinum blond wig and recorded two minutes' worth of the kinds of uncomfortable things white people regularly said to her ("not to sound racist, *but* . . . you can say the N-word, but I can't? . . . this is so ghetto . . . he's so cute for a black guy . . . can I touch it [her hair]?"), and posted it to YouTube.[2] As she explains in her memoir, "it was about all of the seemingly benign comments and expressions of disregard that added up to a constant reminder that I was different from other people, and that my difference was, for some reason, important."[3] Ramsey's video used comedy, parodying an internet meme, to illuminate her own lived experience as a black woman. And it went instantly viral. Within four hours, Ramsey's video had more than a million views—today, it tops 12 million— and Ramsey was catapulted into fame, with interview requests from major media outlets, an audition invitation from *Saturday Night Live*, and countless emails and comments from fans and haters alike. She appeared on *Anderson Live* on CNN, signed with an agent, and quit her graphic design job, bolstered by earnings from the ad views on her YouTube videos. Yet as she soon discovered, she had not only become a YouTube celebrity but also a spokesperson for social justice—or as she terms it in the subtitle of her memoir, "an accidental activist."

However, Ramsey's success as an entertainer was no accident. She had worked hard for years, churning out content on YouTube while working office jobs to pay the bills. She saw YouTube as a proxy for the comedy club scene, via which many comics nurture their craft and amass a following. As she told us, "I started as a stand-up, but I'm also someone who likes to go to bed. So, I felt like YouTube was a great venue for me because no comedy show starts on time, and I had to work; I always had a day job and couldn't perform at 11 or 12 o'clock at night."[4] After "Shit White Girls Say . . . to Black Girls" went viral, she slogged through failed auditions, developed and unsuccessfully pitched a sketch comedy show to 12 networks with no takers, and took a job blogging about social justice for the website Upworthy. Her hustle paid off. By 2014, she was invited by MTV to develop her own web series about race and identity, *Decoded*, and in 2015, she landed a gig as a writer and correspondent on Comedy Central's *The Nightly Show with Larry Wilmore*. These projects cemented her as a major comedic voice on social justice issues. Although *The Nightly Show* was canceled in 2016, she continues to write, produce, and star in *Decoded*, where she uses a combination of sketch comedy and vlogging to humorously break down problematic stereotypes, stigmas, and myths related to racial, ethnic, religious, sexual, and class identity, dissecting topics from white privilege to victim blaming.

Franchesca Ramsey's developing career highlights the relationships and tensions between comedians' creative practice, the changing media environment, the business of entertainment, and social justice. Comedians' perspectives on these intersections animate this chapter. Because it is comedy professionals themselves who shape how comedy functions as a form of cultural production and as an agent of social change, it is critical to know how they conceptualize their role. This chapter draws from in-depth interviews to identify the shared practices, norms, and values of comedy professionals engaged in socially critical comedy in this era of technological and cultural upheaval. How have the particular media, marketplace, and political conditions of the contemporary moment shaped their work? What do they see as the roles and responsibilities of comedy and comedians in the current era? Is there a place for activism in comedy, and how, if at all, can comedy contribute to social change?

We conducted interviews with 17 comedy professionals (see appendix C, table 9) in order to investigate their motivations, experiences, and creative practices vis-à-vis comedy, media, and social justice. While we do not claim to represent an exhaustive landscape of comedy professionals working at the intersection of humor and social justice, we reflect the perspectives of a disparate range of comedy voices, across stand-up, sketch, satirical news, scripted episodic TV, and documentary. We include up-and-coming as well as more established artists, some who have achieved mainstream success with big network projects and others who primarily reach niche audiences through night club performances, online video, stand-up albums, and podcasting. Many, not incidentally, are comedians of color and women.

The interviews surfaced four key themes, around which we structure the chapter. First, contemporary comedians (and comedy) are shaped by the affordances of digital media, which help them hone their individual comedic identities. Second, the current political moment has created both cultural and market imperatives for comedy that focuses on politics and social justice; yet, socially critical comedians continue to face significant market-driven constraints. Third, while not all comedy professionals identify as activists or view their comedy as a form of activism, they still see comedy as functioning in ways that support the conditions for social change. Finally, socially engaged comedy is created with three key practices in mind: providing audiences ways to both laugh and think; punching up, not down; and connecting with audiences through personal storytelling.

COMING OF AGE IN THE YOUTUBE ERA

In today's converged, participatory media culture, individuals and grassroots communities are leveraging digital media to create and share their own creative content, sometimes outside the reach and control of traditional corporate media institutions.[5] For comedians, both aspiring and established, this has opened up new opportunities to develop and test out comic material, while building and interacting with audiences through their social media pages, YouTube channels, and personal blogs and websites. Digital media, because of their openness, visibility, interactivity, and on-demand functionality, offer affordances—particular characteristics and capabilities for action[6]—that shape the practices of contemporary comedians. Franchesca Ramsey's early career path exemplifies the potential of social media and video sharing platforms to elevate marginalized voices and provide a space to talk about issues and perspectives outside of the mainstream. As she explains:

> I quite literally would not have the career that I have if it hadn't been for social media . . . I think social media has removed a lot of the gatekeepers, because not everybody can move to New York or L.A., not everyone can get an agent, not everyone can go to NYU or get a BFA or go to a conservatory to study acting . . . or take $300 improv classes at UCB [Upright Citizens Brigade]. Not everybody has those opportunities or those privileges . . . I think social media has really opened doors—especially for marginalized voices that don't see themselves represented in mainstream media or the representations that they see are so stereotypical and so narrow—so that they have the opportunity to tell their own stories online and then potentially get writing jobs, get acting opportunities, get an agent, get a book deal. We are seeing so much of that, and it's really encouraging, especially right now when it feels like the world is against us.[7]

As Ramsey went on to note, this is not only her story but also the story of Issa Rae, who originally shot her web series, *The Misadventures of Awkward Black Girl*, in college using a cheap web cam. The series was the basis for Rae's now Emmy-nominated, HBO hit, *Insecure*. Donald Glover of *Atlanta* fame also had humble beginnings on YouTube, as did Ilana Glazer and Abbi Jacobson, the creators of Comedy Central's *Broad City*, which began as a web series.

Hasan Minhaj—who achieved renown as a correspondent on *The Daily Show* from 2014–18 and premiered his own Peabody Award–winning political comedy show, *Patriot Act*, on Netflix in 2018—years earlier shaped his work online, together with fellow comedians Fahim Anwar, Asif Ali, and Aristotle Athiras, on their YouTube channel Goatface Comedy. Formed in 2011, Goatface produced comedy sketches about politics and the immigrant experience through the lens of the comedians' Middle Eastern and South Asian identities. As Minhaj sees it, culturally specific comedy can thrive on YouTube "because there are so many people that are like, 'finally,

I've just been waiting for something like this to be created—for me.'"[8] Indeed, audiences are increasingly in control over the process of media consumption; they have come to expect content that is personalized to them, delivered when, where, and how they want it.[9] In turn, they are able to exert their preferences in increasingly visible ways, signaling what they find interesting and entertaining and authentic through their views, likes, shares, and comments. Comedians' understanding of audiences' autonomy and signaling power in the digital age empowers them to create comedy with a particular point of view that resonates with a shared community. In turn, by cultivating their own audiences online, artists are able to establish a viable market for narrowcast comedy from marginalized voices, while asserting their cultural identities. As a case in point, in 2018, Goatface was granted new life—and the potential to reach a mainstream audience—with a comedy special on Comedy Central.

Part and parcel of comedians' coming of age on YouTube and social media is an acute recognition of what their audience wants or needs. As a result, comedians' conceptualization of their audience and the audience's response to their work often shape the content that comedians produce. For example, comedian Jenny Yang sees her role as trying to be "of service" to her social media audience.[10] Likewise, Franchesca Ramsey's audience and its response to "Shit White Girls Say . . . to Black Girls" was what helped her realize her cultural power both as a comedian and as an activist. On *Decoded*, as is the case across the media industry,[11] Ramsey is guided by audience metrics and data:

> I really like looking at numbers and seeing what shares the best and what resonated with people . . . I'm also very fortunate because I have a very active audience and they message me all the time, and they'll send me articles and say, "Have you seen this?" or "I notice you haven't talked about this," or "Here's something you talked about but you didn't get right," or "I wish you would've talked about this more in an episode." We have definitely done episodes that were in direct response to critiques of previous episodes, or just audience suggestions.[12]

In many ways, these practices are no different from what comedians might encounter in a comedy club—calibrating their act in terms of what gets laughs or not—but the digital audience is fundamentally different in its specificity and interactivity, and thus can provide important validation for socially critical and identity-driven humor that may not resonate with the random, eclectic audience members who wander into a comedy club on a given night. As comedian Zahra Noorbakhsh explained, when comedians hone their craft on the club circuit, it reinforces the lowest common denominator—"that antiquated expectation that comedy is universal, that what's funny is funny to everybody"—which oftentimes gives license to tone-deaf or stereotyping humor: "I think that's audience imposed, and I think that now with the internet . . . we have a different sense of audience."[13] In other words, the internet—as an alternative performance space—has helped make clear that there are audiences who dually care about social justice and love comedy, which, in turn, changes the kind of comedy that gets produced and is given a platform.

At the same time, the empowerment of audiences in the digital era demands of performers a level of "relational labor" that was not required in the analog age, as they engage with and relate to their fans and critics, both socially and emotionally, often with limited boundaries between the professional and the personal.[14] Franchesca Ramsey writes in her book about how she has struggled with how much personalized attention to give her fans and critics.[15] Because she is active on social media, she has opened herself up to trolls; while emotionally challenging, this also helps validate and invigorate her creative practice. As she told us:

> One of the downsides of the internet is having tons of people have access to me 24/7 . . . I know an episode is doing well because the harassment I experience just multiplies . . . There are a lot of people who are very threatened by the idea of a woman—let alone a black woman—having any sort of visibility to talk about important issues and to uplift the voices of people who they think are less than them. I think that is very evident in the really overblown responses to my work . . . there are a lot of people who swear that I hate white people or that I'm just like this angry revolutionary who wants to see men enslaved . . . But to me, it says this is the reason why I need to keep doing this work, because if literally just saying police shouldn't kill unarmed black people inspires you to go into a fit of rage, that tells me, "okay, this is a conversation more people need to be having" . . . It's disappointing but it also inspires me to keep moving forward.[16]

Thus, while the openness of social media is a double-edged sword—offering opportunities for marginalized voices while also providing a platform for toxic narratives to flourish—audience feedback and interactivity in the digital age have become essential tools via which socially engaged comedians can find inspiration and validation, even if it means that being a comic with a point of view increasingly requires a steely disposition to endure the inevitable backlash.

A CHANGING ENTERTAINMENT INDUSTRY

At the same time that YouTube and other video-sharing platforms have provided a venue for budding comics to experiment with their craft and connect with audiences, the TV industry has evolved—led by streaming services like Netflix, Amazon, and Hulu—to adopt the on-demand logic and culture of YouTube.[17] Much like YouTube, TV now offers seemingly infinite channels and content catered to specific audience preferences. As the TV audience has splintered across myriad network, cable, and streaming outlets, networks—no longer looking to attract 50 or even 10 million viewers—want new, authentic, narrowly targeted content—and lots of it. Those who produce comedy shows and manage talent see this opportunity most clearly. Joel Church-Cooper, creator and showrunner of the IFC comedy series *Brockmire*, explains how the "thin-slicing of media" has allowed him to do "a very niche show on a very niche channel, where I get to have almost complete creative control."[18] More broadly, he describes how media fragmentation has allowed "for underrepresented voices to finally be heard . . . That opens up doors for Hasan [Minhaj] and other people and *Insecure* and all these great shows. They don't have to be monster hits anymore, because if they are culturally relevant and have 2–3 million fans that are loyal, they can be on for seven seasons, because that's all it takes."[19] Jennie Church-Cooper, who manages Hasan Minhaj, reflects on the benefits of new streaming platforms:

> Ultimately it's more people willing to pay your client to create, and more places to show their content . . . it has helped people, performers, writers, comedians, etc. really be able to hone in on their point of view and explore specificity in what they want to talk about, because we have an ability to access all kinds of content and really hone in as a viewer on what we want to watch. And because there are those opportunities, it has I think encouraged,

particularly comedians, to really bolster their instincts of talking about whatever is meaningful to them, and to trust that the people who are going to respond to what they are saying are now, in this day and age, going to be able to find their content.[20]

Because the business model of streaming services is based on subscriptions rather than ratings per se, this changes the calculus for attracting audiences and allows for more diverse and provocative comedy. As Anne Libera, longtime director at The Second City, observed, "Netflix at this point is not interested in ratings per thing; they're interested in getting heard about and getting people to sign up. So, to bring in a comedian who is maybe controversial is fine, because it will get someone to sign up for Netflix in order to see that comedian, even if they hate them . . . It also opens it up to a variety of voices because it's in their financial interest."[21] This logic can afford comedy professionals greater autonomy. Brent Miller, who produces the Netflix scripted comedy series *One Day at a Time*, noted that "the best thing for me about Netflix is the fact that they bring you on board to do what you do best and they kind of let you do that and support you along the way."[22] With this autonomy, comedians also observed expanded opportunities for creativity and expression. Hasan Minhaj, in reflecting on his show *Patriot Act*—which in its first season took on complex issues like affirmative action, immigration policy, and the U.S.'s relationship with Saudi Arabia—explains, "for a really, really, really long time, I wanted to talk about these things and never really had the platform for it."[23] Thus, the evolving TV industry not only allows comedy creators more freedom but, in so doing, also welcomes new forms of creative storytelling from unique perspectives.

"IT'S COOL TO BE WOKE": A MANDATE FOR SOCIALLY ENGAGED COMEDY

The evolving technologies and platforms of the digital age have coincided with a unique political moment that encompasses ongoing justice challenges exemplified by the Black Lives Matter, Me Too, and March for Our Lives movements, as well as the presidency of Donald Trump. In the Trump era—where public officials govern without regard for facts or truth, where partisan animus rules the day, where marginalized groups, from immigrants to transgender people, are under constant attack—the comedy professionals we interviewed have observed both a cultural and market imperative for comedy that focuses on politics and social justice. As Sara Taksler, former producer for *The Daily Show*, explained, "Before the election, in many ways comedy was a nice-to-have. And in this moment, it's—satire—is a necessity."[24] And as Rachel Dratch observed, today, it's "comedians who are exposing what's really happening."[25] As such, many comedians feel an obligation to speak out and do meaningful work. According to Bethany Hall, "I think right now, because of the climate that we're living in—with so much happening with social justice issues and with politics—I actually think that there is this incredible pressure to write things politically and to have a larger statement."[26] Similarly, Franchesca Ramsey observed that "under a Trump presidency, more people feel compelled to say something. There are a lot of comedians— I would say Patton Oswalt is a really great example—whose work necessarily in the past wasn't very political, but if you go on his Twitter—or even like a Sarah Silverman—they're on Twitter smacking down racists left and right, and reminding people to vote, and calling out Trump at every turn. People feel like now is the time, and I have to say something."[27]

Comedians also noted that comedy focusing on sociopolitical issues— both in response to Trump and more broadly—has become more appealing to audiences and, in turn, to the commercial networks. Comedians thus have license to be riskier, and if they already were being risky, the marketplace is finally ready to reward that. Indeed, W. Kamau Bell now has a forum for his sociopolitical comedy and commentary on major network CNN. Hasan Minhaj has achieved widespread success and attention by sharing his comic perspective as a brown person in America. A web series that deconstructs race and identity is now on-brand for MTV. As comedian Negin Farsad put it, "it's cool to be woke."[28] That is, networks recognize that expanding diversity and incorporating justice-oriented content are going to make them money, because there is an audience for it.

W. Kamau Bell, speaking of his CNN docuseries, *United Shades of America*, reflected, "I think the political moment makes my content more appealing to people—in the sense of 'I don't understand what's going on; can somebody explain this to me? Everybody's telling me that others are wrong; can somebody tell me that other people who are different from me aren't wrong?' Sort of the moment meets the person."[29] Cristela Alonzo observed that people are now trying to educate themselves more in the Trump era by seeking out information about people of color or different demographics that they might not be familiar with or who wouldn't have had a spotlight if it wasn't for Trump and his policies.[30] According to Nato Green, "Since Trump was elected, 20 percent of the U.S. population has participated in a protest. There are a lot of comedians who ... are now putting part of the resistance in their profile and whatnot and trying to do benefit shows ... Because of the level of mobilization and opposition to this historically unpopular president, a lot of comedians feel like it's not career suicide to do that, because there's a constituency for it."[31] As Green further explains, the structural conditions finally support diverse comics doing socially and critically engaged work: "There have been so many people who have been trying so many things and pushing so hard for so long in so many different forums, to advance at least on the level of representation ... that then when the conditions lined up, they were already in position—the external conditions lined up in a way that allowed them to make further advances."[32]

This opening, similar to emerging comics' experiences on YouTube, has in turn helped comics appreciate what it is that their particular perspective can offer to audiences as well as to the wider cultural conversation, encouraging them to assert their cultural identity and use it to their advantage in their comedy. Indeed, we heard from numerous comedians that it was when they embraced their Muslim, Asian American, Latina, Black identities and told their personal stories that they found success. Zahra Noorbakhsh observed that there is "this sense of ownership around identity comedy that is unique, especially for our generation of comedy ... There was a way that previously talking about your identity in comedy pigeonholed you. And I don't think that happens anymore—I think, in fact, it enhances your brand; it's now a way of saying that you have a unique expertise on an experience."[33] This idea—that comics from traditionally underrepresented groups are now able to capitalize on, rather than shy away from, their unique identities and perspectives—is embodied in Hasan Minhaj's reflections on why he decided to create his stand-up show *Homecoming King*: "For me, I really wanted to show in a beautiful, candid, honest way, what the immigrant experience is like for a lot of kids that grew up like me. I hadn't seen that before, and when you think about theater, in that space, there's not a lot of shows that are like my show, there's not a lot of voices like my voice, in that space."[34] Similarly, on his political comedy show *Patriot Act*, he is able to tackle political topics that other mostly white, male late-night hosts wouldn't touch or wouldn't be able to do justice, topics that allow him to speak to his own experiences and perspective:

> Affirmative action is a very messy, complicated topic in America because it's dealing with meritocracy. A lot of our hosts—we have two different late-night hosts named Jimmy. They're white dudes named Jimmy. It's a very complicated thing for them to dive into. So, they're like, "Hey, maybe it's not worth diving into." It's just—when you assess the cost-benefit analysis, they're like, "I don't want to talk about this" . . . that's why, I think, representation matters, because you have people who can provide a perspective that you otherwise can't.[35]

Just as comedians are increasingly rewarded by the market for incorporating their identities into their work, this also places demands on them that are specific to their identities, reflecting their token status within the comedy field and the enduring racial and cultural divides that permeate our society. For comedians from minority groups, their performances are often read through the lens of existing beliefs, stereotypes, and expectations about what comedians of a certain identity should look like or talk about. Comics of color told us that they are often asked to stand in for their cultural group, while being discouraged from doing work that is unrelated to their identity or to social justice. As Franchesca Ramsey observed,

> I'm a comedic person who often says funny things that have nothing to do with identity or activism, and I enjoy that part of my life and my career as well. I'm really at a place now where I'm trying to find a balance, only because as a woman and especially as a black woman, I feel like there are a lot of people who are placing demands on me to constantly educate them. And while I enjoy it, it's quite literally my job but also not my job.[36]

Negin Farsad observed that networks often "trot me out for the brown stuff or the woman stuff," whereas she also would like to do more mainstream things that have nothing to do with her identity.[37] Yet creative decision-makers are often unwilling or unable to see beyond her identity. She explains that she has pitched shows that have no specific race parameters, but "that's not the show that they end up wanting from me. Those shows don't get traction even though I'm dying to make them. Pigeonholing, they call it."[38] Similarly, Zahra Noorbakhsh explained,

> When you're a token you're always speaking on behalf of everybody ... regardless of the fact that I'm Iranian, that I grew up as a California kid, I was always being pinned up in the press as an example of Muslimness against an entire foreign policy world of Muslimness ... When I would get reviews, like "none of this answers for 9/11 ... this is just about her dating life" ... really the expectation was that I would be solving foreign policy for everybody.[39]

These reflections are consistent with research from other professions— dating back to the 1970s, where members of marginalized groups are often expected to represent their cultural group while being typecast into particular roles,[40] and they reveal the problematic assumptions about diversity and representation that are still embedded within the media industry.

A "FICKLE" MARKETPLACE

Even as the marketplace has increasingly opened itself to more diverse comedians and perspectives, socially engaged comedians are not naïve about the media industry's motivations and commitments or about the marketplace's capacity to support social justice–oriented comedy. It is an ongoing challenge for socially critical comedians to be compensated—and compensated well—for the work they do. As Negin Farsad observed, "there are no gold-lined toilets" because of *The Muslims Are Coming!*, despite doing well for a documentary.[41] Likewise, W. Kamau Bell, even with a well-heeded show on CNN, jokingly admitted that "by doing the work that I do, I am naturally limiting my ability to open movies on July Fourth weekend."[42] As Anne Libera of The Second City reflected:

> It's always going to be harder for more marginalized voices of all kinds to get to those really big paydays—the shows, the spaces where the money is really good and the goal is to get as many eyes on them as possible. There's a reason that late-night is primarily white male, because that is still funded by

advertising, and they're looking to get the most viewers . . . My worry is that the gatekeepers are kind of gone . . . the barriers to access are much lower, but it's hard to say whether the barriers to upper levels of power, whether that's the same thing. And then, when you get into the question of who is going to pay for someone to say things that might be unpopular, that's when you get into difficult areas.[43]

In today's polarized political and cultural climate, calls for social justice from within comedy may be unpopular with at least a portion of the potential target audience, even while desirable to others, thereby imposing a commercial penalty for comedians who do this type of work.

The economic realities faced by socially engaged comedians arise from both comedians' unwillingness to compromise in their craft—that is, their personal imperative to remain true to themselves and their values—and the ultimate goal of the market—which is to turn a profit rather than advance social justice. As Nato Green puts it, "The nature of capitalist entertainment is to make money—it's not to end racism or promote social equity or solve the world's problems or anything else. If that happens, it's because they think it's going to make money, not because that's the goal."[44] At the same time, according to Aasif Mandvi, the marketplace is "incredibly fickle . . . you just have to listen to your own internal metronome."[45] W. Kamau Bell recounted a story from 2007 when he met with a manager who warned him not to call himself a "political comedian" because "there's no money in that."[46] And Bell responded, "This is the work. I can't just be another type of comedian; so if you can sell this work, great. Whatever you want to label it . . . I can't do something else. I can't call myself something else because the marketplace says do something different."[47] Bell continued, "At the end of the day, I want the words that come out of my mouth and the art to be really good, because you can't control any of the business stuff."[48] Comedians also understand that they are not selling themselves based on virtue or talent alone; they need to make themselves seem profitable. Nato Green explained, "As a comic, you have to do what you are . . . you have to figure out how to make your own life, and build up your apparatus so that people believe that they can make money off you."[49] Similarly, Joel Church-Cooper observed, "You still have to present yourself as profitable to have a voice in the entertainment industry . . . if you present yourself that way, more creative freedom, possibly more budget, all of it matters."[50]

As cultural studies scholar Graeme Turner has argued, although digital technologies and platforms have opened up the media industry to under-represented social and cultural groups, there is "no necessary connection between the widening of opportunities for participation we are now witnessing and a democratic politics."[51] In his view, just as the comedy practitioners recognized, the media industries are elevating marginalized voices out of self-interest rather than for the sake of social justice. For its part, YouTube—despite its reputation as a democratizing platform and site for participatory culture—has become increasingly less open, prioritizing professionally created content over amateur, user-generated content, while users' discovery of content is governed by corporate-driven algorithms that make certain videos more visible than others.[52] According to media scholar Joanne Morreale, YouTube is "now an arm of the media industry."[53]

Socially critical comedians, including comics of color, are thus operating within a hierarchical commercial media system, attempting to extract value for their work even as they recognize the entrenched power structures and capitalistic priorities that underlie the industry. For example, the creative autonomy that comedians are afforded by streaming platforms, relative to legacy networks, is offered in exchange for the subscribers that the comedians draw to the platform and the brand value or cultural buzz they provide. Still, just as the niche-oriented entertainment industry is monetizing the voices of marginalized and justice-oriented comics, these comedians are leveraging the market—as it avails itself to them—to do the work that they *want* to do—and get paid for it. As Hasan Minhaj trenchantly observes: "As a performer of color in show business now, I'm understanding more and more that if we can control the capital and distribution there's nothing that can stop us. That's really my goal; that's my end game. I'm not gonna ask for my humanity or my dignity or my opportunities, I'm going to take them. That, to me, is the American dream."[54]

CAN COMEDY CHANGE THE WORLD?

Implicit in the work of socially critical comedians who take on social justice issues is the idea that their comedy can have a larger impact. Scholars frequently have conceptualized comedy, and particularly satire, as a form of political activism, in that it highlights injustice, challenges the status quo, raises consciousness, builds community, and sometimes even overtly advocates for change.[55] And in chapter 2, we outlined the key ways in which comedy can contribute to social change through its potential to influence audiences and reshape the public conversation. Yet despite a persistent media narrative attributing activist impulses to contemporary comedians,[56] little is known about how comedy creators themselves actually understand their work—what goals they have when they create socially critical comedy, what influence they think comedy can have on social change, and what place they see, if any, for activism in their work.

In our interviews, we found that there is no concise articulation of what comedians are trying to "do" with their comedy. As W. Kamau Bell explains, "there are different jokes for different reasons."[57] Yet all of the comedians want to do more than make their audiences laugh—they want to provide them with something of value, although entertainment remains a chief goal. The comedians use their humor in various yet intersecting ways—to build empathy, to illuminate, to demystify, to mock power, to instruct and educate, to humanize, to represent and affirm marginalized identities, to create conversation, to provide relief. In scholar Richard Schechner's theory of performance, he proposed an "efficacy-entertainment dyad" in which the two elements occupied opposing ends of a continuum, where entertainment emphasizes "fun" and efficacy emphasizes "results."[58] According to Schechner, both are present in all performances, but one or the other is dominant. We similarly found that comedians' intentions reflect a fluctuating balance between these two poles, prioritizing entertainment but also attending to efficacy to more or less of a degree. In other words, comedians' intentions exist along a spectrum from entertainment to efficacy. Entertainment and efficacy are not mutually exclusive; yet, comedians may give greater weight to one of these elements.

At the most activist, or results-oriented, end of the continuum are those comedians who—in addition to entertaining—seek to mobilize their audience and have a specific goal or change in mind. For example, in July 2018, Negin Farsad, together with comedian Dean Obeidallah, launched the "Boycott Bigotry" campaign. The goal of the comedy-based campaign was

Figure 7 Negin Farsad in Charlottesville, Virginia, during the "Boycott Bigotry" video.

SOURCE / CREDIT: YouTube video screenshot / fair use.

to simultaneously confront Donald Trump's hate and corruption by calling on people to boycott Trump properties. As Farsad told us, "There are two things that bother me about the Trump administration: one is the bigotry, obviously, and the other is the conflicts of interest . . . It's almost like we're paying him to be racist. I just thought, he needs to stop earning money."[59] The grassroots-funded effort, chronicled in a video distributed by progressive advocacy group MoveOn.org,[60] kicked off with a free comedy show in Charlottesville, Virginia, where the comedians staged street actions, like a "Trump venting" booth where people could vent about Trump in exchange for comfort gifts like fuzzy dice; the comedians also hung posters around the city and ran ads in local media with satiric taglines, such as "Trump Winery: Aged with notes of Trump's racism in every bottle . . . Stop spending money on Trump's bigotry."[61] Here, Farsad and Obeidallah deployed comedy with a clear activist mission. Similarly, Israeli comedy writer Omri Marcus endorses an activist style of comedy: "Comedy should stop being a coffee meeting and more like a business meeting where there is an action item at the end."[62]

Yet comedians' activist sensibilities also manifest in less formal ways. Franchesca Ramsey sees herself as a comedic activist, but also as "just a person who wants to see a world where everybody is treated fairly and everyone gets the same opportunities."[63] Ramsey describes her comedy as "a reflection of the world and the world I want to see. Even if on the larger scale, I can't personally change policy, I can't personally open doors for people, I *can* do things that move culture forward and inspire people to do the work that I think we all need to do."[64] Much like Henry Jenkins's concept of the "civic imagination"—which recognizes that the vision for and seeds of change often come from within popular culture[65]—Ramsey sees her comedy as a way to artistically—and humorously—articulate a new and better society unencumbered by racism and other forms of oppression. Ramsey understands comedy as one among many types of activism, all with the goal of creating change: "I think everyone's activism takes different shapes and different forms. There are people who are quite literally marching in the streets and doing really important grassroots work, and then there are people like myself who host a web series. I don't think that one is better than the other; I think that they both serve a purpose."[66]

On the other end of the continuum are comedians who centrally see themselves as storytellers; their goal is to tell an authentic story that resonates with audiences, and any social change outcomes are incidental to that—in contrast to more activist-oriented comedians who also seek to entertain but have deliberate social change aims. For example, Aasif Mandvi, a former correspondent on *The Daily Show* whose latest performance is a one-man off-Broadway show, *Sakina's Restaurant*, about an Indian immigrant who comes to New York in search of the American dream, explains that his chief objective is "to connect with an audience."[67] In describing his 2015 web series *Halal in the Family*, which parodied the classic American sitcom as a way to shed light on Islamophobia, depicting a Muslim family "living in this abject fear of their friends and neighbors thinking they are terrorists," he explains, "Number one, we wanted it to be funny, we wanted it to entertain. And number two, we wanted it to highlight the absurdity and make people think about these topics in a way that they may not have otherwise."[68] Even while Mandvi's comedy calls attention to injustice and shows people what in society needs to change, Mandvi sees a stark difference between the goals and practices of artists and activists: "The artist is ultimately just creating and trying to raise a mirror to the culture in some way . . . the ripple effect of that, whether that creates just waves or a tsunami or whatever that creates, is ultimately not what I'm concerned with—it is to share—whereas I think the activist is much more concerned with the outcome; there is a much more specific agenda for the activist."[69]

Similarly, Joel Church-Cooper, showrunner on *Brockmire*, reflecting on a narrative arc in the show's second season that dealt with institutional racism, explains, "I didn't want to tell that story to be like this is going to change the world . . . But that was a true feeling that I knew to be true from my own life experience, and I wanted to put that into my work and derive comedy from it, mainly just because it was true and I hadn't seen it expressed before—that kind of nuanced take about race in a sports comedy."[70] His goal was "not to be political" but to express "complicated issues that are currently part of our national debate."[71]

Yet despite comedians' differing intentions and the contrasting normative judgments they make about whether comedy counts as activism, they are aligned in terms of what they think comedy actually can accomplish in the context of social change. Comedians—including those who, like Negin Farsad, aspire to change minds—do not necessarily think that comedy can itself produce change; however, they recognize the role comedy can play in laying the groundwork for change—whether by lowering people's defenses, opening up a space for conversation, and/or offering a new perspective. As Farsad reflected with regard to her "Boycott Bigotry" campaign: "I'm not delusional—I know someone's not going to look at my poster and be like, 'she's right; I don't support Trump anymore' . . . But I think that there's a moment where you see something or you hear something and you have a chuckle and it makes you think . . . over time, one chuckle becomes two and three and four, and then we're talking about hundreds of millions of chuckles, which add up to some kind of measurable social change."[72] Quite similarly, Aasif Mandvi explains, "When you're laughing about something, there's an inherent kind of acceptance that happens. If you're willing to relax yourself and your physiology, to the point where you are letting yourself laugh, I feel like you're letting something in. You may not walk away having changed your mind or anything about something, but you have at least allowed yourself to be penetrated by something."[73] Thus, comedians—even if they do not have a particular result in mind—do not see themselves as screaming into the void; they view comedy as a purposeful art form that can open people to new perspectives, which is an important prerequisite for change.

The comedians also identified comedy as a starting point, not an end point, for change. According to W. Kamau Bell, "I think we comedians have the ability to take these complicated things and turn them into jokes and make bigger issues digestible, and can help sort of encourage the conversation, but we don't actually legislate change."[74] Bell observed that despite John Oliver's interventions into the net neutrality debate,

> We are currently losing the battle. It doesn't mean that John Oliver didn't do a good job—just don't rely on the comedian to make this happen . . . he certainly changed the conversation and more people know what net neutrality is now because of him, but if we judge comedy by the results of how the world changes, we are sort of looking at arts to do the wrong thing, where really arts is a better way for us to understand the world.[75]

Like several comedians we interviewed, Hasan Minhaj recognized the role that people play in the process of change: "Art really is just these beautiful pieces of lightning that hopefully strike a chord in your heart, and if it can strike a chord in your heart at the right moment, perhaps it inspires you to change your perspective. But the necessary condition is the people themselves taking initiative."[76]

These perspectives recognize social change as a process within which comedy can play a supportive role. Yet, as in other professions, comedians engage in boundary maintenance,[77] protecting their professional identities as entertainers and artists, distinct from the formal efforts of traditional activists, even if their comedy shares elements of activism. Deflecting responsibility for social change is also a way to account for the uncertainty inherent in audience reactions to their art. Comedians understand that comedy only will have social influence when it engages audiences to learn and feel and share—and sometimes to take some kind of action; and this, for comedians, is unpredictable—that is, they don't know if and how their comedy will resonate. Still, it is clear that comedians see comedy's potential as a catalyst for change.

THE PRACTICE OF SOCIALLY ENGAGED COMEDY

Comedians' ideas about the role comedy can play in social change inform the values that imbue their work. We identified three overarching principles that shaped comedians' creative practice. First is their desire to create comedy that, in the words of Franchesca Ramsey, makes "people laugh but also makes people think;"[78] for these comedians, there needs to be a larger message. As Hasan Minhaj explained, "jokes are just a conduit to saying something significant and meaningful . . . the story and the message and what you're saying and what you're adding to people's lives is far more important than the jokes themselves."[79] Nato Green told us that his performances "are geared toward getting an audience to engage in a conversation about ideas . . . I don't need people to agree with me politically; I just need people to agree we are going to talk about ideas."[80]

Importantly, however, the comedians recognize that jokes—even lowbrow ones—and challenging ideas must go hand in hand. As Aasif Mandvi reflected, "Sometimes people don't want to think; they just want to laugh at poop jokes. The beauty of when I was on *The Daily Show*, what I thought we did really well, was toggle the poop jokes and the smarts . . . A spoonful of poop jokes makes the medicine go down."[81] At the same time, as comedians challenge their audiences to think and engage with difficult topics, they recognize that they cannot be didactic. As Joel Church-Cooper notes, "people engage with stories through empathy, not through 'oh, I see what they are doing, they are challenging the paradigm.'"[82] Indeed, comedians see getting people to laugh as key to getting them to engage deeply with issues. In W. Kamau Bell's Netflix stand-up special, *Private School Negro*, he does a bit about the *Doc McStuffins* cartoon and its importance for representation, for showing young children that black women are doctors. But, as he explains, "I don't go on stage and go 'there's an important TV show called *Doc McStuffins*; here's what happened.' I need to write jokes about it so that people take it seriously because they laughed at it."[83]

The second key value expressed by the comedians is a commitment to punching up, not down—that is, attacking those in power and not diminishing those who already are on the margins. As Nato Green explained, when he and W. Kamau Bell conceived of *Laughter against the Machine* in 2008—a nationally touring comedy show focused on sociopolitical issues—they decided that "we were going to make lots of jokes about painful, difficult subjects, but . . . it was important to us that the perspective not be minimizing or belittling the actual suffering that people were experiencing."[84] Similarly, as Jenny Yang articulated:

To me, truly being funny for the kind of society and America that I want means that we don't pick on the more vulnerable . . . Making fun of the top one percent richest people in the world is very different than making fun of racism, for example, or homeless orphan babies . . . People can make rape jokes that are funny, and there are some really fucked-up rape jokes that are funny . . . To me, it's not about funny; it's about, when you choose targets, you're communicating what your values are and the kind of world you want to live in.[85]

As Franchesca Ramsey elaborates:

People that are marginalized and on the fringes of society or in vulnerable positions have always been susceptible to negative stereotypes or demeaning language and slurs. That's quite literally how they've been put in those positions and kept in them for so long. And so when comedians just regurgitate those ideas, whether it be about women or LGBTQ people or people of color or people with disabilities or fat people . . . it's just to me, very lazy. Those are the same "jokes" that your uncle tells at Thanksgiving—and he's not a comedian, he's just a bigot.[86]

Finally, the comedians emphasized that their best, and often funniest, comedy comes from a personal place, reflecting their own lived experiences and/or issues they care about. Some comedians recognized that sharing their personal stories has a humanizing effect, helping to create a point of connection and build empathy, even across lines of difference. For example, Negin Farsad described how during the "Boycott Bigotry" campaign, she spent twenty minutes talking to a Trump supporter, and at the end of the conversation, she told the woman, "'Oh just so you know, I'm Muslim and I'm from Iran, my family's on the Muslim Ban, so if something ever happens to my parents, their family can't come see them. How does that make you feel?'" Farsad observed, "You could tell she was like, when confronted with something that's so human, you can see the partisanship falling away. She was like 'I'm sorry for you, I'm sorry for you.'"[87] Likewise, Cristela Alonzo described a time when she was performing on college campuses through the National Association for Campus Activities, and while she expected to be most popular in Latinx communities, she ended up being most popular in the Midwest:

I decided to just speak about my life . . . In these towns, I realized that to them I wasn't just Latina. They connected with different parts of my life that connected to them. I was raised Catholic and give Catholic jokes, and Catholics would like my jokes because they connected with them. I would talk about my family and living check to check and not knowing what the future holds. They would get that. Even though we didn't look alike, we were living the same experience.[88]

For Alonzo, talking about her personal experiences also is a way to affirm her identity, "to make sure that people that connect to the kind of upbringing and life I had feel like I can maybe represent a version of their life as well . . . My entire goal with stand-up has always been to represent people like me—and I don't mean Latino necessarily. I mean people that are poor, I mean people in rural areas."[89]

Several comics noted that talking about something deeply personal is a way to make the issues they discuss and the stories they tell more relatable—and funnier. As Aasif Mandvi told us, "I use a lot of personal stuff because I feel like the personal translates into the general. So when you talk about personal things that happened, or when you talk about things that were connected to my life and my experience and my perspective, that can resonate."[90] Bethany Hall similarly elaborated:

When I'm working on a show . . . my goal is to be as open and transparent and honest as possible. My belief is that the more you break down barriers with comedy and the more that you expose the truth of who you are or what you believe, the more funny and the more raw your content is, and because of that, the more relatable it is, the more unique it is. I find that when people do relate to the material that I am part of or have created, it's because I'm talking about something so personal that it somehow becomes universal. Right now, I'm writing a show that . . . tackles the experience of having a miscarriage, which is something that I've experienced personally, and my co-writer has experienced personally, and it's like the more we dig into the honest emotions of what it feels like to have a miscarriage, weirdly the funnier it gets.[91]

That relatability is key, especially in scripted comedy about social justice. As Joel Church-Cooper, showrunner for *Brockmire*, explains: "If it's just a bunch of people white-knighting around and saying the right thing that everyone can applaud for, it's going to be real boring, real predictable. The only chance your message has of actually reaching somebody is if they can relate to your main character and feel the change they're feeling on the screen."[92] Other comedians noted that a focus on the personal is what sustains and supports their creative practice. As W. Kamau Bell told us, "I only can write about and perform about things I care a lot about and feel really deeply connected to. It's not like I have a choice in this. I don't write good jokes about things I don't care about, or I write good jokes, but I can't do them for long because I lose interest."[93]

.   .   .   .   .

By identifying the norms, practices, and values that underlie the production of socially critical comedy, we are better able to understand what it is and how it functions in the context of social change. Scholar Rebecca Krefting, in her articulation of "charged humor," argues that intentionality is key: "Charged humor springs from a social and political consciousness desiring to address social justice issues . . . This kind of humor is intentional, meaning the humorist has designs on an outcome, specific or general—a change in attitudes or beliefs or action taken on behalf of social inequality."[94] We agree with Krefting about the importance of intentionality; however, what we see emerging from our interviews as defining comedy in service of social justice and underlying its potential for change is the intentionality of voice and perspective, of the issues highlighted, not necessarily the intention to produce a distinct change or action in the audience. The comedy professionals profiled in this chapter—leveraging the affordances of new media platforms and emboldened by a changing marketplace and challenging political moment—are using their unique identities and personal experiences to create comedy that offers audiences something of value and takes aim at oppressive power dynamics. Even if comedians don't explicitly identify their work as activism or have clear end goals in mind, they still see their art as functioning in much the same way that activism functions—to spark and/or change the conversation, to challenge the status quo, to call attention to injustice, and to imagine a new and better society. Thus, although there are comedians who engage in traditional activism—by including explicit calls to action in their work, using their star power to raise money for or otherwise bring attention to a cause, or as we detail in the next chapter, collaborating with justice organizations on comedy projects—comedy's wider potential for social change derives from comedians' desire to use their voices and stories and perspectives to intervene in the culture and provide audiences with new frames of reference, new understandings, and new conversations.

7 Creative Collaborations

*❝With social justice, what comedy does is present a certain
issue in a way that doesn't seem like people are getting
attacked. The moment that people feel like they are getting
attacked, they won't listen to you. But if you can make them
laugh, they're willing to listen more.❞*

> Cristela Alonzo, comedian, Define American advisory
> board member[1]

Amanda Nguyen was angry. Her opening remarks to the U.S. Senate
Judiciary Committee were blunt: "On the day that I was raped, I never could
have imagined that a greater injustice awaited me than the one I had already
been forced to endure."[2] Assaulted as a college student, Nguyen was shocked
to learn how difficult her journey to justice would be, thanks to an inadequate criminal justice system—a scenario faced also by millions of Americans.
Crucial medical evidence was routinely destroyed. Case backlogs prevented
the crimes from being investigated. Without basic rights afforded to sexual
assault survivors, including access to their own rape kits containing physical
evidence of the crime, the possibility of justice was minimal.[3]

In 2014, after launching a nonprofit advocacy organization called Rise,
Nguyen set out to change federal and state law in order to expand legal
rights for sexual assault survivors—herself and others: "I started it because
I needed civil rights and nobody else was going to write them, so I decided
to write them myself."[4] Powered by data, motivation, personal stories, and
supportive legislative allies, Rise was methodical. Success—though daunt-

Figure 8 Funny or Die video: "Even Supervillains Think Our Sexual Assault Laws Are Insane."
SOURCE / CREDIT: YouTube video screenshot / fair use.

ing considering the bureaucratic intricacies of legislative advocacy—seemed hopeful. But in 2016, Nguyen and her Rise team—after collaborating with members of Congress to craft federal legislation, the Sexual Assault Survivors' Bill of Rights Act—were stalled. Although momentum had been building for the bill, and despite bipartisan congressional sponsors, it was an election year—a historically difficult time to get things done within the complicated, gridlocked engine of Congress.

Enter comedy. After meeting with Brad Jenkins, former White House official turned director of the D. C. office of Funny or Die, Nguyen decided comedy was worth a try alongside the Rise team's other organizing tactics. The result of their first creative collaboration, a short-form YouTube comedy sketch video produced by Funny or Die, titled "Even Supervillains Think Our Sexual Assault Laws Are Insane," illustrates the stakes: Sitting around a gloomily lit room, five cartoonishly ridiculous and terrible "supervillains," while fiendishly plotting to defeat heroic "Captain Brave" with a litany of evil tactics, reflect on the idea that requiring sexual assault victims to pay for their own rape kits is shockingly "too far"—it's just *too* evil and outrageous for them to even consider as an option in their menu of nefarious machinations.[5]

The timing, comedy content, and accompanying call to action were all strategic. According to Jenkins: "When we did the Senate bill drop, we did it with the Funny or Die video, and it got a ton of attention. First time in the history of Congress . . . Politics and power really do come down to, 'How do I get this person's attention?'"[6] The attention-grabbing video-based campaign humorously skewered and explained the absurdity of the structural challenges facing sexual assault survivors navigating the criminal justice system. With a call to action directed from the Funny or Die video, the accompanying online petition on Change.org garnered thousands of signatures, which the Rise team then delivered to Congress to demonstrate public demand.

On October 7, 2016, President Barack Obama signed the Survivors' Bill of Rights Act of 2016.[7] The new law, unanimously supported by Republicans and Democrats,[8] "codifies a basic set of comprehensive civil rights for at least 25 million rape survivors across the country."[9] Funny or Die and Nguyen continued their creative comedy collaboration as Rise moved next into a state-by-state legislative advocacy effort. To date, at least nine state versions of survivor bill of rights laws have passed, modeled after the federal legislation.[10] In Brad Jenkins's estimation, the comedy elements of the Rise advocacy campaign were vital to the victories, in large part due to the creative collaboration with Nguyen as a social justice leader who wholeheartedly embraced the genre:

> When I tell people we have done this [comedy] for sexual assault—the least funny issue, and the most harrowing and personal issue that you can think of—they are amazed. Amanda is the perfect partner because she thinks comedy is all about empowerment. Sexual assault isn't funny, but what is funny and what we make fun of is the status quo . . . That's where the humor comes in.[11]

In 2018, Amanda Nguyen—the 26-year-old accidental activist and emergent social justice leader—was nominated for the Nobel Peace Prize in recognition of her successful civil rights advocacy, which has effectively transformed decades of ineffective policy to empower millions of sexual assault survivors to pursue justice. Armed with a sophisticated understanding of the interplay between participatory civic practice, public engagement, and policy—and the dynamic role of culture and creativity—she has migrated her efforts onto the world stage, working with the United Nations to pass a global survivors' bill of rights. In her unflinching use of short-form, shareable YouTube comedy videos as an anchor for civic practice alongside traditional advocacy tactics, Nguyen epitomizes a contemporary generation of social justice advocates that seeks "to change the world through any media necessary."[12] For Nguyen, comedy is—and continues to be—a vital cultural tool in her global activism:

> We were able to do this with humor in particular: Basically, it's like taking the medicine with a little sweetener, or taking your vodka with a chaser. This issue is depressing. It's difficult. It is my personal belief that social movements cannot be sustained on anger. Anger will burn out. Rather, they need to be sustained on hope . . . . Humor was a way to entertain people while also hiding a really important message in it, and on top of that, being able to get people to learn about the issue. There is lot of activism fatigue that is happening in today's world. Every issue needs to be worked on. How do you get people to actually care, and get people outside of the low-hanging fruit—[those] who already care? Yes, you're trying to activate them too, but you're also trying to get people who may not be predisposed to care about this to care about it.[13]

The synergistic, creative engagement between Amanda Nguyen's sexual assault policy advocacy initiative and the cultural prowess and cache of Funny or Die illustrates the power and promise of cross-sector collaboration between two disparate professional worlds: social justice advocacy and comedy. In this example, comedy aimed a glaring spotlight onto the outrage of the existing institutional status quo. In so doing, the humorous, critical treatment of a tough issue garnered attention, and its digital dissemination and call to action provided a crucial public engagement mechanism—a way for newly enlightened publics to engage in civic practice, pressuring lawmakers to make a change.

By unpacking this initiative and others, this chapter considers the creative, strategic machinations of contemporary comedy professionals and social justice advocates as they co-create and leverage comedy that engages publics in social challenges. We first position creative cultural strategy for social justice within a participatory, converged media context. Through case studies of collaborations directed by leading contemporary advocacy organizations that have leveraged comedy in their digital-era public engagement strategies, constructed by original interviews with the comedy and social justice professionals who worked together to bring them to life, we illuminate the imperatives and characteristics of this creative and strategic process.

This chapter is anchored by core questions: How do creative-strategic collaborations between social justice groups and comedy manifest—what forms do they take, and how is the comedy made available to the public? Why is comedy collaboration regarded as valuable to the missions of social justice organizations and leaders who have employed it? What are the best practices and shared characteristics of comedians and social justice advocates who worked effectively together to engage the public in serious issues? To imagine comedy that cuts through the message clutter and engages audiences, it is vital to understand how cross-sector creative collaboration manifests—and why it matters.

CULTURAL STRATEGY AND SOCIAL CHANGE: SHAPING CREATIVITY TO ENGAGE AUDIENCES

Convergence Culture and Cultural Resistance

In the contemporary digital era now well past its fledgling years, the boundaries between civic engagement, and entertainment and information consumption, have crumbled. In such a media culture, as scholar Henry Jenkins has eloquently articulated, civic and political practice and engagement in entertaining popular culture are deeply intertwined: "Welcome to convergence culture, where old and new media collide, where grassroots and corporate media intersect, where the power of the media producer and the power of the media consumer interact in unpredictable ways."[14] In Jenkins's conception of participatory culture, audiences interact with one another and with institutions—media, government, corporate—as they consume media messages and entertainment, building buzz and enabling a sense of civic efficacy among them, "bringing the realm of political discourse closer to the everyday experiences of citizens."[15] With the expansion of communication channels and mechanisms for two-way interaction, new voices—and many voices—have the potential to be heard.[16] Engaging with entertaining media products and civic practice may feel like similar activities for audiences who have honed the digital behaviors of choosing what to watch, liking, sharing, tweeting, signing petitions, calling for boycotts of companies, writing emails to Congress or corporations, and registering to vote.

Against this backdrop, entertainment and comedy can also provide a mechanism for individuals and groups to intentionally raise the profile of social justice challenges, and even to take some kind of action. Scholar Stephen Duncombe's idea of cultural resistance is meaningful here—actively creating and leveraging creative culture "to resist and/or change the dominant political, economic and/or social structure."[17] In the participatory media environment, cultural narratives shaped by the entertainment industry, including TV and film, can play a vital role in empowering audiences to actively engage in ideas they care about. Social justice groups in the YouTube era also can create and distribute entertaining cultural products themselves, rather than relying exclusively on the institutional power and reach of the mainstream entertainment industry. The collaborative initiatives highlighted in this chapter consider both realities: the reach of mainstream entertainment comedy produced with the input of social justice groups, along with mediated comedy products created as explicit forms of cultural resistance, as in the case of Rise's collaboration with Funny or Die.

Narrative and Cultural Strategy for Social Justice in the Digital Age

Civic practice and culture are already intertwined in practice; collaboration and co-creation between social justice and creative industries have been well established in historical movements for social change, as scholar Daniel Fischlin and his colleagues articulate: "[I]n the world outside the academy and society's dominant cultural institutions, politics and culture are mutually constitutive. Activists, artists, and intellectuals have long recognized affinities between art and social activism."[18] Leveraging entertainment media for public engagement has been understood by issue advocacy groups, and honed as a practice, for decades beginning in the analog media age,[19] albeit newly in vogue in the participatory, converged media era. In the present day, harnessing the influence of entertainment media for social change is an expanding professional practice labeled as narrative or cultural strategy, which recognizes the amplifying capability of mediated entertainment, alongside its power to shape societal portraits of people and problems. The practice of contemporary cultural and narrative strategy manifests in the following key elements: The attention-getting power of entertainment in the digital age; the ability to mobilize audiences around social justice topics as they appear in entertainment; creating explicit professional connections between social justice advocates and entertainment decision-makers to shape narratives in mainstream entertainment; shifting the power dynamics to ensure that members of traditionally marginalized communities are able to find seats at the decision-making table in the business of entertainment and culture; and the practice of social justice organizations self-producing and distributing original entertainment products.[20]

Notably, contemporary narrative and cultural strategy is fueled entirely by the two-way traits of the converged, participatory media culture, using cultural resistance as an underpinning. The networked participatory culture has bestowed new agency to grassroots ideas, as well as to new voices who have not historically enjoyed access to the legacy media system. Indeed, Henry Jenkins and his colleagues point to new activists and a collective sense of efficacy—"civic agency"—in the participatory era that intersects culture, media, and social justice.[21]

Cultural strategy is not theoretical among social justice advocates, but in full practice, albeit not yet universally adopted across the ecology of social-change organizations. Recent professional and philanthropic interest in popular culture has prompted new opportunities to leverage entertainment for social-change purposes. *Spoiler Alert*, a 2014 multimedia report written by cultural strategist Tracy Van Slyke, urged social justice leaders to leverage pop culture directly as part of their change strategies, as a mechanism to shift "dominant narratives" that reflect and shape cultural values and solutions to social problems.[22] In 2016, two U.S. foundations, Unbound Philanthropy and the Nathan Cummings Foundation, funded an extensive research-based initiative, #PopJustice, which "illuminates the promise and potential of popular culture strategies to advance social change"—including work with comedy.[23] In 2017, eight major global foundations—notably including the Ford Foundation, Open Society Foundations, and Omidyar Networks—pooled resources to create a new funding entity, the Pop Culture Collaborative, to support social change through entertainment media.[24] Inside advocacy groups, narrative and cultural strategists are increasingly recognized as important players in the public engagement process, albeit distinct from traditional strategic communication.

Forms of Creative Collaborations between Advocates and Comedy

Narrative and cultural strategy for social change positions creative collaboration between sectors—social justice and entertainment, including comedy—as a mechanism for shaping new mediated narratives. By working together, social justice and comedy can create influential and entertaining ways to engage publics in issues. As we present through the illustrative initiatives later in this chapter, the collaborations generally manifest in two forms, each with its own foundation of practice and research.

First, social justice groups often act as a resource, supplying issue expertise to entertainment and comedy decision-makers in Hollywood— that is, the writers and producers who may be interested in tackling social issue topics within their stories. The foundation of this practice stems from the rich history and research-based model of Entertainment-Education (E-E), an intentional practice in which prosocial messages are embedded into nondidactic entertainment programming as a mechanism for social change.[25] Among other elements, the E-E approach, which recognizes the unique persuasive power of entertainment storytelling due to an audience's emotional response and involvement with characters, also established the need for a call to action—a mechanism to direct audiences to learn more or do something after watching an entertainment story about a civic or health issue.[26]

Alongside other examples, in the late 1990s, the contemporary practice of E-E in the United States—and progenitor of present-day social change collaborations between philanthropy groups and entertainment media— was shaped in large part through a multiyear HIV-awareness entertainment programming partnership between Viacom's two behemoth youth-serving networks, MTV and Black Entertainment Television (BET), and the Kaiser Family Foundation, a philanthropic public health organization.[27] More recently, a group of social justice groups launched Storyline Partners, which informs and counsels Hollywood writers and producers about topics related to traditionally marginalized individuals and groups.[28] Hollywood, Health & Society, a project of the USC Annenberg Norman Lear Center, has worked since 2002 to provide the entertainment industry with accurate information to develop storylines on health topics.[29] Other nonprofit and advocacy organizations also make collaboration with the entertainment industry an essential part of their strategic practice, meeting with writers and producers to brief them on social and health issues.

As a second form and output of narrative strategy, social justice advocates collaborate with entertainment professionals—writers, performers, and producers—to create and distribute stand-alone original mediated comedy projects designed to engage audiences in their issues. Generally speaking, these creative products, particularly in the context of comedy, are shaped and disseminated as short-form videos or multipart series, often—but not always—as focal points of public engagement campaigns that direct audiences with calls to action. While the comedy collaborations profiled here do not adhere to a strict interpretation of the public-interest advertising approach known as social marketing, we position the model here as a relevant contributing progenitor. As a form of public service advertising, social marketing uses the principles and tactical approach of commercial marketing and advertising, albeit with a distinct goal: to promote positive social change and behavior,[30] serving the social good for "society" or the collective.[31]

Tactically, this form of public interest marketing produces and disseminates media products such as short-form videos and other outputs of traditional commercial advertising. In the context of the participatory media era, funny short-form videos can capitalize on virality, offering advocates the opportunity to reach a wide audience through social media sharing and endorsements, pointing audiences to a website for more information or prescribing a specific way to take action. In this way, short-form comedy videos about social justice topics, when paired with a way to learn or do more, can become "drillable"—that is, empowering and allowing audiences to drill down to learn more, beyond viewers' original exposure to a message encountered in the digital media environment.[32]

In sum, mediated entertainment can serve vital functions in this converged, participatory culture, capturing attention and enabling civil society organizations to reimagine or reframe social problems, thereby acting as a vehicle to raise awareness, shift cultural narratives and public opinion, and encourage public participation in social problems. Comedy, in this context, is both entertainment fodder and cultural resistance. With this backdrop in mind, the collaborative efforts profiled here reveal how social justice organizations have added comedy to their public engagement toolboxes, and why it is valuable.

COMEDY AND ADVOCACY COLLABORATIONS AT WORK

Everytown for Gun Safety: Expanding the Grassroots Base

Everytown for Gun Safety exists because of unthinkable human tragedy. Combining the efforts of two organizations (Mayors Against Illegal Guns and Moms Demand Action for Gun Sense in America) after the 2012 shooting at Sandy Hook Elementary School in Newtown, Connecticut,[33] the grassroots movement that advocates for gun violence prevention was born under the specter of America's gun violence epidemic, which claims the lives of 96 people daily.[34] Everytown's members and leader advocates face persistent roadblocks in the face of a well-funded gun lobby, led by the National Rifle Association (NRA) and its stance against gun reform and regulation.[35] Public engagement in the topic is onerous; the most dedicated spokespeople and advocates are often parents, family members, and friends who have lost beloved people to gun violence. To engage publics and policymakers, gun violence prevention advocates relive and relay painful stories—and they are most readily visible in the public eye during moments of fresh tragedy.

Perhaps not in spite of these public engagement challenges, but because of them, Everytown for Gun Safety embraced cultural strategy—including comedy—from inception. During the movement's early years, Everytown hired Jason Rzepka, a former MTV prosocial entertainment executive, as director of cultural engagement, and the group established a Creative Council, a cadre of visible artists and performers. Cultural and narrative strategy consultant Mik Moore worked with Everytown's in-house cultural strategy and communications leaders to produce and disseminate comedy video content designed as positive fuel for the grassroots movement builders:

Part of our theory for comedy—especially for groups that are working on issues with a lot of tragedy involved—is that folks who do the work, including the activists or donors or community, can get really burnt out on a constant stream of horrific stories and content, and if you want people to be able to have a long-term engagement around an issue like that then you have to find a way to laugh. It can't be just all sadness and anger.[36]

To expand its network of grassroots support with the movement's crucial "mom demographic," the team produced the short-form video PSA parody, "What Could Go Wrong?," inviting comedian Rachel Dratch, a member of the Everytown Creative Council, to star as a kind of "every mom" character, lampooning state policy that allows guns in alcohol-serving bars.[37] The rationale to use comedy was fueled by a desire to energize the grassroots base and skewer gun policies that were, in Jason Rzepka's words, "stranger than fiction"—and thus ripe for comedy—but largely unknown to the public because of the complexity and inaccessibility of policy language. The final video and larger digital engagement tactics were valuable for the movement, according to Rzepka: "This [comedy campaign] platform became a way for deeper engagement, for people to come in, invite their friends in, and helped chapter growth throughout the country."[38] Importantly, comedy provided a mechanism for "evergreen engagement" in gun violence prevention advocacy, not simply crisis engagement around a new mass shooting.

While the YouTube-distributed comedy videos were created as a strategy to inspire the base of grassroots advocates, collaborative work with Comedy Central's Peabody Award–winning program *Inside Amy Schumer* was seen by the Everytown team as a way to engage new audiences. Comedian Amy Schumer, who had been moved to take a public stance against gun violence after a 2015 mass shooting during a screening of her film *Trainwreck*,[39] actively sought Everytown to help her and her team create a funny episode devoted to what they saw as the absurdity of existing gun policy. The *Inside Amy Schumer* and Everytown teams established a collaborative framework to produce the work, according to Erika Soto Lamb, the organization's former chief communications officer: "We played a mediator role and brought the policy experts to the table with the comedy people to explain the policy goals . . . it was a really collaborative effort because we had the same goals—different goals and talents but [both interested in] making a difference on gun violence."[40]

Amy Schumer's 2016 episode about gun safety garnered media attention and hundreds of thousands of viewers for the YouTube-distributed sketch alone.[41] In the lead sketch, "Welcome to the Gun Show," she parodies a QVC/Home Shopping Network on-screen host selling guns; all of the callers who want to buy a gun are prohibited, but, as the sketch unfolds, are able to jump through various policy loopholes.[42] In a twist on the call-to-action idea, the parodied QVC "call now" number was a pipeline by which viewers could call their members of Congress. According to Rzepka:

It was a brilliant way to deliver this information, and it was Amy Schumer at the peak of her cultural relevance, and she wanted to go all-in on this . . . When you called this number [on screen], it was an autodial to Congress where Everytown would give you the top-line script and you'd call into your rep and tell them, "I want a Universal Background Check." It was an Easter egg. Amy and Everytown used this as a vehicle to gain access to legislators— it was a new frontier.[43]

As success indicators, the former Everytown creative cultural team pointed to the public engagement in the Comedy Central program itself, with thousands of calls to Congress, alongside the virality of the funny YouTube videos—but also, the attention-getting creative leadership of Schumer. As Erika Soto Lamb summarized, the cultural reach of the program was profound for their work: "We were doing the research reports about concealed carry and stand your ground laws, but that's not going to reach all Americans in the same way that a really smart sketch show like Amy Schumer will . . . Every moment is meaningful in trying to reach a larger audience."[44]

Define American: Humanizing Immigrant Stories

Over the past few decades, widespread public awareness of immigration-related social justice issues—and polarizing perspectives—have come to the cultural fore in the United States, fostered in part by the visibility of two policy initiatives: The Development, Relief, and Education for Alien Minors (DREAM) Act, an attempted piece of federal legislation first introduced in 2001[45] but not yet passed by Congress,[46] and the Deferred Action for Children Arrivals (DACA) initiative, created by the Obama administration in 2012 as a mechanism to prevent the deportation of some undocumented immigrants brought into the country as children.[47] Culturally American immigrants without U.S. citizenship face emotionally difficult structural roadblocks compounded by negative media framing that often portrays them in othering ways that imply criminality.[48] Perhaps, then, it should come as no surprise that immigrant rights advocacy efforts focus on expanding a public climate of empathy, understanding, and compassion.

Against this backdrop, Jose Antonio Vargas, a Pulitzer Prize–winning journalist, divulged a two-decades-long secret in 2011 when he revealed his undocumented reality in *The New York Times Magazine*[49] and released his documentary memoir, *Documented*,[50] which tells the story of his childhood arrival to the U.S. from the Philippines. In the same year, he created and launched Define American, "a nonprofit media and culture organization that uses the power of story to transcend politics and shift the conversation about immigrants, identity, and citizenship in a changing America."[51] Define American employs cultural strategy and comedy as a creative tactic in its social justice endeavors. Indeed, a stand-up comedian, Cristela Alonzo, serves as a member of the Define American board of advisors and counsels the group on its comedy engagement activities. From Alonzo's perspective, comedy is crucial to Define American's core mission to shape compassionate, humanizing immigrant narratives, given the underrepresentation of marginalized voices in the media system: "When newspeople speak about an issue, it seems like they're speaking from a textbook that they read ... when you are giving stats without any feeling, any kind of heart, it doesn't help anything. It sounds inauthentic. I think that comedy, with regard to social issues, works best when people are willing to put themselves out there and talk about what personally affects their lives."[52]

With creative and entertainment initiatives directed by its in-house cultural strategist —veteran TV producer Elizabeth Grizzle Voorhees— Define American works with mediated comedy in several ways: producing stand-up comedy shows and internally producing and distributing mediated comedy via online platforms, but also serving as a collaborative subject-matter expert with Hollywood TV writers and producers. Voorhees positions the group's cultural and comedy strategy as research-based and symbiotic with policy advocacy:

In order to create public policy change, we have to change the hearts and minds of people in our country first. You can't have effective policy change without changing culture first ... Comedians have a really good sense of how to make things relatable. Immigration can feel very "us vs. them," and very othering of the undocumented population. We never want to do that ... In the storytelling, if there can be hints of humor, it can humanize the stories of immigrants and immigration.[53]

Notably, Define American collaborated with an NBC comedy sitcom, *Superstore*, to help shape a storyline focused on an undocumented character working at a big-box store. In a 2017 episode titled "Mateo's Last Day,"[54] when a character named Mateo, an undocumented immigrant,[55] needs to produce a Social Security card, he panics and tries to leverage an unusual strategy—he comedically tries to encourage his work friends to beat him up, although he is hilariously unsuccessful.[56] The storyline is based on a little-known immigration policy: Undocumented immigrants who are victimized by violent assault can apply for a special "U visa" to remain in the United States.[57] Voorhees described the collaboration as partially inspired by Define American's practice of bringing undocumented comedians into Hollywood meetings to humanize their stories:

We told *Superstore* a funny story about this issue from a friend who was mugged in Boyle Heights, and he was in the hospital when his friends were texting him about how amazing, "congratulations," that now he could get a special kind of visa. How do you make something really tragic and dark funny and light and find the comedy and humor in it? ... They [*Superstore* writers] were able to engage in this finer point of immigration law and still make it funny and educate and teach their audience about how difficult it is to get citizenship.[58]

From Define American's perspective, the tragedy of many immigrant narratives can make it painful for undocumented individuals to share their stories, and hard for audiences to hear them. Precisely because of this difficulty, comedy also plays a role behind the scenes in the group's cultural strategy, says Voorhees: "Even when we go in to consult on crime shows or dramas, like *Grey's Anatomy* and NBC's *Blindspot*, we bring immigrant comedians. We find we do much better in the room with people comfortable sharing their stories and able to share."[59]

Figure 9 Define American video: "Immigrants Pay Taxes."
SOURCE / CREDIT: Facebook video screenshot / fair use.

Define American also produces and disseminates online short-form videos that address various immigrant rights issues. Its first foray into internally produced mediated comedy, a Facebook video titled "Do Undocumented Americans Pay Taxes? [SPOILER ALERT: Of course!]," was created to humorously skewer a damaging myth about undocumented immigrants.[60] With its in-house production team and access to comedians, Define American distributed the funny video in April 2018—"tax season" in the United States. The video features two young people addressing the camera in faux news style, opening with a line that addresses the myth: "A lot of Americans don't think that undocumented immigrants pay taxes, even though there's *a million* explainer videos telling you how we do it," juxtaposed over a montage of the many such serious explainer videos. According to Voorhees, a humorous approach seemed inevitable: "We knew we had to convey boring statistical information and facts—how undocumented immigrants pay taxes, and how it works."[61]

To get audiences to engage with factual information, but in a way that was shareable, memorable, and humanizing, the comedy approach was worth the effort to the team. In a one-year period of public engagement, compared to the organization's other serious short-form online videos, the comedy tax video was the most successful in terms of engagement and shares. As seen by the Define American team, this incremental public engagement is valuable in the context of a long-range social change strategy.

Caring Across Generations: Empowering Invisible Voices

In 2011, when social justice leader Ai-jen Poo co-founded Caring Across Generations, an advocacy effort that aims to ensure human rights protections and fair wages for millions of caregivers in the United States, and to bring care workers and caregiving families together to fight for that cause, she and cofounder Sarita Gupta placed cultural narrative at the core of their strategy.[62] As she puts it: "I lead an organization that seeks to give voice and bring dignity and power to this workforce that works in our homes every day, caring for our children and our parents . . . It's a workforce that works hard—mostly immigrant women and women of color. It is the most undervalued work in our economy—really sort of defined by invisibility."[63]

Poo—a 2014 recipient of a MacArthur Foundation "genius grant" in recognition of her effective, law-changing advocacy on behalf of low-wage domestic workers[64]—positions an authentic, human connection between workers and their employers, and caregivers and those they care for, as a core strategy. With this idea in mind, because the members of this labor class are culturally and politically invisible, lifting up their voices is a vital mechanism for inspiring them, and allied others, to fight for human rights protections.[65] In her experience, by sharing their stories, even seemingly oppositional forces are able to find space for shared values, such as "love" and "respect and dignity" involved in caregiving work.[66]

Among the five coalition-based sectors that define its "Building a Movement" model, Caring Across Generations locates "Culture Makers" on equal footing alongside traditional organizing and advocacy tactics.[67] Comedy is embraced as a collaborative creative strategy within the organization as an attention-getting mechanism, but also because it helps transcend some of the topic's embedded emotional challenges, according to Ishita Srivastava, in-house director of culture change at Caring Across Generations:

> Over some years of experimenting, one thing that was clear was that people don't really want to watch or engage with, or even talk about, issues of caregiving—sickness and death—because they are not happy topics. One thing identified was the need to find ways to talk about these issues that are playful and even humorous. And a lot of the stories from real caregivers were really funny, deeply moving, and sometimes awkward with dark humor and all of that.[68]

As part of its comedy work, Caring Across Generations created a collaborative partnership project with the famed sketch and improv comedy group The Second City, which regularly shapes comedy talent for marketplace hits like *Saturday Night Live*. The comedy initiative emerged out of a dual advocacy challenge: First, caregivers feel their work is isolated and difficult, which can mean sharing their stories to fuel grassroots advocacy is hard. Second, audiences—including policymaking ones—may not want to pay attention to sad, depressing stories inherent in the issue.

Together, Caring Across Generations and The Second City created a comedy improv training initiative to help caregivers tell their stories—which often are funny—and to develop community with one another. Anne Libera, a professor who directs the Comedy Studies program at Columbia College in Chicago and teaches emerging comedians at The Second City, developed a specialized training at the Cleveland Clinic in Las Vegas based in part on her expert understanding of comedy's connecting traits: "I think comedy has a set of unique qualities that help create community, and when we create comedy, we share our lived experience. The minute I can laugh by [hearing] someone who has a very different lived experience than me, I can see them as part of my tribe. It helps with the polarization and marginalization and all of those things."[69] A subsequent pilot effort in Los Angeles brought together caregivers and comedian facilitators to work collaboratively over a six-week period. The Second City's longtime creative executive Kelly Leonard, who leads the organization's partnership projects, emphasized the sense of individual and collective empowerment that was cultivated through the comedy training for caregivers:

Second City has a pedagogy that is completely ensemble-focused, to the extent that one of the great modern improvisers won an award and during his speech he apologized because he stood out from the ensemble. Second City is known for producing individual stars. It's not either/or, it's both. Both of these are true: by empowering the group, you empower the individual, and vice versa ... This was not anything that we discussed overtly with Ai-jen, it just became apparent when we were cultivating our curriculum, and we trusted each other that we would find this. We did, and that's absolutely at play ... The more we have diverse voices speaking to us through comedy, this is the key: seeing one another.[70]

Notably, sharing stories is essential, rather than ancillary, to Caring Across Generations' formal grassroots policy advocacy. As Ai-jen Poo asserts: "Our strategies are also [about] organizing workers all over the country connected to advocacy policy campaigns at the state, local and federal level."[71] Comedy, by training caregivers as spokespeople, and by allowing the kind of light and humor into their narratives to ensure others might hear them, is key to these efforts. According to Srivastava, "[The comedy training] did so much to help them find their voice and identities as caregivers. There was an unexpected outcome in terms of agency and voice to help them prep for their advocacy work—like meeting with policymakers."[72]

Following the collaborative comedy training, Caring Across Generations captured the funny stories and made them available to a nationwide network of advocates as part of its Action Network. In the minds of the group's leaders, a contribution to gradual social change was immediately apparent and will continue to ripple out, embodied in expanding the strength, energy, motivation, and community of the caregiver movement for justice.

NextGen America: Engaging Young People in Policy

Founded in 2013 by activist and billionaire Tom Steyer as NextGen Climate, the grassroots advocacy organization formerly devoted exclusively to the environment rebranded itself as NextGen America in 2017, embracing four core social justice issues: climate, equality, health care, and prosperity (economic inequality).[73] Increasing civic participation and engagement among young people in the United States is key, according to Steyer: "The future of America is dependent on our ability to speak to them [young people] in a way that is meaningful and effective."[74]

Given the mission to encourage young people's participation in policy advocacy, engaging them creatively is prominent among NextGen America's strategic imperatives. James Mastracco, who leads NextGen's creative engagement as vice president of digital, values comedy in public engagement efforts. Inspired by Jon Stewart's pathbreaking intersection of politics and comedy, Mastracco is an example of a generation of young professionals raised on the civic engagement culture of contemporary TV comedy:

> When I was coming of age, as someone who was aware of social issues and becoming aware of politics, and becoming interested in and becoming angry at politics, it was really at this inflection point when Jon Stewart first took over *The Daily Show*. Before then, politics had been left political, and all of a sudden you have this strange mix of biting commentary . . . and it's really funny and they are saying the things that you know are deep in yourself but you couldn't quite find the words: yes, that's exactly what I was trying to think. That sort of shaped my formative years.[75]

In 2016, the NextGen team turned to comedy storytelling to spotlight the human costs of environmental policy in California. The creative inspiration for the project came from a mashup of ideas—the accessible, voyeuristic format of documentary storytelling on Vice, combined with comedy's entertainment value. Mastracco balances the need for entertaining, engaging content that is factually accurate:

> We have this broad array of social and progressive issues that we advocate for, and we hammer politicians who are bad on them and lift up the ones who are good on them. The way we do that in this organization is policy and message. If you work in a creative capacity where you are making things that are public-facing, even at the convergence point, on one side are policy and research teams, communications people paranoid about not wanting to put a tiki torch in an ad, and engineering nerds that are arguing about "this per million policies"; the other side is the public who are like "give me a cat video with the lasers coming out of its eyes" . . . We sit in the middle . . . I need people to be compelled and understand this and need them to be somewhat entertained. It's finding that constant balance.[76]

The creative, strategic ideas for public engagement in California policy advocacy came together in NextGen America's 2016 web-based comedy documentary short-form series, *Spotlight California*. Across five short-form webisodes, hosted on YouTube and a stand-alone website, comedian host Kiran Deol takes viewers on a journey throughout California. Along the way, she meets everyday people and experts, highlighting the human implications of drought and lack of access to water, air pollution and health, oil policy, and more.[77] With an existing comedy fan base, Deol had been previously featured on a Vice series and, according to Mastracco, "She was a great host because she totally fed off people's energy . . . She's clearly a comedian and did all the painful things comedians do, including improv."[78] Her attitude about comedy and its potential connection to social justice was also valuable; as Deol has stated in a media interview: "I think comedy is like 'the gateway drug.' By that, I mean comedy can sometimes serve as a gateway to get you into the other harder drugs of action and activism."[79]

Notably, the NextGen team respected the creative freedom of the process, rather than adopting a dogmatic approach to presenting policy facts within the comedy. In Mastracco's perspective, "When you make a decision to hire someone like Kiran or someone funny to be probing, you're giving up a lot of control. It would be a mistake to go into a project that is driven comedically—at least that's the goal—and really try to control things."[80] To create the webisodes, Ali Hart, *Spotlight California*'s producer, armed with factual policy material from the NextGen America experts, briefed Deol before each "scene" in the documentary. Deol was thus equipped with serious factual information, but her interactions with the subjects in the series were driven also by her comedic sensibilities. According to Hart, this creative input was crucial: "Kiran had a lot of creative control in the comedy—a lesson I learned in the process was to let her do her thing . . . That's her job and that's what comedians do, and that's how you get the gold."[81]

In the end, while the project was challenging given the balance between serious information and entertaining comedy, James Mastracco saw comedy as their only option:

> I think we didn't have a choice [to use comedy]. To talk about a lot of issues related to clean energy, related to the fossil fuel industries . . . we can sound like a crazy person trying to expose conspiracy theories or a blowhard who is ranting and raving. I think comedy was a great way for us to try to make it relatable to people—it was the best choice kind of the only choice when we started to put together the issues that we wanted to talk about.[82]

With an appreciation of its digital-native audience, a spirit of collaboration, and a large dose of creative freedom granted to the comedy, the NextGen America team created a stand-alone entertainment product designed to spark public engagement. Each episode directed viewers to the project's website, where they could learn more and participate through a menu of advocacy options. With attention sparked by a piece of humorous creative resistance and source of public information, viewers signed up to stay in touch with NextGen America's ongoing advocacy efforts.

CHARACTERISTICS OF EFFECTIVE COMEDY-ADVOCACY COLLABORATIONS

Within the converged media culture, comedy as cultural resistance and as a mechanism for public engagement in social issues is on the table in a real way—particularly for digital-native social justice groups. Justice advocates who choose to work with comedy are flexing their "civic imagination" muscles, not only imagining a better world, but believing in themselves as agents of change.[83] Efficacy is fundamental: Social change advocates are innovating with comedy, even if experimentally, because they believe it matters as a way to capture attention, critique a problematic status quo, point out outrage in a funny way, imagine a more optimistic future, and even call for action. Across distinct initiatives and organizations, the highlighted comedy collaborations of this chapter share several characteristics, which help point the way to expanding the practice and study of this form of cultural strategy in social change.

Positioning Comedy within a Social Change Spectrum

The social justice professionals here maintain an expansive articulation of "social change" as they embrace mediated comedy for specific, mission-aligned reasons. Importantly, their rationales for leveraging comedy are not *uniformly* related to behavior change or action on the part of the public, often seen as a kind of holy grail for social change communication. Comedy is not imagined as an all-powerful magic bullet. Rather, the decision-making social justice leaders here think of social change as a multidimensional spectrum and a long game, with comedy as one way to engage publics in that journey. The initiatives and leaders profiled here operate from the perspective that comedy does not replace their other organizing, communication, and advocacy tactics, but that it plays a symbiotic, strategic role alongside traditional means to engage publics and leaders. In other words, they respect that comedy lends something new and different, helping them to accomplish their goals.

For instance, Everytown for Gun Safety leverages comedy to expand its grassroots infrastructure and motivate its base. Define American focuses on humanizing immigrants and using comedy to help the public to connect with them, and to engage audiences beyond tragic stories. Caring Across Generations trains its key storytellers—caregivers, an invisible, vulnerable group—and provides fun and optimism to encourage their advocacy participation. Next GenAmerica embraces comedy and short-form storytelling to engage young audiences in wonky policy information. The founder of Rise sees comedy as deeply embedded in the culture inside the organization, as a way to motivate new activists, not just a way to engage supporters. Regardless of their individual issues and rationale for employing comedy as a collaborative strategy, they are united by the idea that movements for social change cannot sustain attention or momentum without finding ways to inject hope, optimism, and lighthearted outrage into the advocacy mix.

Respecting Comedy's Creative Freedom

Comedy that engages publics in social justice challenges is optimally envisioned and shaped as creative entertainment, not weighed down heavily with didactic messages. In the examples profiled here, the call to action—if it exists—is separate from the comedy. Indeed, cultural strategist Mik Moore points to a major pitfall to avoid in comedy collaborations:

> A challenge is there are lots of groups that either aren't open to using comedy to advance their issue, or insist on making you do it badly. You can have a really great cause and amazing comedians, and a concept that can really work, and typically two things happen with justice groups: (1) there's lots of information and they insist that it all be included in the comedy and the information outweighs the comedy or content, or (2) they get nervous about the humor, so then you dilute the humor, and it's not funny . . . I always say it's important to use the comedy to get their attention, and once you have it, there are lots of ways you can share the serious information. If they don't watch the thing, you've lost. Creating something that's highly watchable that people want to share is critical.[84]

These contemporary social justice advocates respect the very qualities that make comedy powerful—its ability to find humanity or to critique, not to precisely transmit "key messages" and learning points, which are the domain of press releases and fact sheets. Comedy is thus embraced for its artistic, emotional qualities, playing a role alongside traditional strategic communication. In this way, cultural strategy—including work with comedy—is not the same set of controlled-message tactics typically employed in strategic communication. And indeed, thinking of comedy in this way means dooming it to listless work that will fail from inception if it can't capture attention or entertain. The mental model of these collaborations is key; each of the social justice organizations and initiatives profiled here sought out comedy with an open mind, recognizing the ways in which comedy and its creativity could help address the shortcomings of other traditional serious tactics, as well as the challenges baked into the seriousness of their core social issues.

But collaboration between serious social justice topics and comedians can be tricky. A "creative gatekeeper" role is necessary to act as a liaison between the issue experts and the comedy, in order to ensure the comedy does not become didactic. All of the collaborative initiatives here included a professional—usually a cultural/narrative strategist—playing the role of mediator between the comedy and the strategic messages, protecting the entertainment value of the comedy while checking the accuracy of the factual information. This practice was seen as mutually beneficial for the justice advocates and the comedy professionals.

Embracing the Cultural Power of the Converged Media Era

Social justice efforts and organizations launched within the last 15 years are true digital naturals in their DNA and decision-making. This new cohort of social justice leaders understands that relegating *all* public engagement strategies to serious messages means a failure to embrace contemporary grassroots cultural power. They illustrate a way of doing business "by any media necessary," the creative tactics that seize the possibility for new engagement in the participatory, converged media environment.[85] Within this context, digital-native social justice advocates innately understand the role of culture and comedy. Ai-jen Poo, founder of Caring Across Generations, puts it this way:

> When you work with a workforce with so little power and visibility, you have to be really creative. A lot of our typical means to power in this political culture—like voting—are just very challenging and not readily in reach. We have had to be creative about power and the means to build it and that's a little unusual. We believe there are multiple forms of power that require different strategies. Political power—the power to vote and elect and un-elect representatives and push for change through them. There's also economic power, the power to control capital and markets. But the form of power most relevant here is narrative power, which is the power to define reality, or tell the story of why things are the way they are in the world, on your terms . . . The first step is about visibility and presence in the popular imagination, and then the power to define for ourselves the narrative. The progressive movements and social justice advocates often talk about changing hearts and minds, but we mostly work on how to change minds, how to use data and stats and research and make really good rational arguments. But we are as much shaped by our emotional lives and the heart-space than what is rational. We as social justice people have not been as good historically at tapping into that very messy, very unruly part of our minds that can be defined by our emotional lives. That's where we have really challenged ourselves to go.[86]

Thus, they are unafraid to experiment—and to fully embrace comedy collaborations as a part of this exploration—albeit with their serious social justice missions and objectives firmly intact. In other words, embracing comedy and other creative strategies is not seen as ancillary or damaging to their social justice missions, but instead as vital to their work. As NextGen America's James Mastracco puts it: "Let's actually figure out where people are and go to them. You can get people do to a lot of things if you get them engaged—it's about finding people where they are, not this former TV model, as in I'm going to build the big building and we will attract the thing."[87]

Respecting the Professional Expertise of Comedy

Writing and shaping comedy that's really funny is hard work, created by professionals with training and practice. Social justice leaders working with comedy show a deep respect for the creative expertise of comedy writers and performers, crucial to collaborative work. The Second City's Kelly Leonard emphasizes the importance of regarding comedy as a formal enterprise:

> So many people use comedy without a license. Everyone thinks they are funny or that comedy is just innate. That's not the case. What we've seen at Second City is that when you bring people with a lot of comedic skill—if they are developed and mentored and get tons of practice—they can take that skill and turn it into a mastery .... With masterful comedians, we get the feeling that they're letting us see a very true part of themselves that often will connect with a part of ourselves as a viewer or receiver of the comedy.[88]

This kind of professional reverence for comedy, tactically speaking, may manifest in scenarios that are notably different from a pure work-for-hire model, in which a professional is hired to execute a message or campaign strategy precisely as directed. Indeed, according to comedian Rachel Dratch, this respect is vital to creating comedy that entertains and spotlights a social problem: "If the comedian is down with the cause, they're not going to do something that's not good. They're going to try to make the medicine go down well."[89]

Comedy Content That Challenges the Status Quo

Creating and leveraging comedy for social justice engagement does not mean making light of serious issues or making fun of them. The collaborative initiatives here point to a more nuanced articulation of comedy content. Notably, this comedy either critiques the absurdity of the status quo—directly aligned with social justice goals—or creates ways for audiences to experience marginalized people and issues in ways that are funny, humanizing, and non-othering. Rather than making fun of the serious issues themselves, to the contrary, this approach either skewers the outrage of an existing scenario of injustice, or it welcomes audiences to experience people with lightness and humanity. None of the social justice advocates profiled here experienced a public or internal backlash for using comedy, perhaps because of this content approach.

．　　．　　．　　．　　．

There are challenges, of course, in shaping comedy that endeavors to enlighten or inspire or motivate action around social issues. While the case studies here represent a kind of "best practices" scenario—that is, incubating and distributing creative comedy projects born of mutually beneficial relationships between comedy and social justice professionals— they may not reveal as clearly the underlying barriers to cross-sector collaboration between comedy and social change. For example, we know from our own professional work that serious social justice advocates may voice concern about whether or not comedy can be entrusted to not make light of serious issues. Comedians, on the other hand, are uninterested in creating message-heavy comedy that's not entertaining. These are dual questions to be raised on a case-by-case basis, issue by issue, and they are important; that said, the evidence for comedy's influence in social change is presented in chapter 2 for this reason. A certain amount of entrepreneurial spirit comes with comedy—synonymous with innovation. The Second City's Kelly Leonard summarizes the creative process this way: "There's going to be missteps—we all do it—but if we're going to let our shame in that something might get said wrong or may offend one person, you say goodbye to innovation. Goodbye, there will not be any."[90]

Rather than focusing on the barriers, the examples here spotlight how this collaborative process can work and why it is valuable for serious social advocates. Contemporary social justice professionals sought to work with comedy based on an open-minded, yet strategic, understanding of how the creativity, lightness, and deviance of comedy—pointing out the absurdity of the status quo in entertaining and memorable ways—can capture attention and motivate participation in ways that tightly controlled policy- and fact-focused messages may not. In so doing, the practice is seen as symbiotic with, not a replacement for, other public engagement efforts.

We leave this chapter and point toward the future with a different kind of challenge inherent in sparking new practice and study of how comedy and social justice groups can work together: How can social justice groups and comedy professionals more readily find one another to create collaborative creative work? This is an important organizational quandary. As comedian Cristela Alonzo put it: "How do you find one another [justice groups and comedians]? . . . How do we make that happen more often?"[91] As we look forward to the future, we take up this issue in the final chapter.

8 Imagining the Future of Comedy's Role in Social Justice

66 *Flint still doesn't have clean water.* **99**

Michelle Wolf, comedian[1]

If the past roster of humorists invited to perform at the annual White House Correspondents' Association Dinner is any indication, Michelle Wolf was not an avant garde choice in 2018. Following a steady queue of comedy performers incorporated into the elite political news event's seven-decade history, Wolf's comedy pedigree and cultural currency were on par with her predecessors, firmly affixed on the contemporary political pulse. Her ascent in the professional comedy business—a writing job on *Late Night with Seth Myers* in 2013, a correspondent gig with *The Daily Show* in 2016, and a solo HBO stand-up special, *Nice Lady*, in 2017[2]—was nimble and steady, characterized by a distinctive feminist voice and trademark unfiltered takedowns and societal ruminations.

And so, when the established journalism organization welcomed Wolf to lampoon political gridlock and malfeasance on the dais of its First Amendment celebration, her particular mode of creative expression and social critique seemed unquestionably aligned with the bedrock free-speech values of an independent press. To wit, Margaret Talev, then-president of the White House Correspondents' Association, lauded Wolf in a public announcement before the event: "Our dinner honors the First Amendment and strong, independent journalism. Her embrace of these

Figure 10 Michelle Wolf provides comedic entertainment at the 2018 White House Correspondents' Association Dinner.
SOURCE / CREDIT: Stock Image / Shutterstock.com.

values and her truth-to-power style make her a great friend to the WHCA. Her Pennsylvania roots, stints on Wall Street and in science and self-made, feminist edge make her the right voice now."[3]

But the anticipatory praise from the organization was short-lived. As Wolf wrapped her set that night, her concluding words were greeted with stony silence from the audience of newsmakers:

> You guys are obsessed with Trump. Did you used to date him? Because you pretend like you hate him, but I think you love him. I think what no one in this room wants to admit is that Trump has helped all of you. He couldn't sell steaks or vodka or water or college or ties or Eric, but he has helped you. He's helped you sell your papers and your books and your TV. You helped create this monster, and now you're profiting off of him.[4]

To tepid applause, she dropped the proverbial mic with her closing line, referencing the ongoing devastation that plagues residents of Flint, Michigan, victims of lead poisoning in the municipal water supply: "Flint still doesn't have clean water."[5] Later that night, and throughout the following week, the backlash from many in Washington's establishment—notably high-profile journalists from the likes of the *New York Times* and MSNBC and Fox News, alongside President Donald Trump, whose absence from the event broke with decades of tradition—was immediate and ferocious: Wolf's jokes were "over-the-line," they said.[6] From the perspective of some inside the professional vortex of news and politics: She used profane language, she was vulgar, she maligned the White House press secretary.[7] The next day, the White House Correspondents' Association shared an official written statement with its members: "Last night's program was meant to offer a unifying message about our common commitment to a vigorous and free press while honoring civility, great reporting and scholarship winners, not to divide people. Unfortunately, the entertainer's monologue was not in the spirit of that mission."[8] Seven months later, in November 2018, the White House Correspondents' Association announced a change of course for the first time in decades—a historian, not a comedian, as the featured speaker at the annual gala[9]—a decision publicly lauded by President Trump.[10] As the final bookend of a well-trodden cultural moment, Wolf tweeted: "The @whca are cowards. The media is complicit. And I couldn't be prouder."[11]

Was it her vulgar language—echoing President Trump's precise words— that most troubled the assembled cadre of elite, dignified Washington black-tie gala guests? Was it her pointed talk about abortion or slang references to female anatomy that ruffled polite sensibilities? Profanity aside, perhaps Michelle Wolf's most brazen norm violation was her willingness to step into the uncomfortable fray of institutional power, criticizing both political parties and spotlighting the symbiotic relationship between politics and the business of news. Her brutal appraisal of the topic, which dominated her 19-minute act, was missing from dissenting journalists' critical public stances—but others pointed out the irony. As *New York Times* TV critic James Poniewozik wrote:

> Was Ms. Wolf's set vicious? Absolutely . . . But was it gratuitous? Not at all. It drove mercilessly toward its themes: that this administration lies; that its female members are covering for a sexist president; and that journalists have enabled it all with breathless coverage. Those are points of view, and not ones that anyone needs to agree with. But comedy's job is to have a point of view, to pick a hill to die on and defend it with furiously thrown pies. Comedy is not a Page A1 news analysis. It is not its job to call the other side for comment or throw in a "to be sure" paragraph for balance.[12]

The story of Michelle Wolf and the news-agenda-setting frenzy over the 2018 White House Correspondents' Association Dinner is, within the context of comedy and social justice, both paradox and reality, both bitter pill and prescription elixir. Against the backdrop of a climate characterized by increasingly authoritarian political rhetoric, and yet democratized media access to previously unheard voices, the tale illustrates important tensions and opportunities inherent in comedy's intersection with social justice— and the future of these ideas. Perhaps Michelle Wolf chose to disobey an unwritten code of safe verbal conduct for comedians invited to tickle the funny bones of journalists and politicians—power brokers of democracy— when she aimed a bright floodlight onto the profit-centered reality of the commercially dominated news media business. Yet in opting to defy the guise of a hired entertainer dutifully following the bidding of the room, she instead chose to embody a well-established function of comedy in the public sphere—to offer sharp critique and observation that can provide "deeper truths"[13] than those possible from journalism alone, including scrutiny of contemporary news institutions themselves.

We argue that this function of comedy is valuable even while we acknowledge its unpredictability. Comedy, particularly humor that critiques power, can be messy and impolite. It doesn't work for all social issues. Attempting to control comedy creatively is futile—and dilutes its power to galvanize attention and spark debate. And yet, during moments fraught with threats to free expression and democratic functioning, comedy's freedom to be outrageous is crucial. As we look to the future, we argue that social justice leaders who choose to collaborate with comedians must contend with certain paradoxical truths about comedy, along with the potential risks they may incur by aligning with a creative, deviant form of cultural expression. At the same time, we assert that the benefits of embracing comedy for social justice efforts within a changing, diverse climate are well worth the effort. As the future evolves, we consider how and why comedy is positioned to play a role in social change moving forward, where opportunities reside, where critical reflections and challenges remain—and why comedy matters.

COMEDY AND SOCIAL JUSTICE: FORWARD MOMENTUM

Social Consciousness Equals Good (Entertainment) Business

Just over two decades after the premiere of *The Daily Show* and one decade after then-host Jon Stewart's frequent "I'm just a comedian" admonition, its home TV network, Comedy Central, explicitly acknowledged mediated comedy's influence on civic and social issues—a new claim and social change role for a powerhouse commercial outlet focused on making people laugh. In late 2018, Comedy Central announced an unprecedented new position—its first-ever vice president of social impact strategy. Notably, the job wasn't created for a media executive, but it sits instead with a communications and cultural strategy expert with deep roots in civic practice and social justice—Erika Soto Lamb, the political communication professional who guided Everytown for Gun Safety through its inaugural interfaces with comedy. The mission, according to the network, is to "lead and elevate a portfolio of multiplatform social change initiatives that empower Comedy Central's audiences to have an impact on the biggest challenges facing them today."[14] Comedy Central president Kent Alterman announced the effort in a press release as the nexus of comedy and public engagement: "Even though all the divisive issues of our day have seemingly settled into peaceful harmony, we still feel the need to use comedy as a force for good in the world, filling an essential role in the cultural conversation and supporting social change."[15]

Ratings-driven Comedy Central's decision to launch an unprecedented explicit social change enterprise may seem like a natural evolution from the mission-driven pro-social entertainment imprimatur established for decades by its parent company, Viacom. At the same time, the new effort positions comedy and social justice in the evolving and future entertainment business in a significant way. Staying on pace with a young, increasingly diverse audience, Comedy Central is putting financial resources toward a dual bet: Comedy in the entertainment marketplace can be funny and entertaining while reflecting serious social issues, and its audience can—and wants to—be engaged meaningfully in social justice through comedy. Not "either/or," but "both/and."

Comedy Central's social change effort fits within a dominant, recent "social impact" trend in the profit-making business of entertainment broadly—a recognition of a changed audience and market, reflecting a rapidly shifting racial and ethnic demographic reality in the United States. Young people between the ages of 22 and 37, the largest generational cohort since the sprawling post–World War II Baby Boomers, are the most racially and ethnically diverse Americans in history.[16] They are more supportive of social justice issues and equity than older generations and, socialized in the consumer-choice reality of the digital media age, are interested in interacting with brands with socially conscious footprints.[17] A public service mindset alone, while an important authentic motivation, is unlikely to ensure the staying or decision-making power of a social-good effort within a corporate media system. But, the industry's parallel recognition of the changing desires and expectations of contemporary media consumers is potent.

From the enthusiasm of the new audience, which provided millions of YouTube views to validate its generation's most dazzling and diverse new comedy stars—like Issa Rae and Hasan Minhaj and Franchesca Ramsey— the intersection of comedy and social topics has furnished irrefutable evidence of a market shift. In turn, the entertainment industry—which recognizes audience power when it sees it—has increasingly embraced this shifting audience reality by beginning to offer platforms to previously marginalized voices who intersect comedy and social justice topics. Social consciousness and social equity and representation, therefore, are strategic corporate values to reflect back to the contemporary audience. Indeed, over the past decade, major entertainment media companies have launched social impact efforts for their brands and others, from powerhouse talent agencies Creative Artists Agency (CAA) in 2016[18] to William Morris Endeavor (WME),[19] to renewed efforts at NBC Universal.[20] Consulting firm Deloitte has recognized "citizenship and social impact" as a global imperative for corporate enterprises, writing in a 2018 report that Millennial consumers have "sky-high expectations for corporate responsibility."[21] In short, given an audience that embraces social equity and values engaging with socially conscious entertainment and brands, showcasing new comedy voices talking about silly topics alongside social issues may simply be good business— not just social good. As Hasan Minhaj put it from the set of his Netflix comedy public affairs show, *Patriot Act*, "Look, capitalism and virtuous content can happen at the same time. It is possible."[22]

While the formal entertainment industry has a long way to go to achieve fully diverse representation—an issue we address more fully later in this chapter—we are witnessing a notable rise in comedy material from voices that have been traditionally marginalized in media portrayals and comedy, particularly people of color and women. In this way, the comedy professionals' perspectives profiled in this book also represent a crucial additional theme by which we situate the present and future of comedy and social justice in the entertainment marketplace: What happens when traditionally marginalized voices assert real cultural power through comedy—enabled in large part by leveraging digital media platforms to shape their work? Rather than creating comedy narratives to fit or assimilate into a status quo culture, they are asserting their full cultural identities.

Just as the consumer shifts have signaled to a changing entertainment industry that social issue topics and diverse comedy voices make sense for audiences, contemporary comedy professionals understand the imperative for change, as well. Consciousness about the diversity of comedy TV writers' rooms is a through-line, as is a recognition of the digital era's embrace of diverse comedy personalities and voices. From the perspective of Joel Church-Cooper, creator and executive producer of comedy sitcom *Brockmire*:

> Representation behind the scenes is what truly matters to me. It's more important to have representation behind the scenes because that's how you affect the stories you're telling and that's where you get perspective—it's impossible to fake perspective . . . So, that sort of representation on the back end in the writers' room—that kind of perspective and shaping of the story to feel authentic to the lives of people all across this country—they're untapped, new stories. If it's not new in television, no one's going to watch it. There's only one place for new stories to come from—it's the underrepresented, it's the minority perspective.[23]

The entertainment marketplace thus has shifted to embrace new comedy sensibilities and voices, and also to lift them up and make financial bets on them, shaping future forms and audience affections. To be sure, we don't position the future evolution of comedy and social justice entirely at the hands of a changing commercial entertainment marketplace fueled by diverse audiences. We do assert, however, that entertainment industry trends that make good business sense may be more likely to evolve into solid practice—thus, over time, welcoming and embracing comedy voices and perspectives that were missing in the past, reflecting lived experiences that broaden the collective understanding of a society and its challenges.

Civil Society Turns to Comedy

In 2017, as part of the Comedy and Arts Festival hosted annually in Chicago, *The Onion* and its parent network, Fusion Media Group, hosted an unprecedented two-day event funded by the Open Society Foundations, *Rise Up: Comedy for Change*, which brought together "experts, change-makers, creatives, and comedians to explore the role comedy plays in creating social and political change in an increasingly polarized world."[24] The convening curated an unusual cross-section of leading social justice advocates, scholars, philanthropists, comedians, and foundations to discuss perspectives about comedy's function in social change. Comedians shared the stage with human rights groups and philanthropy organizations like WOLA: Advocacy for Human Rights in the Americas, the Harnisch Foundation, and Comic Relief, alongside comedy groups from around the world. At the "Comedy Collaborators" workshop portion of the convening, international comedy groups worked with civil society organizations to build intentional co-created comedy efforts.

While the convening's focus on creative mechanisms to engage publics in social challenges is not new in the humanitarian sector, the urgency and open-mindedness about comedy in a social justice context points to another theme as we consider the future of comedy and social justice: Social justice advocates and civil society organizations are not only embracing cultural and narrative strategy in their public engagement work, but they are considering comedy more intentionally.

In addition to the initiatives and organizations profiled elsewhere in this book, examples are on the rise: The Open Society Foundations, a major funder of civil society groups around the world, raises the possibility of global comedy as a mechanism for civic engagement through convenings like its 2017 gathering: *Comedy, Politics and Social Change: Working at the Intersection of Activism and Humor*.[25] Additionally, the philanthropy funded three comedy groups in Latin America to consider the role of comedy as "creative dissent" in countries noted for political turmoil and closed media systems, partnering with academic researchers to document the creative process.[26] Famed comedy troupe The Second City joined forces with Caring Across Generations to facilitate a social justice variation of Second City's corporate branding program, *Brandstage*,[27] pairing comedy improv players with serious topics in order to find new, lighthearted ways to communicate them. An investigative journalism cooperative, *Dirty Little Secrets*, led by the Center for Investigative Reporting at the University of California Berkeley, facilitated environmental justice reporting in New Jersey and then worked with stand-up comedians to translate the serious work for live comedy audiences, entertaining them and encouraging civic participation.[28] At the University of Colorado Boulder, the *Inside the Greenhouse* project's "Stand Up for Climate Change" initiative hosts an annual international comedy and climate change short-video competition, along with a live performance of comedy featuring students who are mentored in creative climate change communication, including sketch and stand-up, over the course of a semester.[29] The New America Foundation, a serious policy and human rights group, turned to comedy as the focal point of its campaign to capture public attention around unpaid labor, part of its Global Gender Parity initiative.[30] In 2019, the Center for Media & Social Impact, directed by this book's co-author Caty Borum Chattoo, launched a project in collaboration with comedy strategists Moore + Associates and in partnership with Comedy Central, the *Yes, And . . . Laughter Lab*, designed to foster collaborative opportunities among comedy writers, producers, performers, the entertainment industry, and social justice organizations.[31]

Notably, the social justice advocates who are considering comedy collaborations as part of their advocacy and public engagement strategies—and those who have already embraced humor as cultural strategy—acknowledge the crucial need to capture audiences in ways that move well beyond traditional advocacy. They point to the role that creative expression plays as critic of an expanding authoritarian global climate, along with the serious challenges of capturing attention and provoking public engagement amidst a cluttered media environment. They also acknowledge that a sole diet of doom-and-gloom messages may have a limited ability to fully capture public imagination or encourage people to share, learn, and participate. For their part, comedians are embracing a media system that allows them greater access to share their perspectives and comedy, and to cultivate audiences. They are motivated first and foremost by making people laugh and entertaining them, but they also are aware of the power and limelight of comedy—to open conversational doors and help expose seemingly intractable social problems and conditions—even if they don't see themselves as activists or direct agents of change.

This evolution is supported by what we know from research and practice about how comedy can contribute in ways that are strategic for social justice efforts. Together, comedy's ability to meaningfully influence audiences and shape a public and media agenda provide evidence of humor's civic muscle that expands well beyond simple marketing functions of attention alone. Thus, as the social justice sector continues to contemplate ways to engage new audiences with entrenched social justice challenges, comedy is on the table, perhaps in a new way, joining with a parallel trend in the transforming entertainment business that seems increasingly open, relative to the past, to comedic voices speaking truth to power.

CRITICAL REFLECTIONS AND FUTURE OPPORTUNITIES

Despite its unique qualities, comedy is not an airtight, infallible remedy to the challenges faced by social justice advocates both now and in the future. It is not a complete or predictable solution to the complicated business of encouraging publics to engage with social problems—and indeed, nor are other media mechanisms involved in shaping civic information and practice, including journalism. To fully address the promise and complexities of comedy's intersection with social justice, it is imperative to present and wrestle with critical challenges and future opportunities for exploration and learning in this context. We address those here, with an eye toward the future.

Ethical Responsibility and Factual Accuracy in Comedy

When comedians explicitly include social issue topics in their work—whether stand-up, satirical news, scripted sitcoms, sketch, or documentary—they are not bound to the formal ethical standards or responsibilities of journalism, with its long-established practices of fact-checking and editorial scrutiny for accuracy. And yet, comedians are believable and credible, given their seeming authenticity and sometimes, entertaining outrage, as in the case of John Oliver, for example, and his enthusiastic fervor about net neutrality or bail bonds. As scholars Williams and Delli Carpini presciently articulated, comedians' "I'm not a journalist" abdication of responsibility may have had more merit in the broadcast news era, in which a clear separation of "journalism" and "entertainment" was more apparent, but not so in a converged, streaming digital media era.[32] To be sure, comedians *are* entertainers—they are not journalists—so they're not wrong to correct the narrative when asked about their formal roles. But despite the efforts of satirical news hosts and other comedians to deflect responsibility, audiences often perceive their work as indistinguishable from public affairs programming, therefore assuming truth and factual accuracy. Indeed, as Williams and Delli Carpini wrote, while satirical shows can play a positive civic role, the integrity of the process "depends upon little more than the good intentions of their creators, networks, and advertisers. This is a particularly thin reed, given the likelihood of imitators, the explosive growth of cable programming and internet sites on the left and right, and the increasingly blurred line between news and other forms of politically-relevant programming."[33]

To place an even finer point on the issue, not all comedy infused with social justice issues deals with "facts"—much of it is embodied in scenarios and characters and lived experiences, which is not the same as the parody news presentations of *The Daily Show* and its contemporaries. However, other formats of comedy that regularly or occasionally include social-issue themes can imply fact-checking accuracy. Franchesca Ramsey's MTV web series, *Decoded*, regularly uses historical and factual information to help convey a complex understanding of institutional racism, for example. The undocumented immigration storyline and character in NBC's *Superstore* similarly transmitted information about immigration policy. In the case of *Inside Amy Schumer*'s "The Gun Show" episode detailed in chapter 6, an intricate level of detail about gun policy went into creating a funny way to interact with a wonky topic. When PolitiFact examined the script more closely as part of its PunditCheck Truth-O-Meter fact-checking process, it concluded the episode was "half-true," commenting that removing the situational context from the policy-related jokes may have resulted in misleading, or at least incomplete, reflections of gun laws.[34]

What, then, can we make of this reality? Comedians are not likely to make journalistic fact-checking part of their creative enterprises. Still, we argue that an ethical responsibility to approach topics with a desire and process in place to ensure accurate factual information should not be too much to ask of comedians who engage with social topics and the truths behind them. Social justice advocates, who also can't afford to sacrifice accuracy if they hope to engender public support for their causes, are also wise to think about this element as they approach collaborative work.

Interrogating Comedy's Cultural Authority

Comedy talents themselves also are not infallible. Access for newcomers is still controlled, to a large degree, by powerful celebrity comedians. In the #MeToo consciousness-raising moment focused on gender equity and sexual harassment, a public conversation about comedians and their role in criminal or damaging behavior is ongoing. While Bill Cosby's downfall as a convicted sexual predator was unfolding for several years before the 2017 accusations against Hollywood producer Harvey Weinstein opened the door to similar stories, the same cultural protections may have constrained an appropriate response to both Cosby and other comedy celebrities. That is, it may be difficult for a culture to imagine or properly address crimes or transgressions when our devotion to powerful comedians has been so deeply cultivated through a genre that requires emotional affection. Regarding comedy figures with appropriate expectations for human decency and professional integrity, regardless of the lovingly charming characters and personas they create through their entertainment, is an imperative for social progress.

Similarly, comedy as a genre also can be messy—and not necessarily appropriate as an instrument to advance positive, inclusive social justice about every social issue. Indeed, some comedy of the past and present, even while addressing issues like gender equity and racism, has inadvertently promoted deeply entrenched, harmful stereotypes. In her pathbreaking Netflix stand-up comedy special, *Nanette*, lesbian comedian Hannah Gadsby scathingly and memorably turned comedy on its head, asking her audience to see and hear the ways in which self-deprecating humor, when imposed upon marginalized voices, reinforces a damaging status quo and a dominant narrative of power: "Do you understand what self-deprecation means when it come from somebody who already exists in the margins? It's not humility, it's humiliation. I put myself down in order to speak, in order to seek permission to speak, and I simply will not do that anymore, not to myself or anybody who identifies with me."[35]

At the same time, not all comedy aims to lift up disempowered voices or to expand our perspectives on social issues. In fact, comedy—both in mainstream entertainment[36] and in alternative extreme right online communities[37]—is sometimes used to explicitly belittle social justice efforts and target marginalized groups, while appealing to like-minded audiences. Interrogating comedy's power dynamics and understanding who is telling the story—from what vantage point and identity and lived experience, and noting whether the comedy "punches up" at power or punches down at the powerless—is an essential media literacy practice.

Diversity and Representation in the Business of Comedy

In related fashion, despite a seemingly promising trajectory toward more diverse comedy voices, the entertainment industry is still a business with deeply entrenched power dynamics, controlled predominantly by white, male, nondisabled, heterosexual decision-makers. This reality extends to the business of comedy. Indeed, comedy talents hone their work and voices through a distinct, age-old pipeline: Marketplace sensations are still shaped to a large degree by a comedy industry that requires movements through the ranks of live comedy clubs and bars, which may reward comedians who can rely easily on the shared cultural cues of stereotypes, particularly those focused on race, ethnicity, and gender. Hearing and seeing comedy and comedians with diverse life experiences and voices requires alternative spaces and sources of funding to develop their work.[38] Throughout this book, we have illustrated notable exemplars of, and direct perspectives from, comedy professionals who represent a changing portrait, and yet, much progress remains to be made. As Brent Miller, executive producer of Norman Lear's Netflix reboot of the sitcom *One Day at a Time*, stated: "It's insane the number of white men who are still running our business . . . if we are not representing the world as creators of this content, how can we justify that our content is representative of the makeup of this planet?"[39] But entertainment and comedy leaders are increasingly vocal about the imperative to rewrite the script. A forward-looking view may find optimism, then, in public and behind-the-scenes initiatives to change the story.

For instance, in 2016, comedy TV showrunner and *Glee* creator Ryan Murphy launched Half, a foundation housed within his production company. Based on his recognition of the imbalance in representation, and his own assertion that "I personally can do better," Murphy plans to ensure that 50 percent of the director positions on his programs are represented by women, LGBT-identifying, and people of color.[40] Two years later in 2018, shaped as part of Time's Up, a fund focused on gender equity and harassment in the wake of the 2017 #MeToo spotlight on Hollywood[41] (more than a decade after activist Tarana Burke founded the Me Too movement to call attention to sexual assault against African American women[42]), *Transparent* creator Jill Soloway founded 50/50 by 2020, an intersectional initiative that aims to change Hollywood and achieve representational parity among the ranks of creative and business decision-makers—"reimagining leadership to reflect all of us. And our audiences."[43] Working from industry peer group to industry peer group, alongside pressure from external advocacy groups,[44] changing the dynamics of cultural power will remain a crucial enterprise.

Media Platform Power

A critical eye should likewise be trained on the constraints of the democratizing, evolving social media platforms that have played such a vital role in the viral stream of short-form and self-produced comedy in the digital era. The converged, participatory digital media culture, characterized by peer sharing enabled by content aggregators like Facebook, continues to shift in the way of policies and algorithms, affecting audience access and the production practices of comedy producers operating both inside and outside the formal Hollywood entertainment system. Digital-native comedy power players like Funny or Die and CollegeHumor.com gained much of their cultural and brand cache through vast audience reach during the early years of Facebook, where comedy YouTube videos, or videos hosted on other sites' platforms, could achieve a vast number of shares and likes in a matter of days. But expanding experimentation in social-media native video over the past several years (that is, videos created and uploaded in the social media sites themselves, instead of including links to videos hosted elsewhere, like YouTube) has had an acute impact on internet comedy. Now, instead of allowing videos to be shared from YouTube and other hosting sites, videos shared on Facebook must be natively produced for the Facebook platform, and brands must pay to promote content—a departure from the earlier days of "organic" views and traffic allowed from the Facebook algorithm. The impact on digital-native comedy producers has been immediate, leading one media trade publication to dramatically write: "For years, inventive companies like The Onion and Funny or Die capitalized on a culture that just wanted to laugh online. But after massive disruptions in digital advertising and on social media platforms, those companies find themselves imperiled. Did the internet kill its comedy?"[45] The comedy news website *Splitsider* similarly published its own headline: "How Facebook Is Killing Comedy."[46]

In early 2018, Funny or Die announced layoffs, citing the direct challenges from digital advertising and content revenue declines, continuing a downward trend after eliminating 30 percent of its staff in 2016.[47] While the brand has seamlessly evolved into Hollywood long-form film and TV production, the plucky entrepreneurial spirit and viral shareability of its short-form internet comedy—particularly important for comedy that might be produced in collaboration with social justice advocates—will suffer. Innovation and expansion by self-producing comedy groups and individuals, which helped to shape this digital heyday of comedy from new voices, is impaired, even while adjustments will continue to evolve. The success of online comedy ventures, fueled in part by the sharing properties of social media platforms, is thus at least partially reliant on social media giants' policies and algorithms that can either support or hamper the visibility of creative expression produced by noncommercial or less established comedy voices. Thus, efforts to intentionally expand innovation at the intersection of comedy and social justice are wise to also keep an eye on corporate and internet governance and policy.

Philanthropic Funding for Comedy as Art

Mediated comedy is developed nearly exclusively as a commercial practice, within the entertainment industry's economic pipeline. The marketplace for comedy—shaped by stand-up and sketch live stages, distributed by legacy TV and streaming networks—is predominantly nurtured by and for large media corporations. This reality places comedy, and the development of comedy and comedians, in a unique place within the broader arena of art and culture. Other forms of artistic expression, like independent documentary film, for example, also have sources of philanthropic funding to develop work that might not be created optimally within a commercial system—even as the same documentaries are often distributed on commercial media platforms. To develop independent documentary storytelling, a hybrid system of philanthropy and commerce is at work. Theater, as another example, also is funded by nonprofit and government agency sources alongside commercial funding. But comedy is a curious outlier in this regard.

For humor that interrogates social issues, hilariously but intentionally, and for comedy voices who are traditionally marginalized by the commercial marketplace, we suggest the need for new funding opportunities to develop and distribute comedy. Anne Libera from The Second City articulates this idea as comedy shaped by capitalism: "Comedy is popular, literally a popular art form, which means no one gets a grant to write their stand-up routine. So, the jobs available to comedians are defined by the marketplace . . . Capitalism has defined certain forms of comedy."[48] Comedian Bethany Hall proposes philanthropic funding as an optimistic idea to encourage new comedy from comedians who are thinking about social topics:

> An amazing comedian can have a profound idea about how to make a social justice issue digestible for the general public—the challenge for them is like "where do I take this idea because maybe it's not for a mainstream network." How does this comedian find a platform? It's not clear. If there was a clearer path, I think there would be a long line of comedians ready with hilarious content that's ready to be produced, but it doesn't have a home yet. I don't think philanthropists and nonprofits think of comedians . . . Comedians, if they have a passionate idea, they are doing it on their own dime . . . I think that's something that should change.[49]

With our forward-looking lens, based on the examples and interviews featured in this book, we anticipate future opportunities based on this thinking. Major foundations are expressing new interest in comedy in the networked era. With more illustrations of comedy working in service of social justice, perhaps the expansion into philanthropic funding will be organic and inevitable.

Future Inquiry in Comedy Research and Practice

Despite what we know about comedy, a vast scope of untapped explorations at the intersection of comedy and social justice remains. This open space points to areas for future research and practice focused on comedy for social change. To be sure, comedy itself will continue to evolve culturally, experimenting with what's funny and what's not, as well as with form, like the long-form topical storytelling that has recently emerged in stand-up comedy program examples like Hannah Gadsby's *Nanette* or Hasan Minhaj's *Homecoming King* or Chris Gethard's *Career Suicide*. Social-change cultural strategy that incorporates comedy will morph for different topics and audiences as media platforms continue to shift, creating ongoing space to explore comedy and its intersection with social justice. As the practice of humor and social change continues to unfold through the kinds of comedians and collaborations profiled in this book, the opportunity for inquiry about comedy's influence in social change also expands.

We locate multiple ways to examine the cultural impact of comedy as creative expression in social justice, including both qualitative and quantitative research approaches. When social justice organizations choose to work with comedy as part of their public engagement efforts, research can examine the collaborative process across sectors to highlight barriers and shared opportunities. And when public engagement strategies include comedy, research can help to understand audience, media, and policy responses more precisely, thus helping to shape the effectiveness of future social change initiatives. At the moment, this kind of campaign evaluation research is scant—perhaps for reasons of cost or perspectives about the importance of this work. We argue that this research is imperative. Similarly, when comedy in the entertainment marketplace deals with social justice topics, understanding the organic response of the viewing audience will be valuable. Chapter 2's taxonomy of comedy's effects on social change is intended as a helpful framework for this future research— that is, comedy's ability to increase message and issue attention, disarm audiences and lower resistance to persuasion, break down social barriers between groups, stimulate sharing and discussion, and also to influence press coverage and social media discourse, challenge conventional framing of social issues, and provide visibility to alternative ideas and marginalized groups. Original research presented in chapters 4 and 5 shows that comedy's influence works through entertainment value and positive emotions, often not centrally considered in social justice communication efforts.

Generally speaking, much remains to be understood about the complex ways in which audiences make deep political or civic meaning from the full mix of comedy and information they seek out or encounter or share. Notably, the YouTube-socialized youngest audience cohort, the most digital native among us, is not well studied. This offers exciting opportunities for research about comedy's influence on social issues. In terms of comedy's genres, while a well-developed body of research provides deep insights about the civic engagement influence of satirical news programs of *The Daily Show* variety, as well as the sketch comedy from *Saturday Night Live*, parallel inquiries about other humor formats are slim. For example, what do we know about the long-form comedic-style, first-person storytelling examples of *Nanette* and *Homecoming King*? At the moment, not much, which points to research opportunities that can help to inform social justice practice. The presentation of five distinct contemporary comedy genres in the entertainment marketplace, as detailed in chapter 3—that is, satirical news, scripted episodic TV, stand-up, sketch, and comedy documentary—offers a generative foundation for this work.

In terms of cultural and narrative practice, from our ongoing professional work with social justice organizations and comedians, we recognize that the practical realities of finding collaborators in order to shape co-creative work is a challenge. Even if a social justice organization wants to work with comedy professionals, what does this look like? How would the organization locate professional comedy writers and performers? Some of the research described above will help to generate responses to the question of collaboration and best practices, of course, but this particular quandary is rooted in professional practice. Developing practical ways to bring the comedy and social justice sectors together is an ongoing pursuit at the Center for Media & Social Impact, a research center and innovation lab directed by one of this book's authors, alongside other strategists and philanthropists, and an important one, if we value the social change opportunities presented by comedy collaborations.

The global comedy environment also offers an open space for future research inquiry and practice. While this book focuses primarily on cultural conditions and comedy work within the United States, we acknowledge parallel developments happening around the world in places like India, South Africa, Colombia, Mexico, Brazil, Egypt, and beyond, where media platform shifts have democratized access to previously marginalized comedy voices or perspectives. We also see evidence of comedy's influence in civic issues, as well as new conversations from civil society groups about leveraging comedy in their own public engagement work around global social problems. Authoritarian or corrupt government systems, alongside closed or controlled media climates, are crucial contexts for this work, underscoring the imperative to examine the risks of comedy in global regions where institutions of power are particularly threatened by creative expression of dissent. We need look no further than the tale of "the Jon Stewart of Egypt," Bassem Youssef, the wildly successful Egyptian doctor-turned-comedian, whose satirical TV show was seen as such a threat to the ruling power that he was exiled from the country.[50]

Given the changing media climate, the maturation of a transforming streaming-era information and entertainment system, and the networked social movements age, we argue that the timing is optimal for expanding research and practice into the contemporary intersection of comedy and social justice. These observations build upon the evolution of the comedy marketplace and a new generation of comedians, as well as existing research that reveals comedy's civic engagement properties and influences—and yet, these reflections are meant to open entirely new portals to explore.

.   .   .   .   .

The intersection of comedy and social justice is embodied in the voices— particularly the new voices—of comedians who are saying something serious about the world they inhabit, even while they make us laugh. But it also resides in the actions of social justice leaders and organizations who embrace comedy's strategic, artistic ability to grab and hold attention, to persuade, to open a conversation, to welcome new believers or solidify a base of supporters, to focus a critical lens on injustice, to set a media and public agenda, to humanize, and to allow light and optimism into social problems that are seemingly hopeless.

Comedy also can be untidy, unpredictable, offensive, and unapologetic—the very nature of an unorthodox form of artistic expression that observes a state of affairs not only as it is, but as it could or should be. A modicum of tension has always existed, therefore, between dominant institutions and comedy—between controlled messages and artistic entertainment, between polite rhetoric and boundary-pushing expressions of ideas. This delicate relationship will continue. Institutions of power have always regarded comedians with a wary eye because they capture the public imagination so vividly—and indeed, we submit that this is where comedy finds its most potent ability to work alongside or within efforts for social justice. In comedy, social justice advocates and communicators can find a source of power and opportunity to engage publics. After all, when comedy is able to capture attention or spark a conversation, entertainment and funny critique—not predictable or safe messages—are the levers by which people are invited in to participate. Comedy and social justice activism—twin arts and practices that share the values and mannerisms of deviant thinking, encouraging new ways of seeing and new ways of being—are symbiotic.

Under oppressive conditions, open creative expression is at its peak value—not simply to release tension, but to remind a society what's broken and what's possible, to keep citizens alert, to push for participation. The world of the twenty-first century is more connected than ever before, both in its common problems and its shared destiny, facing deep provocations that require the empathetic feelings and active agency of motivated publics to hold institutions of power accountable when they fail to meet—or even imagine—the needs of the people. Comedy lives here, in its time-tested ability to push ideas and invite hope. Meeting the challenges inherent in the complex ebb and flow of social progress is not a simple equation, but embracing creativity to help shape a more just world is one contributing pathway worth taking seriously. With humor, we defy the closed, limited thinking of "no, but," and we choose—with the optimistic, active prospect of "yes, and"—to imagine the possibilities that open up when a comedian and an activist walk into a bar.

Methodological Details and
Full Results from Chapter 4

Sample   We recruited 801 U.S. adults from a national paid opt-in survey panel
through Qualtrics Panels. All participants were between the ages of 18 and 49 to
reflect the relatively younger target audience of Funny or Die. Within that age
range, sampling quotas were used to ensure age, gender, race, and ethnicity
distributions that approximated U.S. census estimates. The mean age of the
sample was 33.7 (SD = 8.9). The sample was 50% female, 67% white, had a
median education level of an Associate's degree, and a median household income
of $40,000–$59,000. Approximately 35% of the sample identified as politically
liberal, 35% as moderate, and 30% as conservative. Approximately 38% of the
sample identified as Democrat, 27% as Republican, and 35% as Independent or
Other.

Dependent Variables (Political Engagement Outcomes)   Efficacy was measured
by averaging participants' level of agreement, from 1 (strongly disagree) to 7 (strongly
agree), with two statements (r = .63, M = 3.79, SD = 1.55): "Government officials pay
attention to what people like me think when they decide what to do about climate
change" and "People like me can influence the government on the issue of climate
change." Climate vote importance was measured with a single question—"How
important will the candidates' positions on climate change be to you when you
decide who you will vote for in the 2018 Congressional election?"—with responses
ranging from 1 (not at all important to my vote) to 7 (extremely important to my
vote) (M = 4.64, SD = 1.91). Discursive action was measured by averaging responses

to three items (Cronbach's α = .92, M = 4.37, SD = 1.87) that asked participants to indicate how likely, from 1 (not at all likely) to 7 (very likely), they would be in the next 12 months to: discuss climate change with family, friends, or acquaintances; look for more information about climate change online or in other media; share information or news stories about climate change on social media or via email. Intended political action averaged responses to five items (Cronbach's α = .93, M = 3.41, SD = 1.82) that asked participants to indicate how likely, from 1 (not at all likely) to 7 (very likely), they would be in the next 12 months to: contact government officials to urge them to take action on climate change, participate in a rally or protest supporting action on climate change, sign a petition supporting action on climate change, join or volunteer with an organization working to reduce climate change, and donate money to an organization working to reduce climate change.

Mediating Variables (Video Processing Variables)   The video enjoyment measure averaged participants' level of agreement, from 1 (strongly disagree) to 7 (strongly agree), with three statements (Cronbach's α = .94, M = 4.97, SD = 1.77): "It was fun for me to watch this video"; "I had a good time watching this video"; and "The video was entertaining." The measure of hopeful emotions combined participants' responses to two items (r = .78, M = 3.24, SD = 1.83) that asked them to indicate how much they felt "hope" and "optimism," respectively, while watching the video, on a scale from 1 (did not feel at all) to 7 (felt very strongly). Fearful emotions averaged responses to two items (r = .76, M = 3.13, SD = 1.93) that asked participants how much they felt "fear" and "worry," respectively, while watching the video, on a scale from 1 (did not feel at all) to 7 (felt very strongly). Counter-arguing averaged participants' level of agreement, from 1 (strongly disagree) to 7 (strongly agree), with two statements (r = .71, M = 2.92, SD = 1.73): "Sometimes I wanted to 'argue back' against what I saw in the video" and "I couldn't help thinking about ways that the information in the video was inaccurate or misleading."

Moderating Variable (Political Orientation)   Political orientation was measured using indicators of both party identification and political ideology. Respondents specified their party identification and its strength, ranging from (1) strong Republican to (7) strong Democrat (M = 3.67, SD = 2.08), and their political ideology, ranging from 1 "very liberal" to 7 "very conservative" (M = 3.85, SD = 1.64). The two variables were highly correlated (r = .62), and were summed to form a 13-point scale ranging from –6 to 6, with negative values indicating liberal, Democratic leanings (M = –0.48, SD = 3.35). For the purpose of analysis, this was recoded into a categorical variable, distinguishing between liberal Democrats (–6 to –2 on summed scale, n = 250, 41.6%), moderate Independents (–1 to 1 on summed scale, n = 170, 28.3%), and conservative Republicans (2 to 6 on summed scale, n = 181, 30.1%).

Covariates   Covariates include basic demographics (age, gender, education, income, race), political orientation, and environmentalism. Environmentalism was measured with a single item that asked respondents to indicate how much they agreed, from 1 (strongly disagree) to 7 (strongly agree), with the statement "I consider myself to be an environmentalist" (M = 4.56, SD = 1.56). Because none of these variables differed significantly across the four experimental conditions (indicating that random assignment was successful), they were not included as covariates in the analyses testing the direct experimental treatment effects (Tables 1 and 4). However, these variables were included as covariates in the regression analyses examining the associations between the processing variables and political engagement outcomes (Table 2) and testing the indirect effects of the treatment variables on the engagement outcomes via the processing variables (Tables 3 and 5).

To test whether political orientation moderated the effects of the video treatment on the dependent and mediating variables, we conducted two-way ANOVAs that interacted the video condition and political orientation. The interaction between the video condition and political orientation was not significant for any of the political engagement outcomes: efficacy $F(6, 789)$ = 1.2,1 p = .30; climate vote importance $F(6, 789)$ = 0.69, p = .66; discursive action $F(6, 789)$ = 1.75, p = .11; political action $F(6, 789)$ = 1.82, p = .09. The interactions were significant for enjoyment $F(4, 592)$ = 2.81, p = .02, η^2 = .016; hope $F(4, 592)$ = 4.56, p = .001, η^2 = .03; and counter-arguing $F(4, 592)$ = 5.15 p < .001, η^2 = .03; but not for fear $F(4, 592)$ = 0.34, p = .85. Estimated means across video conditions and political orientation for enjoyment, hope, and counter-arguing are presented in Table 4.

Table A-1   Estimated Marginal Means for Political Engagement Outcomes and Video Processing Variables across Video Conditions

	Video Treatment				Overall Treatment Effect
	"Old People"	"CCDD"	CNN	Control	
Political Engagement					
Efficacy	4.02 (.11)$_a$	3.76 (.11)$_{a,b}$	3.81 (.11)$_{a,b}$	3.57 (.11)$_b$	$F(3, 797) = 2.86, p = .04, \eta^2 = .01$
Vote Importance	4.70 (.13)$_{a,b}$	4.85 (.13)$_a$	4.73 (.13)$_{a,b}$	4.27 (.13)$_b$	$F(3, 797) = 3.54, p = .01, \eta^2 = .01$
Discursive Action	4.31 (.13)$_{a,b}$	4.63 (.13)$_a$	4.45 (.13)$_{a,b}$	4.09 (.13)$_b$	$F(3, 797) = 3.01, p = .03, \eta^2 = .01$
Political Action	3.33 (.13)$_a$	3.64 (.13)$_a$	3.41 (.13)$_a$	3.28 (.13)$_a$	$F(3, 797) = 1.53, p = .20, \eta^2 = .006$
Processing Variables					
Enjoyment	5.66 (.11)$_a$	5.30 (.11)$_a$	4.14 (.11)$_b$	N/A	$F(2, 598) = 48.42, p < .001, \eta^2 = .14$
Hope	3.57 (.13)$_a$	3.70 (.13)$_a$	2.94 (.13)$_b$	N/A	$F(2, 598) = 10.27, p < .001, \eta^2 = .03$
Fear	2.98 (.13)$_a$	3.12 (.13)$_a$	4.44 (.13)$_b$	N/A	$F(2, 598) = 40.64, p < .001, \eta^2 = .12$
Counter-Arguing	3.01 (.13)$_{a,b}$	3.09 (.13)$_a$	2.63 (.13)$_b$	N/A	$F(2, 598) = 3.84, p = .02, \eta^2 = .01$

note. Results are based on a series of one-way analysis of variance (ANOVA) tests, which assessed the overall effect of the video treatment on each respective outcome and then tested differences in the mean levels of each outcome between all pairwise combinations of video treatments, using the Sidak adjustment for multiple comparisons. Within rows, means with different subscripts are significantly different from one another, $p < .05$, after the Sidak adjustment. Standard errors in parentheses.

Table A-2 OLS Regression Results Predicting Political Engagement from the Video Treatment and Processing Variables

	Efficacy B (SE)	Climate Vote Importance B (SE)	Discursive Action B (SE)	Political Action B (SE)
Video Treatment				
"Old People"	−0.005 (.15)	0.17 (.16)	−0.02 (.15)	0.03 (.15)
"CCDD"	−0.35 (.15)*	0.22 (.16)	0.25 (.14)	0.24 (.15)
Processing Variables				
Enjoyment	0.06 (.04)	0.09 (.04)*	0.16 (.04)***	0.08 (.04)*
Hope	0.24 (.04)***	0.18 (.04)***	0.17 (.04)***	0.21 (.04)***
Fear	0.04 (.03)	0.27 (.04)***	0.30 (.03)***	0.23 (.03)***
Counter-Arguing	0.10 (.03)**	−0.10 (.03)**	−0.06 (.03)	0.005 (.03)
Covariates				
Age	−0.005 (.006)	0.01 (.007)*	−0.01 (.006)*	−0.01 (.006)*
Gender (female)	−0.12 (.11)	−0.09 (.12)	−0.17 (.11)	−0.25 (.11)*
Race (white)	−0.36 (.12)**	−0.19 (.13)	−0.13 (.12)	−0.48 (.12)***
Education	0.08 (.03)*	0.06 (.03)*	0.03 (.03)	0.03 (.03)
Income	0.05 (.02)	−0.04 (.03)	−0.008 (.03)	−0.002 (.03)
Environmentalism	0.27 (.04)***	0.35 (.04)***	0.39 (.04)***	0.39 (.04)***
Liberal Democrats[B]	−0.10 (.14)	0.60 (.15)***	0.36 (.14)***	0.49 (.14)***
Moderate	−0.34 (.14)*	0.17 (.15)	0.04 (.14)	0.27 (.14)
Independents[B]				
Constant	1.31 (.42)**	0.50 (.45)	0.38 (.41)	0.25 (.42)
R^2	.34	.48	.56	.52

NOTE. Unstandardized regression coefficients (B) are reported, with standard errors (SE) in parentheses. $N = 597$. (The unrelated control condition was not included in the analysis.)

[A] CNN is the reference category.

[B] Conservative Republicans are the reference category.

*** $p < .001$; ** $p < .01$; * $p < .05$.

Table A-3 Indirect Effects of Comedy Videos (Compared to News) on Political Engagement via Video Processing Variables

	Political Efficacy		Climate Vote Importance		Discursive Action		Political Action	
Mediator	Indirect Effect (Boot SE)	Boot 95% CI	Indirect Effect (Boot SE)	Boot 95% CI	Indirect Effect (Boot SE)	Boot 95% CI	Indirect Effect (Boot SE)	Boot 95% CI
Enjoyment								
"Old People"[A]	.09 (.07)	−.045, .230	.14 (.08)	−.009, .304	**.25 (.07)**	**.114, .398**	**.13 (.07)**	**.011, .273**
"CCDD"[A]	.07 (.05)	−.032, .174	.10 (.06)	−.007, .220	**.18 (.06)**	**.081, .299**	**.10 (.05)**	**.008, .203**
Hope								
"Old People"[A]	**.17 (.05)**	**.081, .275**	**.13 (.04)**	**.055, .220**	**.12 (.04)**	**.049, .202**	**.15 (.05)**	**.066, .244**
"CCDD"[A]	**.18 (.05)**	**.088, .286**	**.13 (.04)**	**.061, .226**	**.12 (.04)**	**.052, .208**	**.16 (.05)**	**.073, .257**
Fear								
"Old People"[A]	−.05 (.05)	−.156, .048	**−.37 (.07)**	**−.511, −.242**	**−.42 (.07)**	**−.564, −.296**	**−.32 (.06)**	**−.451, −.202**
"CCDD"[A]	−.05 (.05)	−.150, .046	**−.36 (.07)**	**−.501, −.234**	**−.40 (.07)**	**−.542, −.284**	**−.31 (.06)**	**−.435, −.195**
Counter-arguing								
"Old People"[A]	**.04 (.02)**	**.001, .096**	**−.04 (.02)**	**−.088, −.0009**	−.02 (.02)	−.060, .003	.002 (.01)	−.024, .030
"CCDD"[A]	**.05 (.02)**	**.009, .101**	**−.04 (.02)**	**−.101, −.004**	−.03 (.02)	−.070, .002	.002 (.01)	−.030, .031

NOTE. Indirect effects were estimated using the SPSS PROCESS 3.0 macro, developed by Andrew Hayes. Bootstrapped standard errors (Boot SE) and confidence intervals (CI) were computed using 5,000 bootstrap samples. Bold text is used to denote significant effects, $p < .05$. (The unrelated control condition was not included in the analysis.)

[A] CNN is the reference category.

Table A-4 *Estimated Marginal Means for Video Processing Variables across Video Conditions and Political Orientation*

	Video Treatment			Simple Effects of Video Condition Within Each Political Subgroup
	"Old People"	*"CCDD"*	*CNN*	
Enjoyment				
Liberal Democrats	5.98 (.17)$_a$	5.92 (.18)$_a$	4.19 (.17)$_b$	$F(2, 592) = 34.47, p < .001$
Moderate Independents	5.40 (.22)$_a$	5.21 (.20)$_a$	4.09 (.21)$_b$	$F(2, 592) = 11.33, p < .001$
Conservative Republicans	5.42 (.20)$_a$	4.61 (.20)$_b$	4.12 (.21)$_b$	$F(2, 592) = 10.27, p < .001$
Hope				
Liberal Democrats	4.16 (.19)$_a$	4.04 (.20)$_a$	2.71 (.19)$_b$	$F(2, 592) = 17.50, p < .001$
Moderate Independents	3.29 (.25)$_a$	3.86 (.22)$_a$	3.18 (.23)$_a$	$F(2, 592) = 2.53, p = .08$
Conservative Republicans	2.97 (.22)$_a$	3.10 (.22)$_a$	3.03 (.23)$_a$	$F(2, 592) = .095, p = .91$
Counter-Arguing				
Liberal Democrats	2.90 (.18)$_a$	2.42 (.19)$_{a,b}$	1.92 (.18)$_b$	$F(2, 592) = 7.41, p = .001$
Moderate Independents	3.02 (.23)$_a$	2.80 (.21)$_a$	2.65 (.22)$_a$	$F(2, 592) = 0.64, p = .53$
Conservative Republicans	3.16 (.21)$_a$	4.22 (.21)$_b$	3.65 (.22)$_{a,b}$	$F(2, 592) = 6.16, p = .002$

NOTE. Results are based on a series of two-way analysis of variance (ANOVA) tests, which included the video treatment and political orientation as factors. The unrelated control condition was not included in the analyses. Pairwise mean comparisons between treatment conditions were conducted within each political subgroup, using the Sidak adjustment for multiple comparisons. Within rows, means with different subscripts are significantly different from one another, $p < .05$, after the Sidak adjustment. Standard errors in parentheses.

Table A-5   Indirect Effects of Comedy Videos (Compared to News) on Political Engagement via Enjoyment, Hope, and Counter-Arguing across Political Subgroups

Mediator	Political Orientation	Political Efficacy		Climate Vote Importance		Discursive Action		Political Action	
		Indirect Effect (Boot SE)	Boot 95% CI	Indirect Effect (Boot SE)	Boot 95% CI	Indirect Effect (Boot SE)	Boot 95% CI	Indirect Effect (Boot SE)	Boot 95% CI
Enjoyment									
"Old People"[A]	Lib Dem	.10 (.08)	-.043, .253	.15 (.09)	-.010, .332	**.27 (.08)**	**.127, .456**	**.14 (.07)**	**.011, .288**
	Mod Ind	.09 (.07)	-.038, .231	.13 (.08)	-.008, .310	**.24 (.08)**	**.100, .406**	**.13 (.06)**	**.007, .267**
	Cons Rep	.09 (.07)	-.036, .240	.13 (.08)	-.009, .305	**.24 (.08)**	**.100, .418**	**.13 (.13)**	**.008, .263**
"CCDD"[A]	Lib Dem	.09 (.07)	-.041, .245	.15 (.08)	-.009, .318	**.26 (.08)**	**.122, .424**	**.14 (.07)**	**.010, .271**
	Mod Ind	.06 (.05)	-.025, .186	.09 (.06)	-.005, .237	**.17 (.07)**	**.052, .322**	**.09 (.05)**	**.004, .212**
	Cons Rep	.03 (.03)	-.016, .129	.05 (.05)	-.012, .161	.10 (.06)	-.009, .236	.05 (.04)	-.007, .144
Hope									
"Old People"[A]	Lib Dem	**.32 (.08)**	**.169, .502**	**.24 (.08)**	**.114, .407**	**.22 (.07)**	**.100, .371**	**.28 (.08)**	**.140, .453**
	Mod Ind	.07 (.07)	-.079, .219	.05 (.06)	-.061, .174	.05 (.05)	-.055, .155	.06 (.07)	-.070, .195
	Cons Rep	.03 (.07)	-.106, .176	.03 (.06)	-.086, .137	.02 (.05)	-.076, .124	.03 (.06)	-.102, .156
"CCDD"[A]	Lib Dem	**.31 (.08)**	**.166, .464**	**.23 (.07)**	**.109, .384**	**.21 (.06)**	**.100, .344**	**.27 (.07)**	**.138, .426**
	Mod Ind	.13 (.08)	-.016, .300	.10 (.06)	-.013, .227	.09 (.06)	-.015, .212	.11 (.07)	-.010, .259
	Cons Rep	.05 (.07)	-.091, .192	.03 (.05)	-.067, .151	.03 (.05)	-.063, .138	.04 (.06)	-.082, .165
Counter-arguing									
"Old People"[A]	Lib Dem	**.11 (.04)**	**.036, .215**	**-.11 (.05)**	**-.214, -.021**	**-.06 (.04)**	**-.147, -.003**	.006 (.03)	-.062, .078
	Mod Ind	.03 (.04)	-.039, .113	-.03 (.04)	-.108, .036	-.02 (.02)	-.079, .021	.002 (.01)	-.027, .032
	Cons Rep	-.06 (.04)	-.150, .014	.05 (.04)	-.011, .160	.03 (.03)	-.010, .111	-.003 (.02)	-.050, .040
"CCDD"[A]	Lib Dem	**.06 (.03)**	**.014, .133**	**-.06 (.03)**	**-.133, -.008**	-.04 (.02)	-.096, .002	.003 (.02)	-.040, .044
	Mod Ind	.01 (.03)	-.050, .082	-.01 (.03)	-.082, .043	-.008 (.02)	-.058, .027	.0007 (.01)	-.021, .023
	Cons Rep	.05 (.04)	-.024, .152	-.05 (.04)	-.146, .023	-.03 (.03)	-.099, .015	.002 (.019)	-.038, .042

NOTE. Indirect effects were estimated using the SPSS PROCESS 3.0 macro, developed by Andrew Hayes. Bootstrapped standard errors (Boot SE) and confidence intervals (CI) were computed using 5,000 bootstrap samples. Bold text is used to denote significant effects, $p < .05$.
[A] CNN is the reference category. (The unrelated control condition was not included in the analysis.)

APPENDIX B Methodological Overview
and Main Results from
Chapter 5

Full details are available in the original publication:

Caty Borum Chattoo and Lauren Feldman, "Storytelling for Social Change: Leveraging Documentary and Comedy for Public Engagement in Global Poverty," *Journal of Communication* 67 (2017): 678–701, https://doi:10.1111/jcom.12318, used with permission here from Oxford University Press.

A total of 1,258 respondents completed this study. Samples were drawn from four market research sample vendors—Survey Sampling International (SSI), Research Now, uSamp, and Innovate Market Research—in order to minimize potential biases that may be present in any one provider. Respondents were U.S.-based adults between the ages of 18 and 49, with age, gender, and ethnic quotas implemented to ensure a U.S. Census–distributed sample. To ensure nonrejection of similar programming, respondents were asked: "How often do you typically watch each of the following types of TV shows or movies?" Respondents were included only if they indicated at least a "3" on a 1–5 interest scale for any of the following: "documentaries or scripted films about social issues," "investigative reports or journalism," "stories about people from around the world," or "TV shows that focus on social issues." The final sample was 50% female, 79% white, and 12% Hispanic, with a mean age of 33.6 (SD = 8.99). Median education was "some college," and 49% had a bachelor's degree or higher. Median annual household income was $50,000–$59,999.

Table B-1   Means, Standard Deviations, and Treatment Effects for Outcome and Mediating Variables

	Stand Up Planet (N=628)			The End Game (N=630)			Treatment Effect
	Pre-test Mean (SD)	Post-test Mean (SD)	Mean Change (SD)	Pre-test Mean (SD)	Post-test Mean (SD)	Mean Change (SD)	
Outcome Variable							
Government Aid	7.39 (2.4)	8.06 (2.3)	0.67 (1.4)***	7.34 (2.3)	8.06 (2.3)	0.72 (1.5)***	$F(1, 1256) = 0.52$
Awareness	7.12 (2.2)	7.90 (2.0)	0.78 (1.7)***	7.17 (2.2)	7.73 (1.9)	0.56 (1.6)***	$F(1, 1256) = 5.41$*
Knowledge	1.89 (1.2)	3.35 (0.9)	1.45 (1.3)***	2.54 (1.2)	3.54 (0.8)	1.00 (1.2)***	$F(1, 1256) = 39.13$*
Action[A]	1.05 (1.7)	5.70 (2.8)	N/A	0.97 (1.7)	5.31 (2.9)	N/A	$F(1, 1255) = 5.46$*
Mediating Variable							
Transportation	—	3.61 (.91)	—	—	3.79 (.82)	—	$t(1256) = -3.67$***
Relatability	—	3.32 (1.00)	—	—	2.99 (1.04)	—	$t(1256) = 5.65$***
Positive Emotion	—	7.54 (2.5)	—	—	5.70 (3.0)	—	$t(1256) = 11.68$***
Negative Emotion	—	5.53 (2.3)	—	—	6.01 (2.18)	—	$t(1256) = -3.75$***
Entertainment Value	—	9.13 (1.7)	—	—	5.80 (1.7)	—	$t(1256) = 34.80$***

NOTE.   Estimates of treatment effects are based on repeated measures ANOVA for all outcomes except action. For action, ANCOVA with the baseline measure as the covariate was used to test the treatment effect. Treatment effects for mediating variables are based on an independent-samples t-test.
[A] Pre- and post-test variables used different response scales; it is thus not appropriate to compute change scores.
*** $p < .001$; ** $p < .01$; * $p < .05$

Table B-2 OLS Regression Analyses Predicting Outcome Variables

	Govt Aid B (SE)	Awareness B (SE)	Action B (SE)	Knowledge B (SE)
Predictors				
Pre-Test Level	0.69 (.02)***	0.51 (.02)***	0.42 (.04)***	0.16 (.02)***
Stand Up Planet Treatment	−0.26 (.12)*	−0.07 (.12)	−.13 (.19)	−0.04 (.07)
Mediators				
Transportation	0.49 (.06)***	0.33 (.06)***	0.73 (.10)***	0.17 (.04)***
Relatability	0.04 (.04)	0.03 (.05)	0.57 (.07)***	−0.20 (.03)***
Positive Emotion	−0.0008 (.01)	0.04 (.01)*	0.01 (.02)	0.02 (.01)*
Negative Emotion	0.03 (.02)	0.06 (.02)**	0.25 (.03)***	−0.05 (.01)***
Entertainment Value	0.09 (.03)**	0.08 (.03)**	0.16 (.04)***	−0.004 (.02)
Demographic Controls				
Age	0.006 (.004)	0.001 (.004)	−0.02 (.007)**	0.008 (.003)**
Gender (female)	0.04 (.07)	0.15 (.07)*	−0.12 (.12)	0.11 (.05)*
Race (white)	−0.17 (.09)	0.08 (.09)	−0.12 (.15)	0.13 (.06)*
Ethnicity (Hispanic)	0.14 (.11)	0.07 (.11)	0.20 (.18)	−0.11 (.07)
Education	−0.04 (.02)	−0.03 (.02)	0.06 (.04)	0.009 (.02)
Constant	0.36 (.29)	1.48 (.29)***	−1.33 (.46)**	2.74 (.18)***
R^2	.69	.54	.46	.12

NOTE. Unstandardized regression coefficients (B) are reported with standard errors (SE) in parentheses. $N = 1258$.
*** $p < .001$; ** $p < .01$; * $p < .05$.

Table B-3 Indirect Effects of Stand Up Planet Treatment on Outcomes via Mediators

Mediator	Government Aid		Awareness		Knowledge		Action	
	Indirect Effect (Boot SE)	Boot 95% CI	Indirect Effect (Boot SE)	Boot 95% CI	Indirect Effect (Boot SE)	Boot 95% CI	Indirect Effect (Boot SE)	Boot 95% CI
Transportation	**-.09 (.02)**	**-.145, -.048**	**-.06 (.02)**	**-.098, -.025**	**-.02 (.01)**	**-.048, -.006**	**-.14 (.04)**	**-.227, -.070**
Relatability	.01 (.01)	-.012, .044	.01 (.02)	-.024, .045	**-.07 (.01)**	**-.103, -.043**	**.18 (.04)**	**.109, .263**
Positive Emotion	-.001 (.03)	-.059, .055	**.07 (.03)**	**.009, .141**	**.04 (.02)**	**.002, .078**	.02 (.05)	-.079, .115
Negative Emotion	-.014 (.01)	-.038, .002	**-.03 (.01)**	**-.057, -.010**	**.02 (.008)**	**.006, .039**	**-.12 (.03)**	**-.198, -.062**
Entertainment Value	**.31 (.10)**	**.111, .519**	**.27 (.10)**	**.067, .473**	-.01 (.07)	-.142, .116	**.52 (.16)**	**.224, .843**
Total Indirect Effects	**.22 (.11)**	**.001, .431**	**.27 (.10)**	**.062, .469**	-.05 (.07)	-.178, .086	**.46 (.18)**	**.111, .820**

NOTE. Bootstrapped standard errors (Boot SE) and confidence intervals (CI) were computed using 10,000 bootstrap samples. Bold text is used to denote significant effects, $p < .05$.

Comedy Professionals
Interviewed for Chapter 6

All comedy professionals interviewed are listed below. The authors conducted the
interviews by phone or in-person between July and December 2018.

Table C-1

Name	Genre	Role	Major Media Credits
Cristela Alonzo	Stand-up, scripted comedy	Performer, producer	*Lower Classy* (Netflix stand-up special, 2017 — performer) *Cars 3* (animated film, 2017 — cast) *Cristela* (ABC sitcom, 2014–15 — executive producer, creator, cast)
W. Kamau Bell	Stand-up, satirical news, documentary	Stand-up comic, TV host, producer	*United Shades of America with W. Kamau Bell* (CNN docuseries, 2016–present — host, executive producer)

Table C-1 (continued)

Name	Genre	Role	Major Media Credits
			Private School Negro (Netflix stand-up special, 2018 – performer)
			Totally Biased with W. Kamau Bell (FX late-night comedy show, 2012–13 — host, writer, executive producer, creator)
			Laughter against the Machine (comedy tour and documentary, 2008 — performer)
Jennie Church-Cooper		Talent manager, producer	*Patriot Act with Hasan Minhaj* (Netflix satirical news show, 2018–present — executive producer)
			Hasan Minhaj: Homecoming King (Netflix comedy special, 2017 — executive producer)
Joel Church-Cooper	Scripted comedy	Showrunner	*Brockmire* (IFC scripted comedy, 2017–present — executive producer, creator, writer, showrunner)
Rachel Dratch	Sketch	Performer	*Saturday Night Live* (NBC sketch comedy show, 1999–2006 — cast)
Negin Farsad	Stand-up, documentary, scripted comedy	Performer, writer, director, producer	*3rd Street Blackout* (scripted film, 2016 — producer, director, writer, cast)
			The Muslims Are Coming! (documentary, 2013 — producer, director, cast)
Nato Green	Stand-up	Performer, writer	*The Whiteness Album* (standup album, 2018)
			Totally Biased with W. Kamau Bell (FX late-night comedy show, 2012–13 — writer, researcher, cast)

			Laughter against the Machine (comedy tour and documentary, 2008 — performer)
Bethany Hall	Scripted comedy	Performer, writer	*The Chris Gethard Show* (public access, Fusion, and TruTV comedy talk show, 2011–18 — panelist)
			Thanksgiving (The Complex Network scripted comedy series, 2016 — co-creator, writer, executive producer)
Kelly Leonard		Producer	The Second City (comedy theatre and school of improv, 1988–present — Executive Director of Insights and Applied Improvisation)
Anne Libera		Director	The Second City (comedy theatre and school of improv, 1998–present — Director of Comedy Studies)
Aasif Mandvi	Satirical news, scripted comedy	Performer, writer, producer	*Sakina's Restaurant* (one-man off-Broadway show, 2018)
			The Daily Show (Comedy Central satirical news show, 2006–17 — correspondent)
			Halal in the Family (web TV series, 2015 — writer, cast, executive producer)
			The Brink (HBO comedy series, 2015 — writer, producer)
Omri Marcus	Satirical news	Writer	*Eretz Nehederet* (Israeli satirical news program, 2002–06 — writer)
Brent Miller	Scripted comedy	Producer	*One Day at a Time* (Netflix scripted comedy, 2017–present — executive producer)
Hasan Minhaj	Stand-up, sketch, satirical news	Performer, writer, producer	*Patriot Act with Hasan Minhaj* (Netflix comedy talk show, 2018–present — host, creator, writer, executive producer)

Table C-1 (continued)

Name	Genre	Role	Major Media Credits
			Goatface (Comedy Central comedy special, 2018 — cast, writer, executive producer)
			Hasan Minhaj: Homecoming King (Netflix comedy special, 2017 — executive producer, performer, writer)
			The Daily Show (Comedy Central satirical news show, 2014–18 — correspondent)
			Stand-Up Planet (documentary, 2013 — host)
Zahra Noorbakhsh	Stand-up	Performer	*#GoodMuslimBadMuslim* (podcast, 2014–present — co-host)
			Travel Ban (documentary, 2018 — cast)
			The Secret Life of Muslims (Vox docuseries, 2016 — cast)
Franchesca Ramsey	Sketch, satirical news	Performer, writer	*Decoded* (MTV web series, 2015–present — creator, writer, host)
			The Nightly Show with Larry Wilmore (satirical news show, 2015–16 — writer, correspondent)
Sara Taksler	Satirical news, documentary	Producer, director	*The Opposition with Jordan Klepper* (Comedy Central satirical news show, 2017–18 — supervising producer)
			The Daily Show (Comedy Central satirical news show, 2005–07 — producer / senior producer)
			Tickling Giants (documentary, 2016 — director, producer, writer)

Jenny Yang	Stand-up, sketch	Performer, writer, producer	*Busy Tonight* (E! late-night talk show, 2018 — writer and performer)
			Disoriented Comedy (Asian American stand-up comedy tour, 2012–present — producer)
			Digital video creator / collaborator for *BuzzFeed* and *Fusion*

Notes

BOOK EPIGRAPH

"Stand Up Planet Moment: Words of Wisdom from Norman Lear and Carl Reiner," May 16, 2014, video, 0:47, www.youtube.com/watch?v = 8Rf4bjgrFoc.

INTRODUCTION

1. Hasan Minhaj, voice-over narration, in David Munro, *Stand Up Planet*, KCETLink Media and Kontent Films, 2014, www.standupplanet.org/.
2. Brian Montopoli, "Is the U.S. Bail System Unfair?" *CBS News*, February 8, 2013, www.cbsnews.com/news/is-the-us-bail-system-unfair/.
3. Rick Rojas, "New York City to Relax Bail Requirements for Low-Level Offenders," *New York Times*, July 8, 2015, www.nytimes.com/2015/07/09/nyregion/new-york-city-introduces-bail-reform-plan-for-low-level-offenders.html?_r = 0.
4. Hunter Schwartz, "John Oliver's New Target: The Bail Bond Industry and Bounty Hunters," *Washington Post*, June 8, 2015, www.washingtonpost.com/news/the-fix/wp/2015/06/08/john-oliver-on-bail-bonds-and-bounty-hunters/?utm_term = .996fb94e2c65.
5. Scott Eric Kaufman, "John Oliver Gets Results! New York City to Change Bail Requirements for Low-Level Offenders," *Salon*, July 8, 2015, www.salon

.com/2015/07/08/john_oliver_gets_results_new_york_city_to_change_bail_ requirements_for_low_level_offenders/.

6. Colin Gorenstein, "John Oliver Blasts the U.S. Bail System for Locking Up Poor People Regardless of Guilt," *Salon*, June 8, 2015, www.salon.com/2015 /06/08/john_oliver_blasts_the_u_s_bail_system_for_locking_up_poor_people_ regardless_of_guilt/.

7. Schwartz, "John Oliver's New Target."

8. Rojas, "New York City to Relax Bail Requirements"; Kaufman, "John Oliver Gets Results."

9. Ali Kahn, "Preparedness 101: Zombie Apocalypse," Public Health Matters, May 16, 2011, http://blogs.cdc.gov/publichealthmatters/2011/05/preparedness-101-zombie-apocalypse/.

10. Julia David Fraustino and Liang Ma, "CDC's Use of Social Media and Humor in a Risk Campaign—'Preparedness 101: Zombie Apocalypse'," *Journal of Applied Communication Research* 43, no. 2 (March 2015): 222–41, https://doi.org /10.1080/00909882.2015.1019544.

11. Fraustino and Ma, "CDC's Use of Social Media."

12. Pew Research Center, *Beyond Distrust: How Americans View Their Government*, November 23, 2015, www.people-press.org/2015/11/23/beyond-distrust-how-americans-view-their-government/.

13. Amanda D. Lotz, *The Television Will Be Revolutionized*, 2nd ed. (New York: New York University Press, 2014), 42.

14. Lotz, *Television Will Be Revolutionized*, 40–46.

15. Doreen St. Félix, "Hasan Minhaj's 'New Brown America'," *New Yorker*, June 6, 2017, www.newyorker.com/culture/cultural-comment/hasan-minhajs-new-brown-america.

16. Amber Day, *Satire and Dissent: Interventions in Contemporary Political Debate* (Bloomington: Indiana University Press, 2011), 11.

17. Stuart Hall, "Notes on Deconstructing 'The Popular'," in *Cultural Resistance Reader*, ed. Stephen Duncombe (London: Verso, 2002), 185–92, on 192.

18. Isabel Molina-Guzmán, "#OscarsSoWhite: How Stuart Hall Explains Why Nothing Changes in Hollywood and Everything Is Changing," *Critical Studies in Media Communication* 33, no. 5 (November 2016): 438–54, https:// doi.org/10.1080/15295036.2016.1227864.

19. Lotz, *Television Will Be Revolutionized*.

20. Lotz, *Television Will Be Revolutionized*, 37.

21. Nancy Doyle Palmer, "The Muslims Are Coming—to Netflix," *Huffington Post*, January 19, 2014, www.huffingtonpost.com/nancy-doyle-palmer-/the-muslims-are-coming-to_b_4627725.html.

22. Arun Rath with Tanzila Ahmed and Zahra Noorbakhsh, "What Is a 'Good Muslim' Anyway? A Podcast Disrupts the Narrative," May 9, 2015, *All Things*

Considered, NPR, http://www.npr.org/sections/codeswitch/2015/05/09
/405316098/what-is-a-good-muslim-anyway-a-podcast-disrupts-the-narrative.

23. Time Editorial Staff, "Comedians: The Third Campaign," *Time* 76, no. 7
(August 15, 1960): 42.

24. Pew Research Center, *Beyond Distrust*.

25. Megan Garber, "How Comedians Became Public Intellectuals," *The Atlantic*, May 28, 2015, www.theatlantic.com/entertainment/archive/2015/05
/how-comedians-became-public-intellectuals/394277/.

26. See Lauren Feldman, "Cloudy with a Chance of Heat Balls: The Portrayal of
Global Warming on *The Daily Show* and *The Colbert Report*," *International Journal of Communication* 7 (January 2013): 430–51, https://ijoc.org/index.php/ijoc
/article/view/1940; Lauren Feldman, "Learning about Politics from *The Daily Show*: The Role of Viewer Orientation and Processing Motivations," *Mass Communication and Society* 16, no. 4 (March 2013): 586–607, https://doi.org/10.1080/1520
5436.2012.735742; Lauren Feldman, Anthony Leiserowitz, and Edward Maibach,
"The Science of Satire: *The Daily Show* and *The Colbert Report* as Sources of Public
Attention to Science and the Environment," in *The Stewart/Colbert Effect: Essays
on the Real Impact of Fake News*, ed. Amarnath Amarasingam (Jefferson, NC:
McFarland, 2011), 25–46; Dannagal Goldthwaite Young, "The Privileged Role of
the Late-Night Joke: Exploring Humor's Role in Disrupting Argument Scrutiny,"
Media Psychology 11, no. 1 (March 2008): 119–42, https://doi.org/10.1080
/15213260701837073; Dannagal Goldthwaite Young, "Laughter, Learning, or
Enlightenment? Viewing and Avoidance Motivations behind *The Daily Show* and
The Colbert Report," *Journal of Broadcasting and Electronic Media* 57, no. 2 (June
2013): 153–69, https://doi.org/10.1080/08838151.2013.787080; Pew Research
Center, "Journalism, Satire or Just Laughs? 'The Daily Show with Jon Stewart,'
Examined," May 8, 2008, www.journalism.org/2008/05/08/journalism-satire-
or-just-laughs-the-daily-show-with-jon-stewart-examined/#fn1.

27. Pew Research Center, "Journalism, Satire or Just Laughs?"

28. Olivia B. Waxman, "Watch Michelle Obama Rap in a New Video for *College Humor*," *Time*, December 10, 2015, http://time.com/4144403/michelle-
obama-college-humor-rap/.

29. Asawin Suebsaeng, "How Funny or Die Is Changing Politics," *Daily Beast*,
September 20, 2015, www.thedailybeast.com/articles/2015/09/19/how-funny-
or-die-is-changing-politics.html.

30. Christopher Borelli, "Funny or Die's Adam McKay on His Site's Comedy
Influence after Five Years," *Chicago Tribune*, April 28, 2012, www.chicagotribune
.com/entertainment/ct-ent-0430-funny-or-die-main-20120427-story.html.

31. Jeffrey D. Sachs, "From Millennium Development Goals to Sustainable
Development Goals," *Lancet* 379, no. 9832 (June 2012): 2206–11, https://doi.org
/10.1016/S0140-6736(12)60685-0.

CHAPTER 1

1. Richard Zoglin, *Comedy at the Edge: How Stand-Up in the 1970s Changed America*, 1st ed. (New York: Bloomsbury, 2008), 43.

2. "A History of Emmy—The 1940s," Television Academy, accessed January 23, 2019, www.emmys.com/content/history-emmy-1940s.

3. Jon Blistein, "Watch Lena Waithe's Inspiring Emmys 2017 Speech for 'Master of None'," *Rolling Stone*, September 17, 2017, www.rollingstone.com/tv/news/lena-waithes-emmys-2017-speech-for-master-of-none-watch-w503785.

4. Bethonie Butler, "Why Lena Waithe's Historic Emmy Win for 'Master of None' Is So Meaningful," *Washington Post*, September 18, 2017, www.washingtonpost .com/news/arts-and-entertainment/wp/2017/09/18/why-lena-waithes-historic-emmy-win-for-master-of-none-is-so-meaningful/?utm_term = .c3588e561bbb.

5. Elahe Izadi, "How 'Master of None's' Religion Episode Proves That the Show Is Like Nothing Else on TV," *Washington Post*, May 22, 2017, www.washingtonpos t.com/news/arts-and-entertainment/wp/2017/05/22/how-master-of-nones-religion-episode-proves-that-the-show-is-like-nothing-else-on-tv/?utm_term = .5e2afc3818e8.

6. Michael Lev-Ram, "How Netflix Became Hollywood's Frenemy," *Fortune*, June 7, 2016, http://fortune.com/netflix-versus-hollywood/.

7. Lev-Ram, "How Netflix Became Hollywood's Frenemy."

8. Roberto Baldwin, "With *House of Cards*, Netflix Bets on Creative Freedom," *Wired*, February 1, 2013, www.wired.com/2013/02/creative-freedom-cord-cutting/.

9. Amanda D. Lotz, *The Television Will Be Revolutionized*, 2nd ed. (New York: New York University Press, 2014).

10. Butler, "Lena Waithe's Historic Emmy Win."

11. Blistein, "Lena Waithe's Inspiring Speech."

12. Michael X. Delli Carpini and Bruce A. Williams, "Let Us Infotain You: Politics in the New Media Age," in *Mediated Politics: Communication in the Future of Democracy*, ed. W. Lance Bennett and Robert M. Entman (Cambridge: Cambridge University Press, 2001): 160–81.

13. Natalie Jomini Stroud, *Niche News: The Politics of News Choice* (Oxford: Oxford University Press, 2011).

14. Delli Carpini and Williams, "Let Us Infotain You," 160–81.

15. "Three Technology Revolutions," Pew Research Center, accessed January 23, 2019, www.pewinternet.org/three-technology-revolutions/.

16. "Mobile Fact Sheet," Pew Research Center, February 5, 2018, www .pewinternet.1org/fact-sheet/mobile/.

17. "Social Media Fact Sheet," Pew Research Center, February 5, 2018, www .pewinternet.org/fact-sheet/social-media/.

18. Internet Society, *Global Internet Report 2015* (Reston, VA: Internet Society, July 2015), 4, www.internetsociety.org/globalinternetreport/2015/assets /download/IS_web.pdf.

19. Sarah Phillips, "A Brief History of Facebook," *The Guardian*, July 25, 2007, www.theguardian.com/technology/2007/jul/25/media.newmedia.

20. Laura Fitzpatrick, "Brief History YouTube," *Time*, May 31, 2010, http:// content.time.com/time/magazine/article/0,9171,1990787,00.html.

21. Julia Greenberg, "On Its 10th Birthday, a Short History of Twitter in Tweets," *Wired*, March 21, 2016, www.wired.com/2016/03/10th-birthday-short-history-twitter-tweets/.

22. "Three Technology Revolutions."

23. Charles Arthur, "The History of Smartphones: Timeline," *The Guardian*, January 24, 2012, www.theguardian.com/technology/2012/jan/24/smartphones-timeline.

24. Lotz, *Television Will Be Revolutionized*, 6.

25. Lotz, *Television Will Be Revolutionized*, 6–7.

26. Lotz, *Television Will Be Revolutionized*, 70.

27. Lotz, *Television Will Be Revolutionized*.

28. "About Netflix," Netflix, accessed January 24, 2019, https://media.netflix .com/en/about-netflix.

29. "2017 on Netflix—A Year in Bingeing," Netflix, December 11, 2017, https:// media.netflix.com/en/press-releases/2017-on-netflix-a-year-in-bingeing.

30. David Lieberman, "EPIX Signs Streaming Deal with Amazon Prime Instant Video," *Deadline*, September 4, 2012, http://deadline.com/2012/09 /amazon-streaming-deal-epix-328715/.

31. Timothy Stenovec, "Amazon Invests Millions in Original TV Shows to Get You to Buy More Diapers," *Huffington Post*, June 1, 2013, www.huffingtonpost .com/2013/05/31/amazon-tv-shows_n_3362531.html.

32. Natalie Jarvey, "YouTube Grows Up: Inside the Plan to Take on Netflix and Hulu," *Hollywood Reporter*, October 4, 2017, www.hollywoodreporter.com /features/youtube-grows-up-inside-plan-take-netflix-hulu-1045443.

33. Lotz, *Television Will Be Revolutionized*, 75–76.

34. Henry Jenkins, *Convergence Culture: Where Old and New Media Collide* (New York: New York University Press, 2006), 3.

35. Jenkins, *Convergence Culture*, 3.

36. Eun-Ju Lee and Edson C. Tandoc, "When News Meets the Audience: How Audience Feedback Online Affects News Production and Consumption," *Human Communication Research* 43, no. 4 (October 2017): 436–49, https://doi.org /10.1111/hcre.12123.

37. Delli Carpini and Williams, "Let Us Infotain You," 160–81.

38. Delli Carpini and Williams, "Let Us Infotain You," 160–81.

39. Jomini Stroud, *Niche News*, 136–37.

40. Jomini Stroud, *Niche News*, 183.

41. Amber Day, *Satire and Dissent: Interventions in Contemporary Political Debate* (Bloomington: Indiana University Press, 2011), 53.

42. Day, *Satire and Dissent*, 42.

43. Janet L. Finn and Maxine Jacobson, "Social Justice," *Encyclopedia of Social Work*, June 2013, http://socialwork.oxfordre.com/view/10.1093/acrefore /9780199975839.001.0001/acrefore-9780199975839-e-364.

44. Arvind Singhal and Everett M. Rogers, *Entertainment-Education: A Communication Strategy for Social Change* (Mahwah, NJ: Lawrence Erlbaum Associates, 1999), xii.

45. John Dewey, *The Public and Its Problems* (Denver: Alan Swallow, 1927). Also quoted in Patricia Aufderheide, *Documentary Film: A Very Short Introduction* (New York: Oxford University Press, 2007).

46. Dara Z. Strolovitch, "Advocacy in Hard Times: Nonprofit Organizations and the Representation of Marginalized Groups in the Wake of Hurricane Katrina and 9 / 11," in *Nonprofits and Advocacy: Engaging Community and Government in an Era of Retrenchment*, ed. Robert J. Pekkanen, Steven Rathgeb Smith, and Yutaka Tsujinaka (Baltimore: Johns Hopkins University Press, 2014), 137–38.

47. Suzanne Staggenborg, *Social Movements*, 2nd ed. (New York: Oxford University Press, 2016), 6–7.

48. Manuel Castells, *Networks of Outrage and Hope: Social Movements in the Internet Age* (Cambridge: Polity Press, 2012).

49. Castells, *Networks of Outrage and Hope*, 221–28.

50. W. Lance Bennett and Alexandra Segerberg, "The Logic of Connective Action: Digital Media and the Personalization of Contentious Politics," *Information, Communication & Society* 15, no. 5 (July 2012): 739–68, https://doi.org/10 .1080/1369118X.2012.670661.

51. Zeynep Tufekci, "'Not This One': Social Movements, the Attention Economy, and Microcelebrity Networked Activism," *American Behavioral Scientist* 57, no. 7 (March 2013): 848–70, https://doi.org/10.1177%2F0002764213479369.

52. Henry Jenkins et al., *By Any Media Necessary: The New Youth Activism* (New York: New York University Press, 2016), 29.

53. Malcolm Heath, "Aristotelian Comedy," *Classical Quarterly* 39, no. 2 (December 1989): 344–54, https://doi.org/10.1017/S0009838800037411.

54. Cyrus Henry Hoy, "Comedy," *Encyclopædia Britannica*, accessed January 25, 2019, www.britannica.com/art/comedy.

55. Hoy, "Comedy."

56. Sigmund Freud, *Jokes and Their Relation to the Unconscious* (Harmondsworth: Penguin, 1976).

57. John C. Meyer, "Humor as a Double-Edged Sword: Four Functions of Humor in Communication," *Communication Theory* 10, no. 3 (August 2000): 310–31, https://doi.org/10.1111/j.1468–2885.2000.tb00194.x.

58. Simon Critchley, *On Humour* (London: Routledge, 2002), 1, https://doi.org/10.4324/9780203870129.

59. Pamela J. Downe, "Laughing When It Hurts: Humor and Violence in the Lives of Costa Rican Prostitutes," *Women's Studies International Forum* 22, no. 1 (January 1999): 63–78, https://doi.org/10.1016/S0277–5395(98)00109–5.

60. Sophie Quirk, *Why Stand-Up Matters: How Comedians Manipulate and Influence* (London: Bloomsbury Methuen Drama, 2015).

61. Matthew R. Meier and Casey R. Schmitt, eds., *Standing Up, Speaking Out: Stand-Up Comedy and the Rhetoric of Social Change* (New York: Routledge, 2017).

62. Rebecca Krefting, *All Joking Aside: American Humor and Its Discontents* (Baltimore: Johns Hopkins University Press, 2014).

63. Quirk, *Why Stand-Up Matters*, 195.

64. John Limon, *Stand-Up Comedy in Theory, or, Abjection in America* (Durham, NC: Duke University Press, 2000).

65. Quirk, *Why Stand-Up Matters*, 14.

66. Quirk, *Why Stand-Up Matters*, 15.

67. Lawrence E. Mintz, "Standup Comedy as Social and Cultural Mediation," *American Quarterly* 37, no. 1 (Spring 1985): 77, https://doi.org/10.2307/2712763.

68. Quirk, *Why Stand-Up Matters*, 38.

69. Quirk, *Why Stand-Up Matters*, 207.

70. Lacy Lowrey, and Valerie Renegar, "'You Gotta Get Chinky with It!': Margaret Cho's Rhetorical Use of Humor to Communicate Cultural Identity," in *Standing Up, Speaking Out: Stand-Up Comedy and the Rhetoric of Social Change*, ed. Matthew R. Meier and Casey R. Schmitt (New York: Routledge, 2017), 3–17.

71. Abbey Morgan, "'No Damn Mammy, Moms!': Rhetorical Re-invention in the Stand-Up Comedy of Jackie 'Moms' Mabley," in Meier and Schmitt, *Standing Up, Speaking Out*, 40–56.

72. Joanne Gilbert, "Laughing at Others: The Rhetoric of Marginalized Comic Identity," in Meier and Schmitt, *Standing Up, Speaking Out*, 57.

73. Amanda Morris, "Teasing the Funny: Native American Stand-Up Comedy in the 21st Century," in Meier and Schmitt, *Standing Up, Speaking Out*, 111–24.

74. Matthew R. Meier and Chad M. Nelson, "'Would You Want Your Sister to Marry One of Them?': Whiteness, Stand-Up, and Lenny Bruce," in Meier and Schmitt, *Standing Up, Speaking Out*, 92–110.

75. Critchley, *On Humour*, 11.

76. Bambi Haggins, *Laughing Mad: The Black Comic Persona in Post-Soul America* (New Brunswick, NJ: Rutgers University Press, 2007), 211.

77. Mary Stuckey, "Wise Fools: The Politics of Comedic Audiences," in Meier and Schmitt, *Standing Up, Speaking Out*, 185

78. Rebecca Krefting, *All Joking Aside: American Humor and Its Discontents* (Baltimore: Johns Hopkins University Press, 2014).

79. Krefting, *All Joking Aside*, 2.

80. Krefting, *All Joking Aside*, 2.

81. Krefting, *All Joking Aside*, 17.

82. Krefting, *All Joking Aside*, 18.

83. Krefting, *All Joking Aside*, 23.

84. Krefting, *All Joking Aside*, 27.

85. Krefting, *All Joking Aside*, 23.

86. Quirk, *Why Stand-Up Matters*, 207.

87. We note that this is not a full recitation of comedy history in the United States. Instead, we seek here to include relevant details to chart the evolution of technology and culture, along with a focus on notable comedy voices who overtly focused on social justice themes in their work, and thus, paved the path to arrive at today's sociocultural portrait of comedy and the intersection with social justice activism in the streaming era.

88. Charles W. Stein, *American Vaudeville as Seen by Its Contemporaries*, 1st ed. (New York: Knopf, 1984), 3–5.

89. Kliph Nesteroff, *The Comedians: Drunks, Thieves, Scoundrels, and the History of American Comedy* (New York: Grove Press, 2015), 14–15.

90. Nesteroff, *Comedians*, 8.

91. Nesteroff, *Comedians*, 25.

92. Nesteroff, *Comedians*, 24.

93. Nesteroff, *Comedians*.

94. Paul Klein, "Why You Watch When You Watch" (first printed in *TV Guide*, July 1971), reprinted in *TV Guide: The First TV Years*, ed. Jay S. Harris (New York: New American Library, 1978), 186–88.

95. Zoglin, *Comedy at the Edge*.

96. Nesteroff, *Comedians*, 76.

97. Zoglin, *Comedy at the Edge*.

98. Zoglin, *Comedy at the Edge*, 5.

99. This streamlined history snapshot does not attempt an exhaustive recounting or a full decade-by-decade chronicling of comedy's intersection with social justice introduced by distinct personalities, but instead provides highlights of important moments from the crucial decades of the 1960s into the 1980s, which both shaped contemporary mediated comedy genres and established audience interest in comedy focused on social issues.

100. Meier and Schmitt, *Standing Up, Speaking Out*, xxii; and Marc Freeman, "'The Smothers Brothers Comedy Hour' at 50: The Rise and Fall of a Groundbreaking Variety Show," *Hollywood Reporter*, November 25, 2017, www.hollywoodreporter .com/live-feed/smothers-brothers-comedy-hour-oral-history-1060153.

101. See Zoglin, *Comedy at the Edge*; Krefting, *All Joking Aside*; and Nesteroff, *Comedians*.

102. Nesteroff, *Comedians*, 162–63.

103. Zoglin, *Comedy at the Edge*, 11.

104. Nesteroff, *Comedians*, 204.

105. Nesteroff, *Comedians*, 241.

106. Haggins, *Laughing Mad*, 3.

107. Haggins, *Laughing Mad*, 3.

108. Nancy Goldman, "Comedy and Democracy: The Role of Comedy in Social Justice," Animating Democracy, November 2013, http://animatingdemocracy .org/resource/comedy-and-democracy-role-humor-social-justice, 6, highlighting work from Zoglin, *Comedy at the Edge*.

109. Zoglin, *Comedy at the Edge*, 183.

110. Zoglin, *Comedy at the Edge*, 181.

111. Zoglin, *Comedy at the Edge*, 184.

112. Robert Bianco, "King Lear Changed American Television," *USA Today*, August 2, 2015, www.usatoday.com/story/life/tv/columnist/2015/08/01/king-lear/31000883/.

113. Philip Galanes, "Norman Lear and Seth McFarlane and Their TV Families," *New York Times*, June 26, 2015, www.nytimes.com/2015/06/28/style /norman-lear-and-seth-macfarlane-and-their-tv-families.html?_r = 0.

114. Associated Press, "Alan Alda, Norman Lear Honoured at International Emmys," *CBC*, November 20, 2012, www.cbc.ca/news/entertainment/alan-alda-norman-lear-honoured-at-international-emmys-1.1209440; and Maureen Ryan, "'Black-ish' Gets a Visit (and More) from Norman Lear," *Variety*, April 27, 2016, https://variety.com/2016/tv/features/black-ish-norman-lear-1201762355/.

115. Editors of Encyclopædia Britannica, "Rowan & Martin's Laugh In," *Encyclopædia Britannica*, accessed January 25, 2019, www.britannica.com/topic /Rowan-and-Martins-Laugh-in.

116. Jeff Nilsson, "They Socked It to Us," *Saturday Evening Post*, January 19, 2013, www.saturdayeveningpost.com/2013/01/rowan-and-martins-laugh-in/.

117. Lorne Michaels, "Lorne Michaels on the 1970s and the Birth of *Saturday Night Live*," *Vanity Fair*, August 31, 2013, www.vanityfair.com/culture/2013/10 /lorne-michaels-on-the-1970s.

118. Zoglin, *Comedy at the Edge*, 53.

119. See Krefting, *All Joking Aside*; Quirk, *Why Stand-Up Matters*; Zoglin, *Comedy at the Edge*; Nesteroff, *Comedians*; and Haggins, *Laughing Mad*.

120. Stacy L. Smith, Marc Choueiti, and Katherine Pieper, *Inclusion or Invisibility? Comprehensive Annenberg Report on Diversity in Entertainment*, University of Southern California Annenberg, February 2017, https://annenberg.usc.edu/sites/default/files/2017/04/07/MDSCI_CARD_Report_FINAL_Exec_Summary.pdf; and Maureen Ryan, "Showrunners for New TV Season Remain Mostly White andMostlyMale,"*Variety*,June8,2016,http://variety.com/2016/tv/features/diversity-television-white-male-showrunners-stats-fox-nbc-abc-cbs-cw-study-1201789639/.

CHAPTER 2

1. Sara Taksler, in-person interview with author, August 30, 2018.

2. John Dunbar and Dave Levinthal, "Understanding Political Committees, 101," Center for Public Integrity, December 12, 2017, https://publicintegrity.org/federal-politics/political-committees-101/.

3. Lawrence Lessig, *Republic, Lost* (New York: Twelve, 2011).

4. *The Colbert Report*, "Trevor Potter & Stephen's Shell Corporation," Comedy Central, September 29, 2011, www.cc.com/video-clips/3yzu4u/the-colbert-report-colbert-super-pac——trevor-potter——stephen-s-shell-corporation.

5. Bruce W. Hardy et al., "Stephen Colbert's Civics Lesson: How Colbert Super PAC Taught Viewers about Campaign Finance," *Mass Communication and Society* 17, no. 3 (2014): 329–53.

6. Paul R. Brewer, Dannagal G. Young, and Michelle Morreale, "The Impact of Real News about 'Fake News': Intertextual Processes and Political Satire," *International Journal of Public Opinion Research* 25, no. 3 (2013): 323–43; Amber Day, "Shifting the Conversation: Colbert's Super PAC and the Measurement of Satirical Efficacy," *International Journal of Communication* 7 (2013): 414–29.

7. Dave Levinthal, "Colbert Donates Super PAC Funds to Charity," *Politico*, December, 12, 2012, www.politico.com/blogs/media/2012/12/colbert-donates-super-pac-funds-to-charity-151964.

8. A similar framework for comedy's influence was previously proposed in Caty Borum Chattoo, "A Funny Matter: Toward a Framework for Understanding the Function of Comedy in Social Change," *HUMOR: The International Journal of Humor Research* (2018), https://doi.org/10.1515/humor-2018–0004; and Caty Borum Chattoo, *The Laughter Effect: The (Serious) Role of Comedy in Social Change* (Washington, DC: Center for Media & Social Impact, May 2017), https://cmsimpact.org/comedy.

9. Rod A. Martin, *The Psychology of Humor: An Integrative Approach* (Burlington, MA: Academic Press, 2007).

10. Willibald Ruch, "Psychology of Humor," in *The Primer of Humor Research*, ed. Victor Raskin (Berlin: Mouton de Gruyter, 2008), 25.

11. Thomas R. Schultz, "A Cognitive-Development Analysis of Humor," in *Humor and Laughter: Theory, Research, and Applications*, ed. Anthony J. Chapman and Hugh C. Foot (New Brunswick, NJ: Transaction, 1996), 11–36.

12. Schultz, "Cognitive-Development Analysis," 13.

13. Jerry M. Suls, "A Two-Stage Model for the Appreciation of Jokes and Cartoons: An Information-Processing Analysis," in *The Psychology of Humor: Theoretical Perspectives and Empirical Issues*, ed. Jeffrey H. Goldstein and Paul E. McGhee (New York: Academic Press, 1972), 81–100.

14. Mary K. Rothbart, "Incongruity, Problem-Solving and Laughter," in Chapman and Foot, *Humor and Laughter*, 37–54; Ruch, "Psychology of Humor."

15. Michael J. Apter, *The Experience of Motivation: The Theory of Psychological Reversals* (London: Academic Press, 1982).

16. Simon Critchley, *On Humour* (London: Routledge, 2011), 4.

17. Jerry H. Goldstein, Jerry M. Suls, and Susan Anthony, "Enjoyment of Specific Types of Humor Content: Motivation or Salience?," in Goldstein and McGhee, *Psychology of Humor*, 159–72.

18. Michael J. Apter and Mitzi Desselles, "Disclosure Humor and Distortion Humor: A Reversal Theory Analysis," *HUMOR: International Journal of Humor Research* 25, no. 4 (2012): 417–35.

19. Apter, *Experience of Motivation*; Apter and Desselles, "Disclosure Humor."

20. Robert S. Wyer, Jr., and James E. Collins II, "A Theory of Humor Elicitation, *Psychological Review* 99, no. 4 (1992): 663–88.

21. Martin, *Psychology of Humor*.

22. Daniel E. Berlyne, "Humor and Its Kin," in Goldstein and McGhee, *Psychology of Humor*, 43–60.

23. Paul E. McGhee, "The Role of Arousal and Hemispheric Lateralization in Humor," in *Handbook of Humor Research*, ed. Paul E. McGhee and Jeffrey H. Goldstein (New York: Springer, 1983), 13–37.

24. Martin, *Psychology of Humor*, 8.

25. Attila Szabo, "The Acute Effects of Humor and Exercise on Mood and Anxiety," *Journal of Leisure Research* 35, no. 2 (2003): 152–62.

26. Martin Eisend, "A Meta-Analysis of Humor in Advertising," *Journal of the Academy of Marketing Science* 37, no. 2 (2009): 191–203; Stephen R. Schmidt, "The Humour Effect: Differential Processing and Privileged Retrieval," *Memory* 10, no. 2 (2002): 127–38.

27. Madelijn Strick et al., "Humor in the Eye Tracker: Attention Capture and Distraction from Context Cues," *Journal of General Psychology: Experimental, Psychological, and Comparative Psychology* 137, no. 1 (2009): 37–48.

28. Schmidt, "Humour Effect."

29. Kieth A. Carlson, "The Impact of Humor on Memory: Is the Humor Effect about Humor?," *HUMOR: International Journal of Humor Research* 24, no. 1 (2011): 21–41.

30. Barbara L. Fredrickson, "What Good Are Positive Emotions?," *Review of General Psychology* 2, no. 3 (1998): 300–319.

31. Robin L. Nabi, Emily Moyer-Gusé, and Sahara Byrne, "All Joking Aside: A Serious Investigation into the Persuasive Effect of Funny Social Issue Messages," *Communication Monographs* 74, no. 1 (2007): 29–54; Robin L. Nabi, "Laughing in the Face of Fear (of Disease Detection): Using Humor to Promote Cancer Self-Examination Behavior," *Health Communication*, 31, no. 7 (2016): 873–83; Heather L. LaMarre and Whitney Walther, "Ability Matters: Testing the Differential Effects of Political News and Late-Night Political Comedy on Cognitive Responses and the Role of Ability in Micro-Level Opinion Formation," *International Journal of Public Opinion Research* 25, no. 3 (2013): 303–22.

32. Matthew A. Baum, *Soft News Goes to War: Public Opinion and American Foreign Policy in the New Media Age* (Princeton, NJ: Princeton University Press, 2005).

33. Baum, *Soft News Goes to War.*

34. Baum, *Soft News Goes to War.* See also Lauren Feldman, Anthony Leiserowitz, and Edward Maibach, "The Science of Satire: *The Daily Show* and *The Colbert Report* as Sources of Public Attention to Science and the Environment," in *The Stewart/Colbert Effect: Essays on the Real Impacts of Fake News*, ed. Amarnath Amarasingam (Jefferson, NC: McFarland, 2011), 25–46.

35. Michael A. Xenos and Amy B. Becker, "Moments of Zen: Effects of *The Daily Show* on Information Seeking and Political Learning," *Political Communication* 26, no. 3 (2009): 317–32; Lauren Feldman and Dannagal G. Young, "Late-Night Comedy as a Gateway to Traditional News: An Analysis of Time Trends in News Attention among Late-Night Comedy Viewers during the 2004 Presidential Primaries," *Political Communication* 25, no. 4 (2008): 401–22.

36. Baum, *Soft News Goes to War.*

37. Xenos and Becker, "Moments of Zen," 331.

38. Dannagal G. Young, "Late-Night Comedy and the Salience of the Candidates' Caricatured Traits in the 2000 Election," *Mass Communication & Society* 9, no. 3 (2006): 339–66.

39. Young, "Late-Night Comedy."

40. Alex T. Williams and Martin Shelton, "What Drove Spike in Public Comments on Net Neutrality? Likely, a Comedian," Pew Research Center, September 5, 2014, www.pewresearch.org/fact-tank/2014/09/05/what-drove-spike-in-public-comments-on-net-neutrality-likely-a-comedian/.

41. Sam Gustin, "John Oliver Just Crashed the FCC's Website over Net Neutrality—Again," *Vice*, May 8, 2017, https://motherboard.vice.com/en_us/article/3dxdqb/john-oliver-just-crashed-the-fccs-website-over-net-neutralityagain.

42. Dannagal G. Young and Russ M. Tisinger, "Dispelling Late-Night Myths: News Consumption among Late-Night Comedy Viewers and the Predictors of Exposure to Various Late-Night Shows," *Harvard International Journal of*

Press/Politics 11, no. 3 (2006), 113–34; Jeffrey Gottfried, Katerina E. Matsa, and Michael Barthel, "As Jon Stewart Steps Down, 5 Facts about *The Daily Show*," Pew Research Center, August 6, 2015, www.pewresearch.org/fact-tank/2015/08 /06/5-facts-daily-show/.

43. Parkin, "Taking Late Night Comedy Seriously;" Heather LaMarre, "When Parody and Reality Collide: Examining the Effects of Colbert's Super PAC Satire on Issue Knowledge and Policy Engagement across Media Formats," *International Journal of Communication* 7 (2013): 394–413.

44. Hardy et al., "Stephen Colbert's Civics Lesson."

45. Amy B. Becker and Leticia Bode, "Satire as a Source for Learning? The Differential Impact of News Versus Satire Exposure on Net Neutrality Knowledge Gain," *Information, Communication & Society* 21, no. 4 (2018): 612–25.

46. Young Mie Kim and John Vishak, "Just Laugh! You Don't Need to Remember: The Effects of Entertainment Media on Political Information Acquisition and Information Processing in Political Judgment," *Journal of Communication* 58, no. 2 (2008): 338–60.

47. Rebecca L. Collins et al., "Entertainment Television as a Healthy Sex Educator: The Impact of Condom-Efficacy Information in an Episode of Friends," *Pediatrics* 112, no. 5 (2003): 1115–21.

48. Robert Hornik, "The Knowledge–Behavior Gap in Public Information Campaigns: A Development Communication View," in *Information Campaigns: Balancing Social Values and Social Change*, ed. Charles T. Salmon (Newbury Park, CA: Sage, 1989), 113–38.

49. Michael X. Delli Carpini and Scott Keeter, *What Americans Know about Politics and Why It Matters* (New Haven, CT: Yale University Press, 1996).

50. Hardy et al., "Stephen Colbert's Civics Lesson."

51. Timothy C. Brock, "Communication Discrepancy and Intent to Persuade as Determinants of Counterargument Production," *Journal of Experimental Social Psychology* 3, no. 3 (1967): 296–309.

52. Charles S. Taber and Milton Lodge, "Motivated Skepticism in the Evaluation of Political Beliefs," *American Journal of Political Science* 50, no. 3 (2006): 755–69.

53. Richard E. Petty and John T. Cacioppo, "The Elaboration Likelihood Model of Persuasion," in *Advances in Experimental Social Psychology*, ed. Leonard Berkowitz (New York: Academic Press, 1986), 123–205.

54. Nabi, Gusé, and Byrne, "All Joking Aside."

55. Dannagal G. Young, "The Privileged Role of the Late-Night Joke: Exploring Humor's Role in Disrupting Argument Scrutiny," *Media Psychology* 11, no. 1 (2008): 119–42.

56. Emily Moyer-Gusé, "Toward a Theory of Entertainment Persuasion: Explaining the Persuasive Effects of Entertainment-Education Messages," *Communication Theory* 18, no. 3 (2008): 407–25.

57. Rod A. Martin et al., "Humor, Coping with Stress, Self-Concept, and Psychological Well-Being," *HUMOR: International Journal of Humor Research* 6, no. 1 (1993): 89–104.

58. Nabi, "Laughing in the Face of Fear"; Paul Skalski et al., "Effects of Humor on Presence and Recall of Persuasive Messages," *Communication Quarterly* 57, no. 2 (2009): 136–53.

59. Paul Slovic, "If I Look at the Mass I Will Never Act: Psychic Numbing and Genocide," *Judgment and Decision Making* 2, no. 2 (2007): 75–95; Ezra Markowitz, Paul Slovic, Daniel Västfjäll, and Sara Hodges, "Compassion Fade and the Challenge of Environmental Conservation," *Judgment and Decision Making* 8, no. 4 (2013): 397–406.

60. Jessica G. Myrick and Mary Beth Oliver, "Laughing and Crying: Mixed Emotions, Compassion, and the Effectiveness of a YouTube PSA about Skin Cancer," *Health Communication* 30, no. 8 (2015): 820–29.

61. Alexander Vilaythong et al., "Humor and Hope: Can Humor Increase Hope?" *HUMOR: International Journal of Humor* 16, no. 1 (2003): 79–89.

62. Lauren Feldman and P. Sol Hart, "Using Political Efficacy Messages to Increase Climate Activism: The Mediating Role of Emotions," *Science Communication* 38, no. 1 (2016): 99–127.

63. Caty Borum Chattoo and Lauren Feldman, "Storytelling for Social Change: Leveraging Documentary and Comedy for Public Engagement in Global Poverty," *Journal of Communication* 67, no. 5 (2017): 678–701; Paul R. Brewer and Jessica McKnight, "Climate as Comedy: The Effects of Satirical Television News on Climate Change Perceptions," *Science Communication* 37, no. 5 (2015): 635–57; Jody C. Baumgartner, Jonathan S. Morris, and Natasha L. Walth, "The Fey Effect: Young Adults, Political Humor, and Perceptions of Sarah Palin in the 2008 Presidential Election Campaign," *Public Opinion Quarterly* 76, no. 1 (2012): 95–104.

64. Michael Conway and Laurette Dubé, "Humor in Persuasion on Threatening Topics: Effectiveness Is a Function of Audience Sex Role Orientation," *Personality and Social Psychology Bulletin* 28, no. 7 (2002): 863–73; Yong Zhang, "Responses to Humorous Advertising: The Moderating Effect of Need for Cognition," *Journal of Advertising* 25, no. 1 (2013): 15–32; LaMarre and Walther, "Ability Matters"; R. Lance Holbert et al., "Adding Nuance to the Study of Political Humor Effects: Experimental Research on Juvenalian Satire Versus Horatian Satire," *American Behavioral Scientist* 55, no. 3 (2011): 187–211.

65. Nabi, Moyer-Gusé, and Byrne, "All Joking Aside"; Nabi, "Laughing in the Face of Fear"; Christofer Skurka et al., "Pathways of Influence in Emotional Appeals: Benefits and Tradeoffs of Using Fear or Humor to Promote Climate Change-Related Intentions and Risk Perceptions," *Journal of Communication* 68, no. 1 (2018): 169–93; Dannagal G. Young et al., "Fact-Checking Effectiveness as a Function of Format and Tone: Evaluating FactCheck.org and FlackCheck.

org," *Journalism & Mass Communication Quarterly* 95, no. 1 (2018): 49–75; Mark Boukes et al., "At Odds: Laughing and Thinking? The Appreciation, Processing, and Persuasiveness of Political Satire," *Journal of Communication* 65, no. 5 (2015): 721–44.

66. Emily Moyer-Gusé, Chad Mahood, and Sarah Brookes, "Entertainment-Education in the Context of Humor: Effects on Safer Sex Intentions and Risk Perceptions," *Health Communication* 26, no. 8 (2011): 765–74; A. Peter McGraw, Julie Schiro, and Philip Fernbach, "Not a Problem: A Downside of Humorous Appeals," *Journal of Marketing Behavior* 1 (2015): 187–208.

67. Nabi, Moyer-Gusé, and Byrne, "All Joking Aside."

68. Lauren Feldman and Caty Borum Chattoo, "Comedy as a Route to Social Change: The Effects of Satire and News on Persuasion about Syrian Refugees," *Mass Communication and Society* 22, no. 2 (2018).

69. Larry Gross, "Out of the Mainstream: Sexual Minorities and the Mass Media," in *Remote Control: Television, Audiences, and Cultural Power,* ed. Ellen Seiter et al. (New York: Routledge, 2013), 130–49.

70. Gross, "Out of the Mainstream," 131.

71. George Gerbner et al., "Growing Up with Television: Cultivation Processes," in *Media Effects: Advances in Theory and Research, 2nd edition,* ed. Jennings Bryant and Dolf Zillmann (Mahwah, NJ: Lawrence Erlbaum Associates, 2002), 43–67.

72. W. James Potter, "Cultivation Theory and Research: A Conceptual Critique," *Human Communication Research* 19, no. 4 (1993): 564–601.

73. Yuki Fujioka, "Television Portrayals and African-American Stereotypes: Examination of Television Effects When Direct Contact Is Lacking," *Journalism & Mass Communication Quarterly* 76, no. 1 (1999): 52–75.

74. Gordon W. Allport, *The Nature of Prejudice* (Oxford: Addison-Wesley, 1954).

75. See, for example, Fujioka, "Television Portrayals and African-American Stereotypes"; Michelle Ortiz and Jake Harwood, "A Social Cognitive Theory Approach to the Effects of Mediated Intergroup Contact on Intergroup Attitudes," *Journal of Broadcasting & Electronic Media* 51, no. 4 (2007): 615–31; Edward Schiappa, Peter B. Gregg, and Dean E. Hewes, "Can One TV Show Make a Difference? *Will & Grace* and the Parasocial Contact Hypothesis," *Journal of Homosexuality* 51, no. 4 (2006): 15–37; Edward Schiappa, Peter B. Gregg, and Dean E. Hewes, "The Parasocial Contact Hypothesis," *Communication Monographs* 72, no. 1 (2005): 92–115.

76. Schiappa, Gregg, and Hewes, "Parasocial Contact Hypothesis."

77. Schiappa, Gregg, and Hewes, "Can One TV Show Make a Difference?"

78. Albert Bandura, "Social Cognitive Theory of Mass Communication," in Bryant and Zillmann, *Media Effects,* 121–53.

79. Moyer-Gusé, "Toward a Theory of Entertainment Persuasion."

80. Ortiz and Harwood, "Social Cognitive Theory Approach."

81. Strick et al., "Those Who Laugh Are Defenseless"; Madelijn Strick et al., "Humor in Advertisements Enhances Product Liking by Mere Association," *Journal of Experimental Psychology: Applied* 15, no. 1 (2009): 35–45.

82. Ortiz and Harwood, "Social Cognitive Theory Approach."

83. Susan M. Smedema, Deborah Ebener, and Virginia Grist-Gordon, "The Impact of Humorous Media on Attitudes toward Persons with Disabilities," *Disability and Rehabilitation* 34, no. 17 (2012): 1431–37.

84. Thomas E. Ford, "Effects of Stereotypical Television Portrayals of African-Americans on Person Perception," *Social Psychology Quarterly* 60, no. 3 (1997): 266–75; Thomas E. Ford et al., "More Than 'Just a Joke': The Prejudice-Releasing Function of Sexist Humor," *Personality and Social Psychology Bulletin* 34, no. 2 (2008): 159–70.

85. Neil Vidmar and Milton Rokeach, "Archie Bunker's Bigotry: A Study in Selective Perception and Exposure," *Journal of Communication* 24, no. 1 (1974): 36–47.

86. Naomi Rockler, "Race, Whiteness, 'Lightness', and Relevance: African American and European American Interpretations of *Jump Start* and *The Boondocks*," *Critical Studies in Media Communication* 19, no. 4 (2002): 398–418.

87. Jane D. Brown and Carol J. Pardun, "Little in Common: Racial and Gender Differences in Adolescents' Television Diets," *Journal of Broadcasting & Electronic Media* 48, no. 2 (2004): 266–78.

88. Joseph N. Cappella, Hyun Suk Kim, and Dolores Albarracín, "Selection and Transmission Processes for Information in the Emerging Media Environment: Psychological Motives and Message Characteristics," *Media Psychology* 18, no. 3 (2015): 396–424.

89. Jonah Berger and Katherine L. Milkman, "What Makes Online Content Viral?," *Journal of Marketing Research* 49, no. 2 (2012): 192–205.

90. Cappella, Kim, and Albarracín, "Selection and Transmission Processes."

91. Berger and Milkman, "What Makes Online Content Viral?"

92. Henry Jenkins, Sam Ford, and Joshua Green, *Spreadable Media: Creating Value and Meaning in a Networked Culture* (New York: NYU Press, 2013); Karine Nahon and Jeff Hemsley, *Going Viral* (Cambridge: Polity Press, 2013).

93. Limor Shifman, "An Anatomy of a YouTube Meme, *New Media & Society* 14, no. 2 (2012): 187–203.

94. Tim Highfield, "Tweeted Joke Lifespans and Appropriated Punch Lines: Practices around Topical Humor on Social Media," *International Journal of Communication* 9 (2015): 2713–34.

95. Shelly Campo et al., "'Wow, That Was Funny' The Value of Exposure and Humor in Fostering Campaign Message Sharing," *Social Marketing Quarterly* 19, no. 2 (2013): 84–96.

96. Julia Daisy Fraustino and Liang Ma, "CDC's Use of Social Media and Humor in a Risk Campaign—'Preparedness 101: Zombie Apocalypse'," *Journal of Applied Communication Research* 43, no. 2 (2015): 222–41.

97. Geoffrey Baym and Chirag Shah, "Circulating Struggle: The On-Line Flow of Environmental Advocacy Clips from *The Daily Show* and *The Colbert Report*," *Information, Communication & Society* 14, no. 7 (2011): 1017–38.

98. Elihu Katz and Paul F. Lazarsfeld, *Personal Influence: The Part Played by People in the Flow of Mass Communications* (New York: Free Press, 1955); Robert M. Bond et al., "A 61-Million-Person Experiment in Social Influence and Political Mobilization," *Nature* 489 (2012): 295–98; Jason Turcotte et al., "News Recommendations from Social Media Opinion Leaders: Effects on Media Trust and Information Seeking," *Journal of Computer-Mediated Communication* 20, no. 5 (2015): 520–35.

99. S. Shyam Sundar, "The MAIN Model: A Heuristic Approach to Understanding Technology Effects on Credibility," in *Digital Media, Youth, and Credibility*, ed. Miriam Metzger and Andrew J. Flanagin (Cambridge, MA: MIT Press, 2008), 72–100.

100. T. Frankin Waddell and S. Shyam Sundar, "#thisshowsucks! The Overpowering Influence of Negative Social Media Comments on Television Viewers," *Journal of Broadcasting & Electronic Media* 61, no. 2 (2017): 393–409.

101. Solomon Messing and Sean J. Westwood, "Selective Exposure in the Age of Social Media: Endorsements Trump Partisan Source Affiliation When Selecting News Online," *Communication Research* 41, no. 8 (2014): 1042–63.

102. James T. Spartz et al., "YouTube, Social Norms and Perceived Salience of Climate Change in the American Mind," *Environmental Communication* 11, no. 1 (2017): 1–16.

103. Dhavan V. Shah, "Conversation Is the Soul of Democracy: Expression Effects, Communication Mediation, and Digital Media," *Communication and the Public* 1, no. 1 (2016): 12–18.

104. Homero Gil de Zúñiga, Logan, Molyneux, and Pei Zheng, "Social Media, Political Expression, and Political Participation: Panel Analysis of Lagged and Concurrent Relationships," *Journal of Communication* 64, no. 4 (2014): 612–34.

105. Francesca Polletta and Jessica Callahan, "Deep Stories, Nostalgia Narratives, and Fake News: Storytelling in the Trump Era," *American Journal of Cultural Sociology* 5, no. 3 (2017): 392–408.

106. Dannagal G. Young, R. Lance Holbert, and Kathleen H. Jamieson, "Successful Practices for the Strategic Use of Political Parody and Satire: Lessons from the P6 Symposium and the 2012 Election Campaign," *American Behavioral Scientist* 58, no. 9 (2014): 1111–30; Martin, *Psychology of Humor*.

107. Mohamed M. Helmy and Sabine Frerichs, "Stripping the Boss: The Powerful Role of Humor in the Egyptian Revolution 2011," *Integrative Psychological and Behavioral Science* 47, no. 4 (2013): 455.

108. Day, "Shifting the Conversation," 415.

109. Day, "Shifting the Conversation," 417.

110. Lucig H. Danielian and Stephen D. Reese, "A Closer Look at Intermedia Influences on Agenda Setting: The Cocaine Issue of 1986," in *Communication Campaigns about Drugs: Government, Media, and the Public*, ed. Pamela J. Shoemaker (New York: Routledge, 1989), 47–66.

111. Stuart N. Soroka, *"Schindler's List's* Intermedia Influence: Exploring the Role of 'Entertainment' in Media Agenda-Setting," *Canadian Journal of Communication*, 25, no. 2 (2000): 211–30.

112. Day, "Shifting the Conversation."

113. Dannagal G. Young, "Political Entertainment and the Press's Construction of Sarah Feylin," *Popular Communication*, 9, no. 4 (2011): 251–65; Nickie Michaud Wild, "Dumb vs. Fake: Representations of Bush and Palin on *Saturday Night Live* and Their Effects on the Journalistic Public Sphere," *Journal of Broadcasting & Electronic Media* 59, no. 3 (2015): 494–508.

114. Allie VanNest, "Measuring the Impact of 'The John Oliver Effect'," *Parse.ly*, September 8, 2015, https://blog.parse.ly/post/2380/measuring-the-impact-of-the-john-oliver-effect/.

115. Wild, "Dumb vs. Fake," 496.

116. Day, "Shifting the Conversation."

117. Young, "Political Entertainment"; Wild, "Dumb vs. Fake."

118. Seth Abramovitch, "Joe Biden Cites 'Will & Grace' in Endorsement of Same-Sex Marriage," *Hollywood Reporter*, May 6, 2012, www.hollywoodreporter.com/live-feed/joe-biden-cites-will-grace-320724–0.

119. Tessa Berenson, "GOP Senator Says Health Care Bill Must Pass 'The Jimmy Kimmel Test'," *Time*, May 5, 2017, http://time.com/4769236/gop-senator-health-care-bill-jimmy-kimmel-test/.

120. Megan R. Hill and R. Lance Holbert, "Jon Stewart and the 9 / 11 First Responders Health Bill," in *Viewpoints on Media Effects: Pseudo-Reality and Its Influence on Media Consumers*, ed. Carol M. Madere (Lanham, MA: Lexington Books, 2017), 1–18; Catherine Kim, "The Battle over Extending the September 11th Victim Compensation Fund, Explained," *Vox*, July 17, 2019, www.vox.com/2019/6/20/18691670/jon-stewart-9–11-september-11th-victim-compensation-fund-explained.

121. Sara Boboltz, "10 Real-Life Wins for John Oliver's Longest Segments on 'Last Week Tonight'," *Huffington Post*, August 12, 2015, www.huffingtonpost.com/entry/john-oliver-real-life-wins_us_55c8e128e4b0f73b20ba171e; Victor Luckerson, "How the 'John Oliver Effect' Is Having a Real-Life Impact," *Time*,

July 10, 2015, http://time.com/3674807/john-oliver-net-neutrality-civil-forfeiture-miss-america/.

122. Rebecca Krefting, *All Joking Aside: American Humor and Its Discontents* (Baltimore, MD: Johns Hopkins University Press, 2014).

123. Majken Jul Sorensen, "Humor as a Serious Strategy of Nonviolent Resistance to Oppression," *Peace & Change* 33, no. 2 (2008): 167–90.

124. Helmy and Frerichs, "Stripping the Boss."

125. *Saturday Night Live*, "Weekend Update: Tina Fey on Protesting after Charlottesville," NBC, August 17, 2017, www.youtube.com/watch?v = iVvpXZxXWZU.

126. Bethonie Butler, "Tina Fey Ate Cake on *SNL* and It Became a Whole Thing," *Washington Post*, August 18, 2017, www.washingtonpost.com/news /arts-and-entertainment/wp/2017/08/18/ tina-fey-ate-cake-on-snl-and-it-became-a-whole-thing/.

127. Amy Zimmerman, "Tina Fey's 'Eat Cake' Strategy after Charlottesville Is Bad Advice," *Daily Beast*, August 18, 2017, www.thedailybeast.com/tina-feys-eat-cake-strategy-after-charlottesville-is-bad-advice; Megan Garber, "'Let Us Eat Cake': The Tina Fey Effect in 2017," *Atlantic*, August 18, 2017, www .theatlantic.com/entertainment/archive/2017/08/let-us-eat-cake/537294/; Butler, "Tina Fey Ate Cake."

128. Garber, "'Let Us Eat Cake'."

129. John C. Meyer, "Humor as a Double-Edged Sword: Four Functions of Humor in Communication," *Communication Theory* 10, no. 3 (2000): 310–31.

130. Vidmar and Rokeach, "Archie Bunker's Bigotry."

131. Roderick P. Hart and E. Johanna Hartelius, "The Political Sins of Jon Stewart," *Critical Studies in Media Communication* 24, no. 3 (2007): 263–72.

132. Young and Tisinger, "Dispelling Late-Night Myths."

133. Paul Lewis, *Cracking Up: American Humor in a Time of Conflict* (Chicago: University of Chicago Press, 2006), 15.

134. Liisi Laineste, "Can the 'Stripping of the Boss' Be More Than a Joke?," *Integrative Psychological and Behavioral Science* 47, no. 4 (2013): 482.

135. Malcolm Gladwell, "The Satire Paradox," *Revisionist History* (podcast), Season 1, Episode 10 (2016), http://revisionisthistory.com/episodes/10-the-satire-paradox.

136. Garber, "'Let Us Eat Cake'."

137. Alexandra King, "Samantha Bee: There Isn't a 'Smug Liberal Problem'," *CNN*, April 30, 2017, www.cnn.com/2017/04/30/politics/samantha-bee-smug-liberal-problem-cnntv/index.html.

138. Butler, "Tina Fey Ate Cake."

139. Meyer, "Humor as a Double-Edged Sword," 323.

140. Meyer, "Humor as a Double-Edged Sword," 327.

141. Meyer, "Humor as a Double-Edged Sword"; Lewis, *Cracking Up*; Martin, *Psychology of Humor*.

CHAPTER 3

1. Negin Farsad, phone interview with authors, August 15, 2018.

2. Timothy Williams and Mitch Smith, "Cleveland Officer Will Not Face Charges in Tamir Rice Shooting Death," *New York Times*, December 28, 2015, www.nytimes.com/2015/12/29/us/tamir-rice-police-shootiing-cleveland.html.

3. Edyer Peralta and Bill Chappell, "Ferguson Jury: No Charges for Officer in Michael Brown's Death," NPR, November 24, 2014, www.npr.org/sections/thetwo-way/2014/11/24/366370100/grand-jury-reaches-decision-in-michael-brown-case.

4. Emily Nussbaum, "In Living Color," *New Yorker*, April 25, 2016, www.newyorker.com/magazine/2016/04/25/blackish-transforms-the-family-sitcom.

5. Bethonie Butler, "How 'Blackish' Tackled Police Brutality While Staying True to Its Roots," *Washington Post*, February 25, 2016, www.washingtonpost.com/news/arts-and-entertainment/wp/2016/02/25/how-blackish-tackled-police-brutality-while-staying-true-to-its-roots/?utm_term = .ed3acb1bb8cc.

6. Butler, "How 'Blackish' Tackled Police Brutality."

7. Ariana Bacle, "Best of 2016: 'Black-ish' Showrunner Kenya Barris Talks Police Brutality Episode," *Entertainment Weekly*, December 9, 2016, http://ew.com/tv/2016/12/09/best-of-2016-blackish-police-brutality-episode/.

8. Bacle, "Best of 2016."

9. Debbie Emery, "'Black-ish' Episode on Police Brutality Hits Hard on Social Media: 'This Scene Was So Real,'" *The Wrap*, February 24, 2016, www.thewrap.com/black-ish-episode-on-police-brutality-hits-hard-on-social-media-this-scene-was-so-real/.

10. Sandra Gonzalez, "How 'Black-ish' Turned 'Hope' into Emmy Honors," *CNN Entertainment*, July 14, 2016, www.cnn.com/2016/07/14/entertainment/blackish/index.html.

11. Kenya Barris, interview by Terry Gross, "Kenya Barris on 'Black-ish' and What Kids Lose When They Grow Up with More," *Fresh Air*, NPR, May 18, 2016, www.npr.org/2016/05/18/478414550/kenya-barris-on-black-ish-and-what-kids-lose-when-they-grow-up-with-more.

12. David Stamps, "The Social Construction of the African American Family on Broadcast Television: A Comparative Analysis of *The Cosby Show* and *Black-ish*," *Howard Journal of Communication* 28, no. 4 (2017): 405–20, https://doi.org/10.1080/10646175.2017.1315688; Sut Jhally and Justin Lewis, *Enlightened Racism: The Cosby Show, Audiences and the Myth of the American Dream* (Boulder, CO: Westover Press, 1992).

13. Amanda D. Lotz, *The Television Will Be Revolutionized, Second Edition* (New York: New York University, 2014), 40–46.

14. "For Us By Us? The Mainstream Appeal of Black Content," Nielsen, last updated February 2, 2017, www.nielsen.com/us/en/insights/news/2017/for-us-by-us-the-mainstream-appeal-of-black-content.html.

15. Nussbaum, "In Living Color."

16. Daniel Holloway, "Kenya Barris Signs $100 Million Netflix Deal," *Variety*, August16,2018,https://variety.com/2018/tv/news/kenya-barris-100-million-netflix-deal-1202907726/.

17. Peter Petro, *Modern Satire: Four Studies* (Berlin: Mouton, 1982); Avner Ziv, *Personality and Sense of Humor* (New York: Springer, 1984).

18. Jonathan Gray, Jeffrey P. Jones, and Ethan Thompson, "The State of Satire, the Satire of the State," in *Satire TV: Politics and Comedy in the Post-Network Era*, ed. Jonathan Gray, Jeffrey P. Jones, and Ethan Thompson (New York: New York University Press, 2009), 12.

19. Dustin Griffin, *Satire: A Critical Reintroduction* (Lexington: University of Kentucky Press, 1994).

20. Geoffrey Baym, *"The Daily Show*: Discursive Integration and the Reinvention of Political Journalism," *Political Communication* 22, no. 3 (2005): 259–76, https://doi.org/10.1080/10584600591006492.

21. Pew Research Center, *Cable and Internet Loom Large in Fragmented Political News Universe* (Washington, DC: Pew Research Center, 2004), www.people-press.org/2004/01/11/cable-and-internet-loom-large-in-fragmented-political-news-universe/.

22. Lynn Schofield Clark and Regina Marchi, *Young People and the Future of News* (Cambridge: Cambridge University Press, 2017).

23. James Poniewozik, "Jon Stewart, the Fake Newsman Who Made a Real Difference," *Time*, August 4, 2015, http://time.com/3704321/jon-stewart-daily-show-fake-news/; John Oliver, interview by Kelly McEvers, "Is John Oliver's Show Journalism? He Says the Answer Is Simple: 'No,'" *All Things Considered*, NPR, February 12, 2016, www.npr.org/2016/02/12/466569047/is-john-olivers-show-journalism-he-says-the-answer-is-simple-no.

24. Baym, *"Daily Show."*

25. Lance W. Bennett, "Relief in Hard Times: A Defense of Jon Stewart's Comedy in the Age of Cynicism," *Critical Studies in Media Communication* 24, no. 3 (2007): 278–83, https://doi.org/10.1080/07393180701521072.

26. "Televangelists: Last Week Tonight with John Oliver (HBO)," YouTube video, 20:05, posted by LastWeekTonight, August 16, 2015, www.youtube.com/watch?v = 7y1xJAVZxXg.

27. "Government Surveillance: Last Week Tonight with John Oliver (HBO)," YouTube video, 33:13, posted by LastWeekTonight, April 5, 2015, www.youtube.com/watch?v = XEVlyP4_11M.

28. "Miss America Pageant: Last Week Tonight with John Oliver (HBO)," YouTube video, 15:24, posted by LastWeekTonight, September 21, 2014, www.youtube.com/watch?v = oDPCmmZifE8&t = 759s.

29. "Sex Education: Last Week Tonight with John Oliver (HBO)," YouTube video, 21:04, posted by LastWeekTonight, August 9, 2015, www.youtube.com /watch?v = L0jQz6jqQS0.

30. Allie VanNest, "Measuring the Impact of 'The John Oliver Effect,'" *Parse. ly*, September 8, 2015, https://blog.parse.ly/post/2380/measuring-the-impact-of-the-john-oliver-effect/.

31. Leticia Bode and Amy B. Becker, "Go Fix It: Comedy as an Agent of Political Activation," *Social Science Quarterly* 99, no. 5 (2018): 1572–84, https://doi .org/10.1111/ssqu.12521.

32. Alex T. Williams and Martin Shelton, "What Drove Spike in Public Comments on Net Neutrality? Likely, a Comedian," Pew Research Center, last updated September 5, 2014, www.pewresearch.org/fact-tank/2014/09/05 /what-drove-spike-in-public-comments-on-net-neutrality-likely-a-comedian/.

33. Ben Brody, "The Story behind the Clip That Launched 45,000 Comments on the FCC's Website," *Bloomberg*, February 26, 2015, www.bloomberg.com /news/articles/2015-02-26/how-john-oliver-transformed-the-net-neutrality-debate-once-and-for-all.

34. Dannagal G. Young, *Irony and Outrage: The Polarized Landscape of Rage, Fear, and Laughter in the U.S.* (New York: Oxford University Press, forthcoming).

35. Amy Mitchell et al., *Political Polarization & Media Habits* (Washington, DC: Pew Research Center, 2014), www.journalism.org/2014/10/21/political-polarization-media-habits/.

36. Amal Ibrahim and Nahed Eltantawy, "Egypt's Jon Stewart: Humorous Political Satire and Serious Culture Jamming," *International Journal of Communication* 11 (2017): 19.

37. Pamala S. Deane, "Sitcom," in *St. James Encyclopedia of Popular Culture, Volume 4*, ed. Tom Pendergast and Sara Pendergast (Detroit: St. James Press, 2000), 418–19.

38. Edward Schiappa, Peter B. Gregg, and Dean E. Hewes, "Can One TV Show Make a Difference? *Will & Grace* and the Parasocial Contact Hypothesis," *Journal of Homosexuality* 51, no. 4 (2006): 15–37, https://doi.org/10.1300 /J082v51n04_02; Edward Schiappa, Peter B. Gregg, and Dean Hewes, "The Parasocial Contact Hypothesis," *Communication Monographs* 72, no. 1 (2005): 92–115, https://doi.org/10.1080/0363775052000342544; Michelle Ortiz and Jake Harwood, "A Social Cognitive Theory Approach to the Effect of Mediated Intergroup Contact on Intergroup Attitudes," *Journal of Broadcasting & ElectronicMedia* 51, no. 4 (2007): 615–31, https://doi.org/10.1080/08838150701626487; Emily Moyer-Gusé, "Toward a Theory of Entertainment Persuasion: Explaining

the Persuasive Effects of Entertainment-Education Messages," *Communication Theory* 18, no. 3 (2008): 407–25, https://doi.org/10.1111/j.1468-2885.2008.00328.x; Jonathan Cohen, "Defining Identification: A Theoretical Look at the Identification of Audiences with Media Characters," *Mass Communication and Society* 4, no. 3 (2001): 245–64, https://doi.org/10.1207/S15327825MCS0403_01.

39. Melanie C. Green and Timothy C. Brock, "The Role of Transportation in the Persuasiveness of Public Narrative," *Journal of Personality and Social Psychology* 79, no. 5 (2009): 701–21, https://doi.org/10.1037/0022-3514.79.5.701.

40. Matthew Pittman and Kim Sheehan, "Sprinting a Media Marathon: Uses and Gratification of Binge-Watching Television through Netflix," *First Monday* 20, no. 10 (2015); Maeva Flayelle, Pierre Maurage, and Joël Billeux, "Toward a Qualitative Understanding of Binge-Watching Behavior: A Focus Group Approach," *Journal of Behavioral Addictions* 6, no. 4 (2017): 457–71, https://doi.org/10.1556/2006.6.2017.060; Hongjin Shim and Ki Joon Kim, "An Exploration of the Motivations for Binge-Watching and the Role of Individual Differences," *Computers in Human Behavior* 82 (2018): 94–100, https://doi.org/10.1016/j.chb.2017.12.032; Yoon Hi Sung, Eun Yeon Kang, and Wei-Na Lee, "Why Do We Indulge? Exploring Motivation for Binge Watching," *Journal of Broadcasting & Electronic Media* 62, no. 3 (2018): 408–26, https://doi.org/10.1080/08838151.2018.1451851.

41. Emily Moyer-Gusé and Robin L. Nabi, "Explaining the Effects of Narrative in an Entertainment Television Program: Overcoming Resistance to Persuasion," *Human Communication Research* 36, no. 1 (2010): 26–52, https://doi.org/10.1111/j.1468-2958.2009.01367.x; Moyer-Gusé, "Toward a Theory of Entertainment Persuasion."

42. George Gerbner et al., "Growing Up with Television: Cultivation Process," in *Media Effects: Advances in Theory and Research, Volume 2*, ed. Jennings Bryant and Dolf Zillman (Mahwah, NJ: L. Erlbaum Associates, 2002), 43–67.

43. Riva Tukachinsky, Dana Mastro, and Moran Yarchi, "The Effect of Prime Time Television Ethnic/Racial Stereotypes on Latino and Black Americans: A Longitudinal National Level Study," *Journalism of Broadcasting & Electronic Media* 61, no. 3 (2017): 538–56, https://doi.org/10.1080/08838151.2017.1344669.

44. Deane, "Sitcom," 419.

45. Emily Nussbaum, "The Great Divide," *New Yorker*, April 7, 2014, www.newyorker.com/magazine/2014/04/07/the-great-divide-emily-nussbaum.

46. Lotz, *Television Will Be Revolutionized*.

47. Amanda D. Lotz, *We Now Disrupt This Broadcast: How Cable Transformed Television and the Internet Revolutionized It All* (Cambridge, MA: MIT Press, 2018).

48. Joe Otterson, "487 Scripted Series Aired in 2017, FX Chief John Landgraf Says," *Variety*, January 3, 2018, https://variety.com/2018/tv/news/2017-scripted-tv-series-fx-john-landgraf-1202653856/.

49. Darnell Hunt et al., *Hollywood Diversity Report 2018: Five Years of Progress and Missed Opportunities* (Los Angeles: UCLA College of Social Sciences Institute for Research on Labor and Employment, 2018), https://socialsciences.ucla.edu/hollywood-diversity-report-2018/.

50. GLAAD, *Where We Are on TV '17—'18* (New York: GLAAD Media Institute, 2017), www.glaad.org/whereweareontv17; Hunt et al., *Hollywood Diversity Report 2018*; Stacy L. Smith, March Choueiti, and Katherine Pieper, *Inclusion or Invisibility? Comprehensive Annenberg Report on Diversity in Entertainment* (Los Angeles: Institute for Diversity and Empowerment at Annenberg, 2016), https://annenberg.usc.edu/sites/default/files/CARDReport_FINAL.pdf.

51. Hunt et al., *Hollywood Diversity Report 2018*.

52. Amanda D. Lotz, "*Fresh Off the Boat* and the Rise of Niche TV," *The Conversation*, March 6, 2015, https://theconversation.com/fresh-off-the-boat-and-the-rise-of-niche-tv-37451.

53. Kevin Fallon, "*Modern Family*'s Big, Gay (and Important) Wedding," *Daily Beast*, May 22, 2014, www.thedailybeast.com/modern-familys-big-gay-and-important-wedding.

54. Alyssa Rosenberg, "'Modern Family' and Gay Marriage: It's Complicated," *Atlantic*, October 12, 2010, www.theatlantic.com/entertainment/archive/2010/10/modern-family-and-gay-marriage-its-complicated/64397/; Yoonj Kim, "When Race Is the Punchline on Prime Time," *Slate*, May 25, 2018, https://slate.com/culture/2018/05/american-sitcoms-are-dealing-more-openly-with-race-but-not-always-getting-it-right.html.

55. Tad Friend, "Donald Glover Can't Save You," *New Yorker*, March 5, 2018, www.newyorker.com/magazine/2018/03/05/donald-glover-cant-save-you.

56. GLAAD, *Where We Are on TV*.

57. Lisa Moore, "*The Marvelous Mrs. Maisel* Might Be Set in the 1960s but the Story Is Still True for Female Comedians Today," *The Conversation*, December 14, 2017, https://theconversation.com/the-marvelous-mrs-maisel-might-be-set-in-the-1960s-but-the-story-is-still-true-for-female-comedians-today-87282.

58. Smith, Choueiti, and Pieper, *Inclusion or Invisibility?*

59. Aymar Jean Christian, *Open TV: Innovation beyond Hollywood and the Rise of Web Television* (New York: New York University Press, 2018), 108.

60. Oliver Double, *Getting the Joke: The Inner Workings of Stand-Up Comedy, Second Edition* (London: Bloomsbury, 2014).

61. Ian Brodie, "Stand-Up Comedy as a Genre of Intimacy," *Ethnologies* 30, no. 2 (2008): 153, https://doi.org/10.7202/019950ar.

62. Brodie, "Stand-Up Comedy," 154.

63. Bambi Haggins, *Laughing Mad: The Black Comic Persona in Post-Soul America* (New Brunswick, NJ: Rutgers University Press, 2007), 78.

64. Ian Brodie, *A Vulgar Art: A New Approach to Stand-Up Comedy* (Jackson: University Press of Mississippi, 2014), 41.

65. Haggins, *Laughing Mad*.

66. Haggins, *Laughing Mad*, 60.

67. Jaclyn Michael, "American Muslims Stand Up and Speak Out: Trajectories of Humor in Muslim American Stand-Up Comedy," *Contemporary Islam* 7, no. 2 (2013): 129–53, https://doi.org/10.1007/s11562-011-0183-6.

68. Michael, "American Muslims Stand Up," 149.

69. Kim Reid, Edy Hammond Stoughton, and Robin M. Smith, "The Humorous Construction of Disability: 'Stand-Up' Comedians in the United States," *Disability & Society* 21, no. 6 (2006): 635, https://doi.org/10.1080/09687590600918354.

70. Jean-Philippe Laurenceau, Paula R. Pietromonaco, and Lisa Feldman Barrett, "Intimacy as an Interpersonal Process: The Importance of Self-Disclosure, Partner Disclosure, and Perceived Partner Responsiveness in Interpersonal Exchanges," *Journal of Personality and Social Psychology* 74, no. 5 (1998): 1238–51; Harry T. Reis and Phillip Shaver, "Intimacy as an Interpersonal Process," in *Handbook of Personal Relationships: Theory, Research and Intervention*, ed. Steve Duck et al. (Oxford: John Wiley & Sons, 1988), 367–89.

71. Schiappa, Gregg, and Hewes, "Can One TV Show Make a Difference?;" Patrick Corrigan et al., "Does Humor Influence the Stigma of Mental Illness?" *Journal of Nervous and Mental Disease* 202, no. 5 (2014): 397–401, https://doi.org/10.1097/NMD.0000000000000138.

72. Jesse David Fox, "Netflix Will Release a Series of 15-Minute Stand-Up Specials in 2018," *Vulture*, January 22, 2018, www.vulture.com/2018/01/netflix-15-minute-stand-up-specials-exclusive.html; Jeffrey Fleishman, "Netflix Is Expanding Its Stand-Up Comedy Reach with Specials Focusing on Emerging and Global Voices," *LA Times*, July 26, 2018, www.latimes.com/entertainment/tv/la-ca-netflix-standup-comedy-20180726-story.html#.

73. Kliph Nesteroff, *The Comedians: Drunks, Thieves, Scoundrels and the History of American Comedy* (New York: Grove Press, 2015), 241.

74. Larry Rohter, "Second City Looks Back in Laughter," *New York Times*, December 15, 2009, www.nytimes.com/2009/12/16/arts/16second.html?action = click&contentCollection = Book%20Review&module = RelatedCoverage&region = Marginalia&pgtype = article.

75. Sam Wasson, *Improv Nation: How We Made a Great American Art* (New York: Houghton Mifflin Harcourt, 2017).

76. Wasson, *Improv Nation*.

77. Joanna Robinson, "S. N. L. Struggles to Find Its Identify in the Era of Trump," *Vanity Fair*, May 17, 2018, www.vanityfair.com/hollywood/2018/05/saturday-night-live-season-review-trump-fatigue-ratings.

78. Jeffrey P. Jones, "Politics and the Brand: *Saturday Night Live*'s Campaign Season Humor," in Saturday Night Live *and American TV*, ed. Nick Marx, Matt Sienkiewicz, and Ron Becker (Bloomington: Indiana University Press, 2013), 77–91.

79. Jones, "Politics and the Brand."

80. Racquel Gates, "Bringing the Black: Eddie Murphy and African American Humor on *Saturday Night Live*," in Marx et al., Saturday Night Live *and American TV*, 151–72.

81. Jody C. Baumgartner, Jonathan S. Morris, and Natasha L. Walth, "The Fey Effect: Young Adults, Politics Humor, and Perception of Sarah Palin in the 2008 Presidential Election Campaign," *Public Opinion Quarterly* 76, no. 1 (2012): 95–104, https://doi.org/10.2307/41345969.

82. Amy B. Becker, "Trump Trumps Baldwin? How Trump's Tweets Transform *SNL* into Trump's Strategic Advantage," *Journal of Political Marketing* (2017): 1–19, https://doi.org/10.1080/15377857.2017.1411860.

83. "About Funny or Die," Funny or Die, www.funnyordie.com/.

84. KC Ifeanyi, "How *Funny or Die* Plans to Conquer TV Comedy," *Fast Comedy*, November 27, 2017, www.fastcompany.com/40498675/how-funny-or-die-plans-to-conquer-tv-comedy.

85. Brian Raftery, "*Funny or Die* at 10: An Oral History of a Comedy Juggernaut," *Wired*, April 2, 2017, www.wired.com/2017/04/an-oral-history-of-funny-or-die/.

86. Aaron Blake, "'Between Two Ferns' Video Leads to 40 Percent More Visits to HealthCare.gov," *Washington Post*, March 12, 2014, www.washingtonpost .com/news/post-politics/wp/2014/03/12/between-two-ferns-video-leads-to-40-percent-more-visits-to-healthcare-gov/.

87. Brad Jenkins, phone interview with authors, September 7, 2018.

88. Bill Nichols, *Introduction to Documentary, Second Edition* (Bloomington: Indiana University Press, 2010), 6.

89. Patricia Aufderheide, *Documentary: A Very Short Introduction* (New York: Oxford University Press, 2007).

90. Caty Borum Chattoo, "Documentary and Communication," in *Oxford Bibliographies in Communication*, ed. Patricia Moy (New York: Oxford University Press, 2018), https://doi.org/10.1093/OBO/9780199756841–0207.

91. Borum Chattoo, "Documentary and Communication."

92. Heather L. LaMarre and Kristen D. Landreville, "When Is Fiction as Good as Fact? Comparing the Influence of Documentary and Historical Reenactment Films on Engagement, Affect, Issue Interest, and Learning," *Mass Communication and Society* 12, no. 4 (2009): 537–55, https://doi.org/10.1080 /15205430903237915.

93. Caty Borum Chattoo and Lauren Feldman, "Storytelling for Social Change: Leveraging Documentary and Comedy for Public Engagement in Global Poverty," *Journal of Communication* 67, no. 5 (2017): 678–701, https://doi.org/10.1111 /jcom.12318; LaMarre and Landreville, "When Is Fiction as Good as Fact?"

94. John Corner, "Documentary: The Transformation of a Social Aesthetic," in *Television and Common Knowledge*, ed. Jostein Gripsrud (London: Routledge, 1999), 182.

95. "Documentary," Box Office Mojo, www.boxofficemojo.com/genres /chart/?id = documentary.htm.

96. Amber Day, *Satire and Dissent: Interventions in Contemporary Political Debate* (Bloomington: Indiana University Press, 2011), 99.

97. John Corner, *The Art of Record: A Critical Introduction to Documentary* (Manchester: Manchester University Press, 1996); Day, *Satire and Dissent*; Steven Mintz, "Michael Moore and the Re-Birth of the Documentary," *Film & History: An Interdisciplinary Journal of Film and Television Studies* 35, no. 2 (2005), 10–11, https://doi.org/10.1353/flm.2005.0049.

98. Caty Borum Chattoo and Will Jenkins, *Movies & Grassroots Community Engagement: Documentary Films State and Local Public Policy in the United States* (Washington, DC: Center for Media and Social Impact, 2018), 13.

99. Ellen McGirt, "CNN's 'United Shades of American with W. Kamau Bell' Is Back and Ready to Listen," *Fortune*, last updated April 29, 2018, http://fortune.com/2018/04/29/cnns-united-shades-of-america-with-w-kamau-bell-is-back-and-ready-to-listen/.

CHAPTER 4

1. George Carlin, *Jammin' in New York* (HBO Comedy Special), 1992; full transcript from https://scrapsfromtheloft.com/2017/04/06/george-carlin-jamming-new-york-1992-full-transcript/.

2. "Old People Don't Care about Climate Change," Facebook video, posted by Funny or Die, April 22, 2016, www.facebook.com/funnyordie/videos /10154082817033851/.

3. Alicia Prevost, phone interview with authors, July 25, 2018.

4. Cary Funk, Brian Kennedy, Meg Hefferon, and Mark Strauss, "Majorities See Government Efforts to Protect the Environment as Insufficient," Pew Research Center, May 14, 2018, www.pewinternet.org/2018/05/14/majorities-see-government-efforts-to-protect-the-environment-as-insufficient/. For a different perspective, see Shruti Kuppa, *Do Millenials See Climate Change as More Than Just a Meme?*, Johns Hopkins University, Energy Policy and Climate Program, 2018, www.climatechangecommunication.org/wp-content/uploads/2018 /05/Do-Millennials-See-Climate-Change-as-More-Than-Just-a-Meme.pdf.

5. "Voter Turnout Demographics," United States Elections Project, accessed October 30, 2018, www.electproject.org/home/voter-turnout/demographics.

6. David Ockwell, Lorraine Whitmarsh, and Saffron O'Neill, "Reorienting Climate Change communication for Effective Mitigation: Forcing People to be Green or Fostering Grass-Roots Engagement?," *Science Communication* 30, no. 3 (2009): 305–27.

7. T. F. Stocker et al., "IPCC, 2013: Summary for Policymakers," in *Climate Change 2013: The Physical Science Basis. Contribution of Working Group I to the Fifth Assessment Report of the Intergovernmental Panel on Climate Change* (Cambridge: Cambridge University Press, 2013), www.ipcc.ch/pdf/assessment-report/ar5/wg1/WG1AR5_SPM_FINAL.pdf; Jerry M. Melillo, Terese Richmond, and Gary W. Yohe, eds., *Climate Change Impacts in the United States: The Third National Climate Assessment*, U. S. Global Change Research Program, 2014, https://nca2014.globalchange.gov/report.

8. "Global Temperature," *NASA Global Climate Change: Vital Signs of the Planet*, accessed October 30, 2018, https://climate.nasa.gov/vital-signs/global-temperature/; "Climate at a Glance: Global Time Series," NOAA National Centers for Environmental Information, October 2018, www.ncdc.noaa.gov/cag/.

9. Myles Allen et al., *IPCC Special Report on Global Warming of 1.5°C, Summary for Policymakers*, Intergovernmental Panel on Climate Change, October 6, 2018, http://report.ipcc.ch/sr15/pdf/sr15_spm_final.pdf.

10. National Academies of Sciences, Engineering, and Medicine, *Attribution of Extreme Weather Events in the Context of Climate Change* (Washington, DC: National Academies Press, 2016), https://doi.org/10.17226/21852; Stephanie C. Herrig et al., eds., "Explaining Extreme Events of 2016 from a Climate Perspective," *Special Supplement to the Bulletin of the American Meteorological Society* 99, no. 1 (2018), S1–S157; James P. Kossin, "A Global Slowdown of Tropical-Cyclone Translation Speed," *Nature* 558, no. 7708 (2018): 104–7; Geert Jan van Oldenborgh et al., "Attribution of Extreme Rainfall from Hurricane Harvey, August 2017," *Environmental Research Letters* 12, no. 12 (2017): 124009.

11. Allison Crimmins et al., "Executive Summary," in *The Impacts of Climate Change on Human Health in the United States: A Scientific Assessment* (Washington, DC: U. S. Global Change Research Program, 2016), 1–24, http://dx.doi.org/10.7930/J0OP0WXS.

12. Robin Mearns and Andrew Norton, "Equity and Vulnerability in a Warming World: Introduction and Overview," in *The Social Dimensions of Climate Change: Equity and Vulnerability in a Warming World*, ed. Robin Mearns and Andrew Norton (Washington, DC: World Bank, 2009), 7.

13. Mearns and Norton, "Equity and Vulnerability," 7.

14. Janet L. Gamble et al., "Ch. 9: Populations of Concern," in *The Impacts of Climate Change on Human Health* (Washington, DC: U. S. Global Change Research Program, 2016), 247–86, http://dx.doi.org/10.7930/J0Q81B0T; Barry S. Levy and Jonathan A. Patz, "Climate Change, Human Rights, and Social Justice," *Annals of Global Health* 81, no. 3 (2015): 310–22.

15. Justin Gillis and Nadja Popovich, "The U.S. Is the Biggest Carbon Polluter in History. It Just Walked Away from the Paris Climate Deal," *New York Times*, June 1, 2107, www.nytimes.com/interactive/2017/06/01/climate/us-biggest-carbon-polluter-in-history-will-it-walk-away-from-the-paris-climate-deal.html.

16. Brady Dennis, Michael Laris, and Juliet Eilperin, "Trump Administration to Freeze Fuel-Efficiency Requirements in Move Likely to Spur Legal Battle with States," *Washington Post*, August 2, 2018, www.washingtonpost.com/national /health-science/2018/08/01/90c818ac-9125-11e8-8322-b5482bf5e0f5_story.html.

17. Pew Research Center, "Public's 2019 Priorities: Economy, Health Care, Education and Security All Near Top of List," January 24, 2019, www.people-press.org/2019/01/24/publics-2019-priorities-economy-health-care-education-and-security-all-near-top-of-list/.

18. Anthony Leiserowitz et al., *Climate Change in the American Mind: December 2018*, Yale University and George Mason University (New Haven, CT: Yale Program on Climate Change Communication, 2018), http://climatecommunication .yale.edu/publications/climate-change-in-the-american-mind-december-2018/.

19. Cary Funk and Brian Kennedy, "The Politics of Climate," Pew Research Center, October 4, 2016, www.pewinternet.org/2016/10/04/public-views-on-climate-change-and-climate-scientists/.

20. Leiserowitz et al., *Climate Change in the American Mind*.

21. Anthony Leiserowitz et al., *Politics and Global Warming, December 2018*, Yale University and George Mason University (New Haven, CT: Yale Program on Climate Change Communication, 2018), http://climatecommunication.yale.edu /publications/politics-global-warming-december-2018/.

22. Alexa Spence, Wouter Poortinga, and Nick Pidgeon, "The Psychological Distance of Climate Change," *Risk Analysis: An International Journal* 32, no. 6 (2012): 957–72.

23. Richard J. Lazarus, "Super Wicked Problems and Climate Change: Restraining the Present to Liberate the Future," *Cornell Law Review* 94 (2008): 1153–234; Kelly Levin et al., "Overcoming the Tragedy of Super Wicked Problems: Constraining Our Future Selves to Ameliorate Global Climate Change," *Policy Sciences* 45, no. 2 (2012): 123–52.

24. Deborah L. Guber, "Partisan Cueing and Polarization in Public Opinion about Climate Change," in *The Oxford Research Encyclopedia of Climate Science*, ed. Matthew Nisbet (New York: Oxford University Press, 2017), https://doi .org/10.1093/acrefore/9780190228620.013.306.

25. Riley E. Dunlap and Aaron M. McCright, "Organized Climate Change Denial," in *The Oxford Handbook of Climate Change and Society*, ed. John S. Dryzek, Richard R. Norgaard, and David Scholsberg, 144–60 (Oxford: Oxford University Press, 2011).

26. Leiserowitz et al., *Politics and Global Warming*.

27. Charles S. Taber and Milton Lodge, "Motivated Skepticism in the Evaluation of Political Beliefs," *American Journal of Political Science* 50, no. 3 (2006): 755–69.

28. P. Sol Hart and Erik C. Nisbet, "Boomerang Effects in Science Communication: How Motivated Reasoning and Identity Cues Amplify Opinion

Polarization about Climate Mitigation Policies," *Communication Research* 39, no. 6 (2012): 701–23.

29. Lauren Feldman, "The Effects of TV and Cable News Viewing on Climate Change Opinion, Knowledge, and Behavior," in *Oxford Encyclopedia of Climate Change Communication*, ed. Matthew C. Nisbet (New York: Oxford University Press, 2018).

30. Maxwell T. Boykoff and Jules M. Boykoff, "Balance as Bias: Global Warming and the US Prestige Press," *Global Environmental Change* 14, no. 2 (2004): 125–36; Maxwell T. Boykoff, "Lost in Translation? United States Television News Coverage of Anthropogenic Climate Change, 1995–2004," *Climatic Change* 86, nos. 1–2 (2008): 1–11.

31. Maxwell T. Boykoff, "Flogging a Dead Norm? Newspaper Coverage of Anthropogenic Climate Change in the United States and United Kingdom from 2003 to 2006," *Area* 39, no. 4 (2007): 470–81.

32. Lauren Feldman, P. Sol Hart, and Tijana Milosevic, "Polarizing News? Representations of Threat and Efficacy in Leading US Newspapers' Coverage of Climate Change," *Public Understanding of Science* 26, no. 4 (2017): 481–97.

33. Frederick W. Mayer, *Stories of Climate Change: Competing Narratives, the Media, and U.S. Public Opinion 2001–2010*, Joan Shorenstein Center on the Press, Politics, and Public Policy Discussion Paper Series #D-72 (Boston, MA: Harvard University, 2012), http://shorensteincenter.org/wp-content/uploads /2012/03/d72_mayer.pdf.

34. Feldman, Hart, and Milosevic, "Polarizing News?"

35. "Letters to the Editor—Comments: Week of July 24, 2017," *New York Magazine*, July 23, 2017, http://nymag.com/nymag/letters/comments-2017-07-24/.

36. Michael Svoboda, "Cli-Fi on the Screen(s): Patterns in the Representations of Climate Change in Fictional Films," *Wiley Interdisciplinary Reviews: Climate Change* 7, no. 1 (2016): 43–64.

37. Saffron O'Neill and Sophie Nicholson-Cole, "Fear Won't Do It: Promoting Positive Engagement with Climate Change through Visual and Iconic Representations," *Science Communication* 30, no. 3 (2009): 355–79.

38. Lauren Feldman and P. Sol Hart, "Using Political Efficacy Messages to Increase Climate Activism: The Mediating Role of Emotions," *Science Communication* 38, no. 1 (2016), 99–127; Lauren Feldman and P. Sol Hart, "Is There Any Hope? How Climate Change News Imagery and Text Influence Audience Emotions and Support for Climate Mitigation Policies," *Risk Analysis* 38, no. 3 (2018): 585–602.

39. Leiserowitz et al., *Climate Change in the American Mind*.

40. Connie Roser-Renouf et al., "Engaging Diverse Audiences with Climate Change: Message Strategies for Global Warming's Six Americas," in *The Routledge Handbook of Environment and Communication*, ed. Robert Cox and Anders Hansen (New York: Oxford University Press, 2015), 368–86.

41. Lauren Feldman, Anthony Leiserowitz, and Edward Maibach, "The Science of Satire: *The Daily Show* and *The Colbert Report* as Sources of Public Attention to Science and the Environment," in *The Stewart/Colbert Effect: Essays on the Real Impacts of Fake News*, ed. Amar Amarasingam (Jefferson, NC: McFarland, 2011), 25–46; Ashley A. Anderson and Amy B. Becker, "Not Just Funny after All: Sarcasm as a Catalyst for Public Engagement with Climate Change," *Science Communication* 40, no. 4 (2018): 524–40; Paul R. Brewer and Jessica McKnight, "A Statistically Representative Climate Change Debate: Satirical Television News, Scientific Consensus, and Public Perceptions of Global Warming," *Atlantic Journal of Communication* 25, no. 3 (2017): 166–80.

42. Leiserowitz et al., *Climate Change in the American Mind*.

43. Roser-Renouf et al., "Engaging Diverse Audiences with Climate Change."

44. Christofer Skurka et al., "Pathways of Influence in Emotional Appeals: Benefits and Tradeoffs of Using Fear or Humor to Promote Climate Change–Related Intentions and Risk Perceptions," *Journal of Communication* 68, no. 1 (2018): 169–93.

45. Nadia Y. Bashir et al., "The Ironic Impact of Activists: Negative Stereotypes Reduce Social Change Influence," *European Journal of Social Psychology* 43, no. 7 (2013): 614–26.

46. Lauren Feldman, "Cloudy with a Chance of Heat Balls: The Portrayal of Global Warming on *The Daily Show* and *The Colbert Report*," *International Journal of Communication* 7 (2013): 430–51.

47. Pew Research Center, "Journalism, Satire or Just Laughs? 'The Daily Show with Jon Stewart', Examined," Project for Excellence in Journalism, May 8, 2008, www.journalism.org/node/10953.

48. Feldman, "Cloudy with a Chance of Heat Balls"; Paul R. Brewer, "Science: What's It Up To? *The Daily Show* and the Social Construction of Science," *International Journal of Communication* 7 (2013): 452–70.

49. Feldman, "Cloudy with a Chance of Heat Balls."

50. Paul R. Brewer and Jessica McKnight, "Climate as Comedy: The Effects of Satirical Television News on Climate Change Perceptions," *Science Communication* 37, no. 5 (2015): 635–57.

51. Kevin Kalhoefer, "How Broadcast TV Networks Covered Climate Change in 2017," Media Matters for America, February 12, 2018, www.mediamatters.org/research/2018/02/12/how-broadcast-tv-networks-covered-climate-change-2017/219277.

52. Emily Atkin, "John Oliver Is the Best Climate Change Reporter on Television," *New Republic*, October 30, 2017, https://newrepublic.com/minutes/145563/john-oliver-best-climate-change-reporter-television.

53. "Floods: Last Week Tonight with John Oliver (HBO)," YouTube video, 19:28, posted by LastWeekTonight, October 29, 2017, https://youtu.be/pf1t7cs9dkc.

54. "Paris Agreement: Last Week Tonight with John Oliver (HBO)" YouTube video, 20:57, posted by LastWeekTonight, June 4, 2017, https://youtu.be /5scez5dqtAc.

55. "Climate Change Debate: Last Week Tonight with John Oliver (HBO)," YouTube video, 4:26, posted by LastWeekTonight, May 11, 2014, https://youtu .be/cjuGCJJUGsg.

56. *Modern Family*, "Under Pressure," ABC, January, 15, 2014.

57. *30 Rock*, "Greenzo," NBC, November 8, 2007.

58. *30 Rock*, "Greenzo."

59. *30 Rock*, "Greenzo."

60. *30 Rock*, "Sun Tea," NBC, November 19, 2009.

61. "Weekend Update: U.N.'s Climate Change Report—*SNL*," YouTube video, posted by *Saturday Night Live*, October 13, 2018, www.youtube.com/watch?v = 07oe1m67eik.

62. Laura Gabbert and Justin Schein, dirs., *No Impact Man* (Eden Wurmfeld Films and Shadowbox Films, 2009).

63. Marilyn DeLaure, "Environmental Comedy: *No Impact Man* and the Performance of Green Identity," *Environmental Communication: A Journal of Nature and Culture* 5, no. 4 (2011): 447–66.

64. DeLaure, "Environmental Comedy," 458.

65. Ali Hart, phone interview with authors, July 20, 2018.

66. *Spotlight California*, "In Our Air" (episode 3), February 9, 2016, https:// spotlightcalifornia.com/.

67. Andrew J. Hoffman, "Talking Past Each Other? Cultural Framing of Skeptical and Convinced Logics in the Climate Change Debate," *Organization & Environment* 24, no. 1 (2011): 3–33.

68. "Climate Change Denial Disorder," YouTube video, posted by Funny or Die, April 16, 2015, www.youtube.com/watch?v = fZTTI_0mHN0.

69. "Facts First: Climate Change Is Real," YouTube video, posted by CNN, January 18, 2018, www.youtube.com/watch?v = gXQSyqNGLcI&t = 2s.

70. "Overheard LA with Nina Dobrev," YouTube video, posted by Funny or Die, April 7, 2017, www.youtube.com/watch?v = _GTBHWqu9TI.

71. Full methodological details and results are reported in appendix A.

72. This latter finding is surprising, as we had expected counter-arguing to interfere with effects on engagement (as it did in the case of climate vote importance). One possible explanation is that the *act* of counter-arguing made people feel more politically empowered.

73. We also found that liberal Democrats were more likely to counter-argue the "Old People" video than the CNN video. Given that liberal Democrats also enjoyed the "Old People" video more than the CNN video, we suspect that liberal Democrats were "arguing back" against the actors' *explicit* statements suggest-

ing that climate change isn't concerning, rather than contesting the implied satiric message that climate change *is* important.

74. It is somewhat surprising that conservative Republicans were less likely to enjoy and more likely to counter-argue the "CCDD" video, even though the video's direct effects on climate vote importance and discursive action occurred without regard to political orientation. One possibility is that the "CCDD" video motivated conservative Republicans to consider climate change in their vote and engage discursively, but in support of candidates and perspectives that are not accepting of climate science.

75. Not all climate change news will necessarily arouse fear. News that emphasizes solutions to climate change is likely to elicit more hope and less fear than news focused only on climate impacts. See Feldman and Hart, "Using Political Efficacy Messages"; Feldman and Hart, "Is There Any Hope?"

76. Feldman and Hart, "Using Political Efficacy Messages"; Feldman and Hart, "Is There Any Hope?"

77. Mia Costa, Brian F. Schaffner, and Alicia Prevost, "Walking the Walk? Experiments on the Effect of Pledging to Vote on Youth Turnout," *PloS One* 13, no. 5 (2018), https://doi.org/10.1371/journal.pone.0197066.

78. Leiserowitz et al., *Climate Change in the American Mind.*

CHAPTER 5

1. David Paul Meyer, *You Laugh But It's True*, Day 1 Films, 2011, www.youlaughbutitstrue.com/.

2. David Munro, *Stand Up Planet*, KCETLink Media and Kontent Films, 2014, www.standupplanet.org/.

3. Munro, *Stand Up Planet.*

4. Munro, *Stand Up Planet.*

5. Munro, *Stand Up Planet.*

6. World Health Organization, *Inheriting a Sustainable World? Atlas on Children's Health and the Environment* (Geneva: World Health Organization, 2017); "Pollution, Poor Sanitation Kill India's Under-5 Kids," *Times of India*, last updated March 7, 2017, https://timesofindia.indiatimes.com/life-style/health-fitness/health-news/pollution-poor-sanitation-kill-indias-under-5-kids/articleshow/57510617.cms.

7. Harmeet Shah Singh, "Why Are So Many Children Dying in India?" *CNN*, September 1, 2015, www.cnn.com/2015/08/31/asia/india-child-deaths/index.html.

8. United Nations Inter-agency Group for Child Mortality Estimation, *Levels & Trends in Child Mortality* (New York: United Nations Children's Fund, 2017), 4–5.

9. United Nations, *Levels & Trends in Child Mortality*, 3.

10. Rufus B. Akindola, "Towards a Definition of Poverty: Poor People's Perspectives and Implications for Poverty Reduction," *Journal of Developing Societies*, 25, no. 2 (2010): 121, https://doi.org/10.1177/0169796X0902500201.

11. United Nations, "About the Sustainable Development Goals," accessed January 27, 2019, www.un.org/sustainabledevelopment/sustainable-development-goals/.

12. Susan Rice, Corinne Graff, and Carlos Pascual, eds., *Confronting Poverty: Weak States and U.S. National Security* (Washington, DC: Brookings Institution Press, 2010).

13. Nandita Dogra, *Representations of Global Poverty: Aid, Development and International NGOs* (London: I. B. Tauris, 2012).

14. United Nations, "Sustainable Development Goals," Sustainable Development Knowledge Platform, accessed January 27, 2019, https://sustainabledevelopment.un.org/sdgs; United Nations, "Goal 1: End Poverty in All Its Forms Everywhere," Sustainable Development Goals, accessed January 27, 2019, www.un.org/sustainabledevelopment/poverty/.

15. United Nations Human Rights, "'American Dream Is Rapidly Becoming American Illusion,' Warns UN Rights Expert on Poverty," December 15, 2017, https://www.ohchr.org/EN/NewsEvents/Pages/DisplayNews.aspx?NewsID = 22546.

16. Jessica L. Semega, Kayla R. Fontenot, and Melisa A. Kollar, *Income and Poverty in the United States: 2016* (Washington, DC: U.S. Census Bureau, 2017), 11.

17. Semega, Fontenot, and Kollar, *Income and Poverty in the United States*, 14.

18. Elise Gould, *The State of American Wages 2017* (Washington, DC: Economic Policy Institute, 2018).

19. Elise Gould, Alyssa Davis, and Will Kimball, *Broad-Based Wage Growth Is a Key Tool in the Fight against Poverty* (Washington, DC: Economic Policy Institute, 2015).

20. Scot Haller, "Africa's Sick and Hungry Kids Are All in the Family for Actress Sally Struthers," *People*, April 18, 1983, https://people.com/archive/africas-sick-and-hungry-kids-are-all-in-the-family-for-actress-sally-struthers-vol-19-no-15/.

21. Tracey Jenson, "Welfare Commonsense, Poverty Porn and Doxosophy," *Sociological Research Online* 19, no. 3 (2014): 1–7, https://doi.org/10.5153/sro.3441.

22. Nathaniel Whittemore, "The Rise and Fall of Poverty Porn," *Fast Company*, January 1, 2012, www.fastcompany.com/90185706/the-rise-and-fall-of-poverty-porn.

23. Whittemore, "Rise and Fall of Poverty Porn"; Dogra, *Representations of Global Poverty*.

24. Taniesha A. Woods, Beth Kurtz-Costes, and Stephanie J. Rowley, "The Development of Stereotypes About the Rich and Poor: Age, Race, and Family

Income Differences in Beliefs," *Journal of Youth and Adolescence* 34, no. 5 (2005): 437, https://doi.org/10.1007/s10964-005-7261-0.

25. Woods, Kurtz-Costes, and Rowley, "Development of Stereotypes," 437.

26. Judith A. Chafel, "Society Images of Poverty: Child and Adult Beliefs," *Youth & Society* 28, no. 4 (1997): 432–63, https://doi.org/10.1177%2F0044118X97028004003.

27. Woods, Kurtz-Costes, and Rowley, "Development of Stereotypes," 438.

28. Heather E. Bullock, Karen Fraser Wyche, and Wendy R. Williams, "Media Images of the Poor," *Journal of Social Issues* 57, no. 2 (2001): 229–46, https://doi.org/10.1111/0022-4537.00210.

29. Bullock, Fraser Wyche, and Williams, "Media Images of the Poor," 243.

30. Bullock, Fraser Wyche, and Williams, "Media Images of the Poor," 229–46.

31. Philip Alston, "Statement on Visit to the USA," Statement by United Nations Special Rapporteur on Extreme Poverty and Human Rights, Washington, DC, December 15, 2017, www.ohchr.org/EN/NewsEvents/Pages/DisplayNews.aspx?NewsID = 22533&LangID = E.

32. Dogra, *Representations of Global Poverty*, 5.

33. Larry Minear, "The Other Missions of NGOs: Education and Advocacy," *World Development* 15, no. 1 (1987): 201–21, https://doi.org/10.1016/0305-750X(87)90158-6.

34. Noam Unger and Abigail Jones, "Global Development 2.0: An Expanding Ecosystem," *Monday Developments* (March 2009): 23–24.

35. John D. Cameron, "Can Poverty Be Funny? The Serious Use of Humour as a Strategy of Public Engagement for Global Justice," *Third World Quarterly* 36, no. 2 (2015): 274–90, https://doi.org/10.1080/01436597.2015.1013320.

36. "About ONE," ONE, accessed January 27, 2019, www.one.org/international/about/.

37. "Homepage," Malaria No More, accessed January 27, 2019, www.malarianomore.org/; "Homepage," Save the Children, www.savethechildren.org/; "Homepage," Oxfam, accessed January 27, 2019, www.oxfamamerica.org/.

38. Cameron, "Can Poverty Be Funny?" 277.

39. Dogra, *Representations of Global Poverty*.

40. Cameron, "Can Poverty Be Funny?" 277; Dogra, *Representations of Global Poverty*.

41. Nandita Dogra, *Representations of Global Poverty*.

42. Cameron, "Can Poverty Be Funny?" 276.

43. Cameron, "Can Poverty Be Funny?" 279.

44. Cameron, "Can Poverty Be Funny?" 274–90.

45. "The Homeless Homed," *The Daily Show*, last updated January 7, 2015, www.cc.com/video-clips/lntv3q/the-daily-show-with-jon-stewart-the-homeless-homed.

46. "Homeless Homed," *The Daily Show*.

47. Eleanor Goldberg, "'Daily Show' Schools Us on Why Homeless Aren't Actually 'Moochers' Who Cost Taxpayers," *Huffington Post*, last updated January 1, 2018, www.huffingtonpost.com/2015/01/08/daily-show-homelessness_n_6437644.html.

48. "'Poor' in America," *The Colbert Report*, last updated July 26, 2011, www.cc.com/video-clips/zq2rpw/the-colbert-report—poor—in-america.

49. "39 Cents—SNL," *Saturday Night Live*, YouTube, last updated October 12, 2014, www.youtube.com/watch?time_continue = 4&v = MEb_epsuLqA.

50. "Radi-Aid," SAIH, Campaigns, accessed January 27, 2019, https://saih.no/english/our-work/campaign/radiaid-africa-for-norway.

51. "Let's Save Africa!—Gone Wrong," SAIH Norway, YouTube, last updated November 8, 2013, www.youtube.com/watch?v = xbqA6o8_WC0.

52. "Homepage," Radi-Aid, accessed January 27, 2019, www.radiaid.com/.

53. John Hendel, "Showtime's 'Shameless' New Show about Poverty," *Atlantic*, January 8, 2011, www.theatlantic.com/entertainment/archive/2011/01/showtimes-shameless-new-show-about-poverty/69108/.

54. Hank Stuever, "What's the Best Show about Poverty, Crime and Crazy Sex? It's 'Shameless,'" *Washington Post*, January 7, 2016, www.washingtonpost.com/entertainment/tv/whats-the-best-show-about-poverty-crime-and-crazy-sex-its-shameless/2016/01/07/.

55. English Taylor, "How 'Shameless' Reinvented the Working-Class-Family TV Show," *The Atlantic*, February 2, 2012, www.theatlantic.com/entertainment/archive/2012/02/how-shameless-reinvented-the-working-class-family-tv-show/252851/.

56. Stacey Wilson Hunt, "The Gallaghers Are Back for *Shameless*'s First Post-Trump Season," *Vulture*, November 2, 2017, www.vulture.com/2017/11/shamelesss-first-post-trump-season.html.

57. Dannagal G. Young, R. Lance Holbert, and Kathleen Hall Jamieson, "Successful Practices for the Strategic Use of Political Parody and Satire: Lessons from the P6 Symposium and the 2012 Election Campaign," *American Behavioral Scientist* 58, no. 9 (2013): 1111–30. https://doi.org/10.1177/0002764213506213.

58. "About Comic Relief," Comic Relief, www.comicrelief.com/about-comic-relief.

59. Dominic Harris, "Comic Relief Raises £75m with Fun and Stunts," *The Guardian*, March 16, 2013, www.theguardian.com/tv-and-radio/2013/mar/17/comic-relief-raises-75m.

60. The Deadline Team, "Red Nose Day Charity Special Coming to NBC with Comic Relief, Funny or Die," *Deadline Hollywood*, July 13, 2014, https://deadline.com/2014/07/red-nose-day-charity-special-nbc-funny-or-die-comic-relief-803447/.

61. "The Red Nose Day Special," NBC, accessed January 27, 2019, www.nbc.com/the-red-nose-day-special?nbc = 1.

62. "Comic Relief Channel," Comic Relief, accessed January 27, 2019, YouTube, www.youtube.com/channel/UCdF5u0ggeSETozc8fsprjcw.

63. "Red Nose Day 2018 Was a Huge Success!" Red Nose Day, Impact, accessed January 27, 2019, https://rednoseday.org/impact.

64. "World Toilet Day November 19," United Nations, accessed January 27, 2019, http://www.un.org/en/events/toiletday/.

65. Marc Silver, "Mr. Toilet and Mr. Condom Think Jokes Will Save the World," NPR, April 20, 2015, www.npr.org/sections/goatsandsoda/2015/04/20 /400990919/mr-toilet-and-mr-condom-think-jokes-will-save-the-world.

66. Morgan Clendaniel, "Meet Mr. Toilet: The Man Trying to Make Commodes a Global Status Symbol," *Fast Company*, November 15, 2013, www .fastcompany.com/2679219/meet-mr-toilet-the-man-trying-to-make-commodes-a-global-status-symbol.

67. Clendaniel, "Meet Mr. Toilet."

68. "Meet Mr. Toilet, Jessica Yu," Forward Focus Films, Vimeo, last updated January 9, 2012, https://vimeo.com/34792993; Jessica Yu, "Meet Mr. Toilet," Full Frame Documentary Film Festival, last updated 2013, www.fullframefest .org/film/meet-mr-toilet/; Jessica Yu, *Focus Forward: Meet Mr. Toilet*, IDFA and Forward Focus Films, 2012, www.idfa.nl/en/film/6fbd869b-6c82–47f9–8b27-e0f49fe97913/focus-forward-meet-mr-toilet.

69. "UN Designates November 19 as UN World Toilet Day," World Toilet Organization, last updated November 19, 2013, http://worldtoilet.org/un-designates-november-19-as-un-world-toilet-day/.

70. Munro, *Stand Up Planet*.

71. The producing credits for *Stand Up Planet* include, in alphabetical order: Caty Borum Chattoo, Xandra Castleton, Mark Decena, Wendy Hanamura, Teri Heyman, Craig Minassian, David Munro, and Ashley Scales. *Stand Up Planet* was created by David Munro and Xandra Castleton, and directed by David Munro and co-directed by Daniel Marracino. *Stand Up Planet* was funded by a grant from the Bill & Melinda Gates Foundation.

72. Arvind Singhal and Everett M. Rogers, *Entertainment-Education: A Communication Strategy for Social Change* (Mahwah, NJ: Lawrence Erlbaum Associates, 1999).

73. "Press Release: Children Dying Daily Because of Unsafe Water Supplies and Poor Sanitation and Hygiene, UNICEF Says," UNICEF Press Centre, last updated March 22, 2013, www.unicef.org/media/media_68359.html.

74. South Africa HIV epidemic profile (Reports), 2014, www.unaids.org/en /regionscountries/countries/southafrica.

75. Robin L. Nabi, Emily Moyer-Gusé, and Sahara Byrne, "All Joking Aside: A Serious Investigation into the Persuasive Effect of Funny Social Issue Messages," *Communication Monographs* 74, no. 1 (2007): 50, https://doi.org/10.1080 /03637750701196896.

76. Character involvement also features prominently as a mechanism that helps explain an audience's engagement with entertainment narratives, including comedy. Although we considered character involvement in this research, it did not figure prominently in our findings; thus, we do not discuss it at length here. However, an overview is provided in chapter 2.

77. Melanie C. Green and Timothy C. Brock, "The Role of Transportation in the Persuasiveness of Public Narrative," *Journal of Personality and Social Psychology* 79, no. 5 (2009): 701–21, https://doi.org/10.1037/0022–3514.79.5.701.

78. Green and Brock, "Role of Transportation," 701–21; Michael D. Slater and Donna Rouner, "Entertainment-Education and Elaboration Likelihood: Understanding the Processing of Narrative Persuasion," *Communication Theory* 12, no. 2 (2002): 173–91, https://doi.org/10.1111/j.1468–2885.2002.tb00265.x; Emily Moyer-Gusé, "Toward a Theory of Entertainment Persuasion: Explaining the Persuasive Effects of Entertainment-Education Messages," *Communication Theory* 18, no. 3 (2008): 407–25, https://doi.org/10.1111/j.1468–2885.2008.00328.x.

79. Moyer-Gusé, "Toward a Theory of Entertainment Persuasion," 407–25; Sheila T. Murphy et al., "Involved, Transported, or Emotional? Exploring the Determinants of Change in Knowledge, Attitudes, and Behavior in Entertainment-Education," *Journal of Communication* 61, no. 3 (2011): 407–31, https://doi.org/10.1111/j.1460–2466.2011.01554.x; Sheila T. Murphy et al., "Narrative versus Nonnarrative: The Role of Identification, Transportation, and Emotion in Reducing Health Disparities," *Journal of Communication* 63, no. 1 (2013): 116–37, https://doi.org/10.1111/jcom.12007.

80. Paul Slovic et al., "The Affect Heuristic," *European Journal of Operational Research* 177, no. 3 (2007): 1333–52, https://doi.org/10.1016/j.ejor.2005.04.006.

81. Heather L. LaMarre and Kristen D. Landreville, "When Is Fiction as Good as Fact? Comparing the Influence of Documentary and Historical Reenactment Films on Engagement, Affect, Issue Interest, and Learning," *Mass Communication and Society* 12, no. 4 (2009): 537–55, https://doi.org/10.1080/15205430903237915.

82. Murphy et al., "Narrative versus Nonnarrative," 116–37.

83. Singhal and Rogers, *Entertainment-Education*.

84. Georges E. Khalil and Lance S. Rintamaki, "A Televised Entertainment-Education Drama to Promote Positive Discussion about Organ Donation," *Health Education Research* 29, no. 2 (2014): 284–96, https://doi.org/10.1093/her/cyt106; Frank M. Schneider et al., "Learning from Entertaining Online Video Clips? Enjoyment and Appreciation and Their Differential Relationships with Knowledge and Behavioral Intentions," *Computers in Human Behavior* 54, no. C (2016): 4745–82, https://doi.org/10.1016/j.chb.2015.08.028.

85. "The End Game," *Al Jazeera*, Lifelines: The Quest for Global Health, last updated November 19, 2014, www.aljazeera.com/programmes/lifelines/2014/01/end-game-20141291063664974.html

86. Viewers of *Stand Up Planet* also found the characters more relatable than viewers of *The End Game*, although character involvement was inconsistently related to the outcome variables (i.e., it was positively related to intended action, but negatively related to knowledge).

87. Emily Moyer-Gusé, Sarah Brookes, and Chad Mahood, "Entertainment-Education in the Context of Humor: Effects of Safer Sex Intentions and Risk Perceptions," *Health Communication* 26, no. 8 (2011): 765–74, https://doi.org /10.1080/10410236.2011.566832.

88. Singhal and Everett M. Rogers, *Entertainment-Education*.

89. Cameron, "Can Poverty Be Funny?," 274–90.

CHAPTER 6

1. Jenny Yang, phone interview with authors, August 8, 2018.

2. Franchesca Ramsey, "Shit White Girls Say . . . to Black Girls," YouTube video, 2:01, posted by @checsaleigh, January 4, 2012, www.youtube.com /watch?v = ylPUzxpIBe0.

3. Franchesca Ramsey, *Well, That Escalated Quickly: Memoirs and Mistakes of an Accidental Activist* (New York: Grand Central, 2018), 20.

4. Franchesca Ramsey, phone interview with authors, July 26, 2018.

5. Henry Jenkins, *Convergence Culture: Where Old and New Media Collide* (New York: New York University Press, 2006).

6. danah boyd, *It's Complicated: The Social Lives of Networked Teens* (New Haven, CT: Yale University Press, 2014), 10.

7. Ramsey, phone interview.

8. Hasan Minhaj, in-person interview with author, November 1, 2018.

9. Philip W. Napoli, *Audience Evolution: New Technologies and the Transformation of Media Audiences* (New York: Columbia University Press, 2011).

10. Yang, phone interview.

11. Napoli, *Audience Evolution*; Caitlin Petre, "The Traffic Factories: Metrics at Chartbeat, Gawker Media, and the New York Times," *Tow Center for Digital Journalism*, May 7, 2015, www.cjr.org/tow_center_reports/the_traffic_factories_ metrics_at_chartbeat_gawker_media_and_the_new_york_times.php.

12. Ramsey, phone interview.

13. Zahra Noorbakhsh, phone interview with authors, July 30, 2018.

14. Nancy K. Baym, *Playing to the Crowd: Musicians, Audiences, and the Intimate Work of Connection* (New York: New York University Press, 2018), 16–22.

15. Ramsey, *Well, That Escalated Quickly*.

16. Ramsey, phone interview.

17. José Van Dijck, *The Culture of Connectivity: A Critical History of Social Media* (New York: Oxford University Press, 2013), 122.

18. Joel Church-Cooper, phone interview with authors, November 7, 2018.

19. Ibid.

20. Jennie Church-Cooper, phone interview with author, August 30, 2018.

21. Anne Libera, phone interview with authors, July 30, 2018.

22. Brent Miller, phone interview with authors, December 21, 2018.

23. Hasan Minhaj, in-person interview with author, November 1, 2018.

24. Sara Taksler, in-person interview with author, August 30, 2018.

25. Rachel Dratch, phone interview with authors, November 16, 2018.

26. Bethany Hall, phone interview with authors, July 30, 2018.

27. Ramsey, phone interview.

28. Negin Farsad, phone interview with authors, August 15, 2018.

29. W. Kamau Bell, phone interview with authors, August 20, 2018.

30. Cristela Alonzo, phone interview with authors, August 15, 2018.

31. Nato Green, phone interview with authors, August 9, 2018.

32. Green, phone interview.

33. Noorbakhsh, phone interview.

34. Minhaj, in-person interview.

35. Minhaj, in-person interview.

36. Ramsey, phone interview.

37. Farsad, phone interview.

38. Farsad, phone interview.

39. Noorbakhsh, phone interview.

40. Rosabeth Moss Kanter, "Some Effects of Proportions on Group Life: Skewed Sex Ratios and Responses to Token Women," *American Journal of Sociology* 82, no. 5 (1977): 965–99; Yolanda F. Niemann and John F. Dovidio, "Relationship of Solo Status, Academic Rank, and Perceived Distinctiveness to Job Satisfaction of Racial / Ethnic Minorities," *Journal of Applied Psychology* 83, no. 1 (1998): 55–71; Richard Shafer, "What Minority Journalists Identify as Constraints to Full Newsroom Equality," *Howard Journal of Communications* 4, no. 3 (1993): 195–208.

41. Farsad, phone interview.

42. Kamau Bell, phone interview.

43. Libera, phone interview.

44. Green, phone interview.

45. Aasif Mandvi, phone interview with authors, November 30, 2018.

46. Kamau Bell, phone interview.

47. Kamau Bell, phone interview.

48. Kamau Bell, phone interview.

49. Green, phone interview.

50. Joel Church-Cooper, phone interview.

51. Graeme Turner, *Understanding Celebrity* (London: Sage, 2013), 91.

52. Van Dijck, *Culture of Connectivity*, 115–16; Joanne Morreale, "From Homemade to Store Bought: *Annoying Orange* and the Professionalization of YouTube," *Journal of Consumer Culture* 14, no. 1 (2014): 113–28.

53. Morreale, "From Homemade to Store Bought," 126.

54. Minhaj, in-person interview.

55. See, for example, Amber Day, *Satire and Dissent: Interventions in Contemporary Political Debate* (Bloomington: Indiana University Press, 2011); Elizabetta Ferrari, "Fake Accounts, Real Activism: Political Faking and User-Generated Satire as Activist Intervention," *New Media & Society* 20, no. 6 (2018): 2208–23.

56. Megan Garber, "John Oliver, Activist," *The Atlantic*, November 14, 2016, www.theatlantic.com/entertainment/archive/2016/11/john-oliver-activist-comedian/507599/; Michael Stahl, "Comedians as Activists in the Era of Trump," *Vulture*, January 20, 2017, www.vulture.com/2017/01/comedians-as-activists-in-the-era-of-trump.html

57. Kamau Bell, phone interview.

58. Richard Schechner, *Performance Theory* (New York: Routledge, 1988).

59. Farsad, phone interview.

60. Negin Farsad and Dean Obeidallah, "Boycotting Bigotry: Comedians Combat Trump's Corruption and Hate," YouTube video, 10:57, posted by MoveOn, August 8, 2018, www.youtube.com/watch?v = nMDv2jQGGv0.

61. Farsad and Obeidallah, "Boycotting Bigotry."

62. Omri Marcus, phone interview with authors, August 10, 2018.

63. Ramsey, phone interview.

64. Ramsey, phone interview.

65. Henry Jenkins et al., *By Any Media Necessary: The New Youth Activism* (New York: New York University Press, 2016), 29–30.

66. Jenkins et al., *By Any Media Necessary*.

67. Aasif Mandvi, phone interview with authors, November 30, 2018.

68. Mandvi, phone interview.

69. Mandvi, phone interview.

70. Joel Church-Cooper, phone interview.

71. Joel Church-Cooper, phone interview

72. Farsad, phone interview.

73. Mandvi, phone interview.

74. Kamau Bell, phone interview.

75. Kamau Bell, phone interview.

76. Minhaj, in-person interview.

77. Seth C. Lewis, "The Tension between Professional Control and Open Participation: Journalism and Its Boundaries," *Information, Communication & Society* 15, no. 6 (2012): 836–66.

78. Ramsey, phone interview.

79. Minhaj, in-person interview.

80. Green, phone interview.

81. Mandvi, phone interview.

82. Joel Church-Cooper, phone interview.

83. Kamau Bell, phone interview.

84. Green, phone interview.

85. Yang, phone interview.

86. Ramsey, phone interview.

87. Farsad, phone interview.

88. Alonzo, phone interview.

89. Alonzo, phone interview.

90. Mandvi, phone interview.

91. Hall, phone interview.

92. Joel Church-Cooper, phone interview.

93. Kamau Bell, phone interview.

94. Rebecca Krefting, *All Joking Aside: American Humor and Its Discontents* (Baltimore: John Hopkins University Press, 2014), 25.

CHAPTER 7

1. Cristela Alonzo, phone interview with authors, August 15, 2018.

2. "Amanda Nguyen Senate Testimony," C-SPAN, June 26, 2018, www.c-span .org/video/?c4737608/amanda-nguyen-senate-testimony.

3. Diana Pearl, "How a 24-Year-Old Rape Survivor Is Pushing Congress to Change the Way the U. S. Handles Sexual Assault," *People*, August 30, 2016, https://people.com/celebrity/amanda-nguyen-and-rise-profile-passing-sexual-assault-bill-of-rights/.

4. Amanda Nguyen, phone interview with authors, November 16, 2018.

5. Rise, Erin Richards, Funny or Die, and Courtney Davis, "Even Supervillains Think Our Sexual Assault Laws Are Insane," produced by Rob Hatch-Miller and Eleanor Winkler, Funny or Die, February 24, 2016, video, 2:58, www .funnyordie.com/2016/2/24/18114547/even-supervillains-think-our-sexual-assault-laws-are-insane.

6. Brad Jenkins, phone interview with authors, September 7, 2018.

7. Survivors' Bill of Rights Act of 2016, Pub. L. No. 114–236, 130 Stat. 966, www.gpo.gov/fdsys/pkg/PLAW-114publ236/html/PLAW-114publ236 .htm.

8. Amanda Nguyen, "Letter from the Founder," Rise, accessed January 27, 2019, www.risenow.us/letter/.

9. Nguyen, "Letter from the Founder."

10. Olivia Messer, "States Rush to Introduce Sexual-Assault Survivor 'Bill of Rights'," *Daily Beast*, January 26, 2018, www.thedailybeast.com/states-rush-to-introduce-sexual-assault-survivor-bill-of-rights.

11. Jenkins, phone interview.

12. Henry Jenkins et al., *By Any Media Necessary: The New Youth Activism* (New York: New York University Press, 2016), 9.

13. Nguyen, phone interview.

14. Henry Jenkins, *Convergence Culture: Where Old and New Media Collide* (New York: New York University Press, 2006), 2.

15. Jenkins, *Convergence Culture*, 219.

16. Jenkins, *Convergence Culture*, 219.

17. Stephen Duncombe, "Introduction," in *Cultural Resistance Reader*, ed. Stephen Duncombe (London: Verso, 2002), 5.

18. Daniel Fischlin, Ajay Heble, and George Lipsitz, *The Fierce Urgency of Now: Improvisation, Rights, and the Ethics of Cocreation* (Durham, NC: Duke University Press, 2013), 147.

19. Kathryn C. Montgomery, *Target: Prime Time Advocacy Groups and the Struggle over Entertainment Television* (Oxford: Oxford University Press, 1990).

20. *#PopJustice Report Series: Executive Brief.* See full report series: "#Pop-Justice: Social Justice and the Promise of Pop Culture Strategies," Liz Manne Strategy, Unbound Philanthropy, The Nathan Cummings Foundation, www.unboundphilanthropy.org/sites/default/files/%23PopJustice%20Executive%20Brief_FINAL%20with%20full%20credits%20%287%29_0.pdf.

21. Jenkins et al., *By Any Media Necessary*, 31.

22. Tracy Van Slyke, *Spoiler Alert*, accessed January 31, 2019, https://center-formediajustice.org/wp-content/uploads/2015/10/SpoilerAlert.compressed.pdf.

23. "Pop Culture for Social Change," Unbound Philanthropy, accessed January 27, 2019, www.unboundphilanthropy.org/announcing-popjustice-report-series.

24. "Partners," Pop Culture Collab, accessed January 28, 2019, http://popcollab.org/partners/.

25. Arvind Singhal et al., *Entertainment-Education and Social Change: History, Research, and Practice* (Mahwah, NJ: Lawrence Erlbaum Associates, 2004; New York: Routledge, 2010).

26. Suruchi Sood, Amy Henderson Riley, and Kristine Cecile Alarcon, "Entertainment-Education and Health and Risk Messaging," *Oxford Research Encyclopedia, Communication*, May 2017, https://oxfordindex.oup.com/view/10.1093/acrefore/9780190228613.013.245.

27. Matt James et al., "Leveraging the Power of the Media to Combat HIV/AIDS," *Health Affairs* 24, no. 3 (May/June 2005), www.healthaffairs.org/doi/full/10.1377/hlthaff.24.3.854; Henry J. Kaiser Family Foundation, *Entertainment Education and Health in the United States*, 2004, https://kaiserfamilyfoundation.files

.wordpress.com/2013/01/entertainment-education-and-health-in-the-united-states-issue-brief.pdf.

28. Storyline Partners, accessed January 28, 2019, www.storylinepartners .com/.

29. "Hollywood, Health & Society," Norman Lear Center, accessed January 28, 2019, https://learcenter.org/project/hollywood-health-society-2/.

30. Nancy R. Lee and Philip Kotler, *Social Marketing: Changing Behavior for Good*, 5th ed. (Thousand Oaks, CA: SAGE, 2016).

31. Lee and Kotler, *Social Marketing*, 12.

32. Jason Mittell, "Forensic Fandom and the Drillable Text," Spreadable Media, accessed January 28, 2019, http://spreadablemedia.org/essays/mittell/# .XE9z6817lhE.

33. "We Are Everytown for Gun Safety," Everytown, accessed on January 28, 2019, https://everytown.org/who-we-are/.

34. "Gun Violence in America," Everytown for Gun Safety, last modified January 25, 2019, https://everytownresearch.org/gun-violence-america/. Data from Centers for Disease Control and Prevention, WISQARS Fatal Injury Reports. Data reflect a five-year average (2012–16) of gun deaths by intent.

35. Adam Winkler, *Gunfight: The Battle over the Right to Bear Arms in America* (New York: W.W. Norton, 2011).

36. Mik Moore, phone interview with authors, July 20, 2018.

37. "What Could Go Wrong?" Moms Demand Action for Gun Sense in America, January 28, 2016, video, 1:44, www.youtube.com/watch?v = abwqlggNsNI.

38. Jason Rzepka, phone interview with authors, August 16, 2018.

39. Cassidy Hopkins, "Amy Schumer on Gun Violence and the 'Trainwreck' Theater Shooting," *Hollywood Reporter*, November 18, 2015, www.hollywood reporter.com/news/amy-schumer-gun-violence-trainwreck-842027.

40. Erika Soto Lamb, phone interview with authors, November 16, 2018.

41. Megan Garber, "*Inside Amy Schumer*, Guns, and Comedy's Fifth Wall," *The Atlantic*, April 28, 2016, www.theatlantic.com/entertainment/archive/2016 /04/amy-schumer-guns-and-comedys-fifth-wall/480516/.

42. "Welcome to the Gun Show!" *Inside Amy Schumer*, video, 4:33, April 28, 2016, www.cc.com/video-clips/nnli8o/inside-amy-schumer-welcome-to-the-gun-show-.

43. Rzepka, phone interview.

44. Soto Lamb, phone interview.

45. DREAM Act, S. 1291, 107th Cong. (2001), www.congress.gov/bill/107th-congress/senate-bill/1291.

46. American Immigration Council, *The Dream Act, DACA, and Other Policies Designed to Protect Dreamers*, September 2017, www.americanimmigrationcouncil .org/sites/default/files/research/the_dream_act_daca_and_other_policies_ designed_to_protect_dreamers.pdf.

47. American Immigration Council, *Dream Act.*

48. Reidar Ommundsen, Knud S. Larsen, Kees van der Veer, and Dag-Erik Eilertsen, "Framing Unauthorized Immigrants: The Effects of Labels on Evaluations," *Psychological Reports* 114, no. 2 (April 1, 2014): 461–78, https://doi.org/10.2466/17.PR0.114k20w0; Emily M. Farris and Heather Silber Mohamed, "Picturing Immigration: How the Media Criminalizes Immigrants," *Politics, Groups, and Identities* 6, no. 4 (June 18, 2018): 814–24, https://doi.org.10.1080/21565503.2018.1484375.

49. Jose Antonio Vargas, "My Life as an Undocumented Immigrant," *New York Times*, June 22, 2011, www.nytimes.com/2011/06/26/magazine/my-life-as-an-undocumented-immigrant.html.

50. *Documented*, accessed January 28, 2019, https://documentedthefilm.com/.

51. "About," Define American, accessed January 28, 2019, https://defineamerican.com/about/.

52. Alonzo, phone interview.

53. Elizabeth Voorhees, phone interview with authors, July 27, 2018.

54. "Mateo's Last Day," *Superstore*, NBC, aired March 23, 2017, www.imdb.com/title/tt6091698/.

55. Michael Conti, "NBC's 'Superstore' Reveals That One Character Is Undocumented," Define American (blog), August 20, 2016, https://defineamerican.com/blog/nbcs-superstore-reveals-that-one-character-is-undocumented/.

56. "Mateo's Last Day," *Superstore*, NBC, www.nbc.com/superstore/video/mateos-last-day/3485641.

57. "Green Card for a Victim of a Crime (U Nonimmigrant)," U.S. Citizenship and Immigration Service, last modified May 23, 2018, www.uscis.gov/green-card/other-ways-get-green-card/green-card-victim-crime-u-nonimmigrant.

58. Voorhees, phone interview.

59. Voorhees, phone interview.

60. Define American, "Do Undocumented Americans Pay Taxes? [Spoiler Alert: Of Course!]" Facebook video, April 17, 2018, www.facebook.com/Define American/videos/1660631074019306/.

61. Voorhees, phone interview.

62. Laura Flanders, "Can 'Caring Across Generations' Change the World?" *The Nation*, April 30, 2012, www.thenation.com/article/can-caring-across-generations-change-world/.

63. Ai-jen Poo, phone interview with authors, August 14, 2018.

64. "Ai-jen Poo," MacArthur Fellows Program, MacArthur Foundation, accessed January 28, 2019, www.macfound.org/fellows/924/.

65. Jay Newton-Small, "Ai-jen Poo Wants to Make You See Invisible People," *Time*, July 18, 2016, http://time.com/collection-post/4402890/ai-jen-poo-national-domestic-workers-alliance/.

66. Flanders, "Change the World."

67. Caring Across Generations, accessed January 28, 2019, https:// caringacross.org/.

68. Ishita Srivastava, phone interview with authors, July 24, 2018.

69. Anne Libera, phone interview with authors, July 30, 2018.

70. Kelly Leonard, phone interview with authors, July 24, 2018.

71. Poo, phone interview.

72. Srivastava, phone interview.

73. "Our Story," NextGen America, accessed January 28, 2019, https:// nextgenamerica.org/our-story/.

74. Jim Newell, "How to Turn Out Young Voters? Remind Them of Their Power," *Slate*, August 9, 2018, https://slate.com/news-and-politics/2018/08 /tom-steyers-nextgen-america-releases-major-new-research-on-motivating-young-voters.html.

75. James Mastracco, phone interview with authors, August 16, 2018.

76. Mastracco, phone interview.

77. Spotlight California, YouTube (channel), accessed January 28, 2019, www .youtube.com/channel/UChpiT2xdTjjqISbdcMkY84A.

78. Mastracco, phone interview.

79. Megan Rummler, "Short-Form Comedy Documentary and the Immigration Experience: 'American Haze' and Comedy as the Gateway Drug to Common Ground," Laughter Effect, May 9, 2018, https://thelaughtereffect.com/short-form-comedy-documentary-and-the-immigration-experience-b0ff0a226f68.

80. Mastracco, phone interview.

81. Ali Hart, phone interview with authors, July 20, 2018.

82. Mastracco, phone interview.

83. Jenkins et al., *By Any Media Necessary*, 29.

84. Moore, phone interview.

85. Jenkins et al., *By Any Media Necessary*.

86. Poo, phone interview.

87. Mastracco, phone interview.

88. Leonard, phone interview.

89. Rachel Dratch, phone interview with authors, November 16, 2018.

90. Leonard, phone interview.

91. Alonzo, phone interview.

CHAPTER 8

1. Emily Stewart, "Wonder What Michelle Wolf Said to Make Everyone So Mad? Read It Here," *Vox*, April 30, 2018, www.vox.com/policy-and-politics

/2018/4/30/17301436/michelle-wolf-speech-transcript-white-house-correspondents-dinner-sarah-huckabee-sanders.

2. Lara Zarum, "Michelle Wolf Is the Voice Comedy Needs Right Now," *Village Voice*, November 30, 2017, www.villagevoice.com/2017/11/30/michelle-wolf-is-the-voice-comedy-needs-right-now/.

3. "2018 Dinner," White House Correspondents' Association, accessed January 28, 2019, www.whca.press/dinner/2018-dinner/.

4. Stewart, "What Michelle Wolf Said."

5. Stewart, "What Michelle Wolf Said."

6. Michael M. Grynbaum, "Did Michelle Wolf Kill the White House Correspondents' Dinner?" April 30, 2018, www.nytimes.com/2018/04/30/business/media/michelle-wolf-white-house-correspondents-dinner.html.

7. Alex Johnson and Phil McCausland, "Correspondents Group Criticizes Comedian Michelle Wolf for Remarks at Annual Dinner," *NBC News*, April 29, 2018, www.nbcnews.com/politics/white-house/comedian-michelle-wolf-sparks-fury-debate-roast-correspondents-dinner-n869931; Grynbaum, "Michelle Wolf."

8. Johnson and McCausland, "Correspondents Group Criticizes."

9. "WHCA Announces Acclaimed Author Ron Chernow as Featured Speaker for 2019 Dinner," White House Correspondents' Association, accessed January 29, 2019, www.whca.press/2018/11/19/whca-announces-acclaimed-author-ron-chernow-as-featured-speaker-for-2019-dinner/.

10. Donald J. Trump (@realDonaldTrump), Twitter, November 20, 2018, https://twitter.com/realDonaldTrump/status/1065088330969305089.

11. Greg Evans, "White House Correspondents' Dinner Ditches Comics; Michelle Wolf Calls Association 'Cowards'," *Deadline*, November 19, 2018, https://deadline.com/2018/11/white-house-correspondents-dinner-serious-ron-chernow-no-comedian-host-1202504736/.

12. James Poniewozik, "Michelle Wolf Did Her Job: It's the Correspondents' Dinner That Is the Problem," *New York Times*, April 30, 2018, www.nytimes.com/2018/04/30/arts/television/michelle-wolf-white-house-correspondents-dinner.html.

13. Jeffrey P. Jones, *Entertaining Politics: Satiric Television and Political Engagement* (Plymouth, UK: Rowman & Littlefield, 2010), 168.

14. "Comedy Central Names Erika Soto Lamb Vice President, Social Impact Strategy," Comedy Central, accessed January 29, 2019, https://press.cc.com/press-release/2018/09/13/press-erika-soto-lamb-named-vice-president-social-impact-strategy.

15. "Comedy Central Names Erika Soto Lamb."

16. "The Generation Gap in American Politics," Pew Research Center, March 1, 2018, www.people-press.org/2018/03/01/the-generation-gap-in-american-politics/.

17. Meredith Ferguson, "Dollars & Change: Young People Tap Brands as Agents of Social Change," May 13, 2018, https://medium.com/dosomething strategic/dollars-change-young-people-tap-brands-as-agents-of-social-change-2612b717e5f7.

18. Anita Busch, "CAA Launches Social Impact Consultancy," *Deadline*, September 15, 2016, https://deadline.com/2016/09/caa-launches-social-impact-consultancy-will-be-led-by-former-caa-marketing-exec-1201820555/.

19. Anita Busch, "WME/IMG Partners with UNICEF in Global Social Impact Strategy," *Deadline*, January 11, 2017, https://deadline.com/2017/01/wme-img-unicef-global-social-impact-strategy-1201883039/.

20. "Erase The Hate Announces 'Change Makers' Selected for Social Impact Campaign's Innovative Accelerator Program," *Cision PR Newswire*, February 5, 2018, www.prnewswire.com/news-releases/erase-the-hate-announces-change-makers-selected-for-social-impact-campaigns-innovative-accelerator-program-300593730.html.

21. Dimple Agarwal et al., "Citizenship and Social Impact: Society Holds the Mirror: 2018 Global Human Capital Trends," *Deloitte Insights*, March 28, 2018, www2.deloitte.com/insights/us/en/focus/human-capital-trends/2018/corporate-citizenship-social-impact.html.

22. Hasan Minhaj, in-person interview with author, November 1, 2018.

23. Joel Church-Cooper, phone interview with authors, November 7, 2018.

24. David Ford, "'RiseUp: Comedy for Change' Agenda Announced," *Fusion Media Group*, May 26, 2017, https://fmg.kinja.com/agenda-for-riseup-comedy-for-change-conference-annou-1795585218.

25. "Comedy, Politics, and Social Change: Working at the Intersection of Activism and Humor," Open Society Foundations, accessed January 29, 2019, www.opensocietyfoundations.org/events/comedy-politics-and-social-change-working-intersection-activism-and-humor.

26. Caty Borum Chattoo and Amy Henderson Riley, *Comedy as Creative Dissent in Latin America: Lessons from Cross-Sector Creative Collaborations in Brazil, Colombia and Mexico* (Washington, DC: Center for Media & Social Impact, American University School of Communication, Washington, DC), https://cmsimpact.org.

27. "Brandstage Grows Your Brand in New and Unexpected Ways," Second City Works, accessed January 29, 2019, www.secondcityworks.com/partners/brandstage.

28. Caty Borum Chattoo and Lindsay Green-Barber, "An Investigative Journalist and a Stand-up Comic Walk into a Bar: The Role of Comedy in Public Engagement with Environmental Journalism," *Journalism* (March 2018), https://doi.org/10.1177%2F1464884918763526.

29. Max Boykoff and Beth Osnes, "A Laughing Matter: Confronting Climate Change through Humor," *Political Geography* 68 (2019): 154–63, https://doi.org/10.1016/j.polgeo.2018.09.006.

30. Zuzana Boehmová and Elizabeth Weingarten, "Working for Free Is Pretty Funny, Right?" *Slate*, March 8, 2018, https://slate.com/human-interest/2018/03/unpaid-labor-is-hilarious.html.

31. Yes, And Laughter Lab, Center for Media & Social Impact and Moore + Associates, www.yesandlaughterlab.com/.

32. Bruce A. Williams and Michael X. Delli Carpini, "Real Ethical Concerns and Fake News: *The Daily Show* and the Challenge of the New Media Environment," in *The Stewart/Colbert Effect: Essays on the Real Impacts of Fake News*, ed. Amarnath Amarasingam (Jefferson, NC: McFarland, 2011).

33. Williams and Delli Carpini, "Real Ethical Concerns," 185.

34. Lauren Carroll, "Fact-Checking Amy Schumer's 'Welcome to the Gun Show'," *PunditFact*, PolitiFact, April 29, 2016, www.politifact.com/punditfact/statements/2016/apr/29/amy-schumer/fact-checking-amy-schumers-welcome-gun-show/.

35. Jenny Hollander, "13 Hannah Gadsby 'Nanette' Quotes You Won't Be Able to Stop Thinking About," *Marie Claire*, July 20, 2018, https://www.marieclaire.com/culture/a22502991/hannah-gadsby-nanette-quotes/.

36. Harmon Leon, "Right-Wing Comedy: Is It the Fine Art of Punching Down?," *The Observer*, May 14, 2019, https://observer.com/2019/05/nick-di-paolo-chad-prather-right-wing-comedy/; Joseph Bernstein, "The Alt-Right Has Its Very Own TV Show on Adult Swim," *BuzzFeed*, August 25, 2016, www.buzzfeednews.com/article/josephbernstein/the-alt-right-has-its-own-comedy-tv-show-on-a-time-warner-ne.

37. Viveca S. Greene, "'Deplorable' Satire: Alt-Right Memes, White Genocide Tweets, and Redpilling Normies," *Studies in American Humor* 5, no. 1 (2019), 31–69, www.jstor.org/stable/10.5325/studamerhumor.5.1.0031.

38. Zahra Noorbakhsh, phone interview with authors, July 30, 2018.

39. Brent Miller, phone interview with authors, December 21, 2018.

40. Lacey Rose, "Ryan Murphy Launches Foundation to Tackle Hollywood's Diversity Problem (Exclusive)," *Hollywood Reporter*, February 3, 2016, www.hollywoodreporter.com/news/ryan-murphy-launches-foundation-tackle-861436.

41. Cara Buckley, "Powerful Hollywood Women Unveil Anti-Harassment Action Plan," *New York Times,* January 1, 2018, www.nytimes.com/2018/01/01/movies/times-up-hollywood-women-sexual-harassment.html.

42. Sandra E. Garcia, "The Woman Who Created #MeToo Long before Hashtags," *New York Times*, October 20, 2017, www.nytimes.com/2017/10/20/us/me-too-movement-tarana-burke.html.

43. 50/50 by 2020, accessed January 29, 2019, https://site.5050by2020.com/home.

44. See, for example, Color of Change's *Race in the Writers' Room* report and initiative: https://hollywood.colorofchange.org/.

45. Alison Herman and Victor Luckerson, "Dying Laughing," *The Ringer*, March 26, 2018, www.theringer.com/2018/3/26/17157020/online-comedy-the-onion-funny-or-die-digital-media.

46. Herman and Luckerson, "Dying Laughing"; Sarah Aswell, "How Facebook Is Killing Comedy," *Vulture*, February 6, 2018, www.vulture.com/2018/02/how-facebook-is-killing-comedy.html.

47. Dade Hayes, "Funny or Die Sets New Round of Layoffs," *Deadline*, January 23, 2018, https://deadline.com/2018/01/funny-or-die-sets-new-round-of-layoffs-1202267461/.

48. Anne Libera, phone interview with authors, July 30, 2018.

49. Bethany Hall, phone interview with authors, July 30, 2018.

50. Andrew Marantz, "Heckling the Jon Stewart of Egypt," *New Yorker*, March 13, 2017, www.newyorker.com/magazine/2017/03/13/heckling-the-jon-stewart-of-egypt.

About the Authors

Caty Borum Chattoo is Director of the Center for Media & Social Impact at American University's School of Communication in Washington, D. C., where she is also Assistant Professor.

Lauren Feldman is Associate Professor in the School of Communication & Information at Rutgers University.

Index

Founded in 1893,
UNIVERSITY OF CALIFORNIA PRESS
publishes bold, progressive books and journals
on topics in the arts, humanities, social sciences,
and natural sciences—with a focus on social
justice issues—that inspire thought and action
among readers worldwide.

The UC PRESS FOUNDATION
raises funds to uphold the press's vital role
as an independent, nonprofit publisher, and
receives philanthropic support from a wide
range of individuals and institutions—and from
committed readers like you. To learn more, visit
ucpress.edu/supportus.